Performing Masculinity

Also by Rainer Emig

MODERNISM IN POETRY: MOTIVATIONS, STRUCTURES AND LIMITS

W.H. AUDEN: TOWARDS A POSTMODERN POETICS

STEREOTYPES IN CONTEMPORARY ANGLO-GERMAN RELATIONS (*edited*)

KRIEG ALS METAPHER IM ZWANZIGSTEN JAHRHUNDERT

ULYSSES: NEW CASEBOOK (*edited*)

GENDER ↔ RELIGION (*edited with Sabine Demel*)

HYBRID HUMOUR: COMEDY IN TRANSCULTURAL PERSPECTIVES (*edited with Graeme Dunphy*)

Also by Antony Rowland

THE POETRY OF CAROL ANN DUFFY: 'CHOOSING TOUGH WORDS' (*edited with Angelica Michelis*)

HOLOCAUST POETRY

SIGNS OF MASCULINITY (*edited with Emma Liggins and Eriks Uskalis*)

THE FUTURE OF MEMORY (*edited with Rick Crownshaw and Jane Kilby*)

THE LAND OF GREEN GINGER

TONY HARRISON AND THE HOLOCAUST

Performing Masculinity

Edited by

Rainer Emig

Antony Rowland

First published 2010 by
PALGRAVE MACMILLAN

Palgrave Macmillan in the UK is an imprint of Macmillan Publishers Limited,
registered in England, company number 785998, of Houndmills, Basingstoke,
Hampshire RG21 6XS.

Palgrave Macmillan in the US is a division of St Martin's Press LLC,
175 Fifth Avenue, New York, NY 10010.

Palgrave Macmillan is the global academic imprint of the above companies
and has companies and representatives throughout the world.

Palgrave® and Macmillan® are registered trademarks in the United States,
the United Kingdom, Europe and other countries.

ISBN-13: 978–0–230–57798–5 hardback

This book is printed on paper suitable for recycling and made from fully
managed and sustained forest sources. Logging, pulping and manufacturing
processes are expected to conform to the environmental regulations of the
country of origin.

A catalogue record for this book is available from the British Library.

Library of Congress Cataloging-in-Publication Data
Performing masculinity / edited by Rainer Emig, Antony Rowland.
      p.   cm.
   Includes bibliographical references and index.
   ISBN 978–0–230–57798–5 (alk. paper)
   1. Masculinity in literature.   2. Literature, Modern—History and
criticism.   3. Masculinity in popular culture.   I. Emig, Rainer, 1964–
II. Rowland, Antony.
   PN56.M316P37 2010
   809′.933521—dc22   2009048424

10   9   8   7   6   5   4   3   2   1
19   18   17   16   15   14   13   12   11   10

Printed and bound in Great Britain by
CPI Antony Rowe, Chippenham and Eastbourne

Contents

Preface

What might it mean to perform masculinity? I raise this question not simply because all of the essays gathered in this engaging volume provide a wide range of historically and theoretically inflected answers to it. Every contributor to the lively pages that follow shows little hesitation in assuming that the forms of maleness that he or she investigates are the result of complex performances that often involve intense struggles with maintaining a desirable gender identity. Yet it is perhaps timely to remember that only 20 years ago the idea of a scholarly collection titled *Performing Masculinity* would most probably have sounded somewhat unusual to readers located outside the field of dramatic studies. The view that all masculinities are continuously making and unmaking themselves through performative acts – ones rooted in material practices and psychic formations – would most likely have struck researchers exploring the gendering of male bodies as largely the preserve of stage and screen. To suggest that masculinity, in all its endless variants, was constitutively performed at each and every historical moment would have made it sound as if the piecing together of manhood were purely a matter of appropriate props, particular dress styles, and types of bodily comportment. Such a formulation would have made masculinity look as if it were more or less a matter of dressing up that could, since it was performed, be entertaining too. More to the point, the emphasis on performance might well have suggested that if a person could find the clothes, accent, and body style to pass for a particular type of man, that individual could do so by choice. Two decades ago, the concept of performing a specific gender would have resonated with perhaps too many connotations of pleasure-seeking consumerism for any researcher in the more empirically based disciplines to take it with much seriousness.

If we look back at some of the earliest path-breaking studies of masculinity dating from the 1970s and 1980s, it becomes evident from their titles that the male sex was by and large not something to be embraced. Books such as *Men's Liberation* (1975) by Jack Nichols point urgently to the need for men to be freed from their gender. Equally striking is Andrew Tolson's pioneering *Limits of Masculinity* (1977), where manhood appears as both a restrictive and restricted concept. Once we open the covers of books such as Joan Mellen's *Big Bad Wolves* (1977) and Paul

Hoch's *White Hero, Black Beast* (1977), we recognize that the paternalistic and racist manifestations of maleness in Hollywood film and popular culture are the ones under sharpest critique. And when we encounter Jeff Hearn's *Gender of Oppression* (1987), we know for sure that the masculinity that researchers had been subjecting to scrutiny had very little charm or appeal. The unquestionable problem with masculinity was that it embodied the worst imaginable face of a white, heterosexist, and patriarchal society in which it seemed unable to transform in line with the progressive demands and desires of the feminist movement and Gay Liberation. Everything about it proved pretty loathsome, since it revelled in the self-glorifying ideology of its unconquerable, brutal, phallic supremacy.

Yet by the time the early 1990s came around, there was a sufficiently large body of thoughtful writing on gender and sexuality for critics to see that critiquing masculinity in such terms appeared as rigid as the manhood they deplored. As the editors of the present volume acknowledge, it was the appearance of Judith Butler's astonishing *Gender Trouble* (1990) that helped recast our critical insights into the cultural, psychic, and social production of gender. No longer could anyone dedicated to understanding how human beings acquire styles of masculinity or femininity avoid engaging with the performative aspects of gender. This fresh emphasis on performance, which cultural and literary critics took up with great responsiveness, opened our eyes to the possibility that masculinity might not even need a male body to make itself manifest. No sooner had leading scholars such as Sue-Ellen Case reminded us that in lesbian performance the butch-femme dialectic was one enjoyed between women than discussions of gender underwent a most welcome denaturalization. From this point on, masculinity did not have to be predicated on a sexed male body. As a result, these new paths of inquiry led to innovative works such as Judith Halberstam's *Female Masculinity* (1999) and Jay Prosser's *Second Skins* (1998), which – for all their methodological differences – emerged at a crucial moment when scholars engaged more urgently than ever before with pressing debates about transgender and transsexual subjectivities.

At the same time, the gathering strength of LGBT studies, the advent of queer theory and an authoritative series of fine analyses of the racial and ethnic components of masculinity unravelled manhood to such a degree that it became no longer possible to talk complacently about this previously uniform concept in the singular. These days books appear with titles such as *Oh Boy! Masculinities and Popular Music* (2007). By this point, as the exclamation mark insists, men have not only been pluralized; they have also become much more exciting to discuss. But as with all refreshing developments in the study of gender, these shifts of emphasis should not distract from an enduring problem. Even if, as *Performing Masculinity* shows, researchers have grown adept in talking about the intricate ways in which types of maleness emerge in diverse cultures, no one can claim that we have at last managed – at least critically – to emancipate ourselves from them. Even if we now know that there are different masculinities that have always been competing for cultural attention, it is still the case that we must continue to critique, rather than just celebrate, their performances of gender.

Joseph Bristow
University of California, Los Angeles
October 2009

Notes on Contributors

Anthony Bateman is Honorary Visiting Research Fellow at the International Centre for Sports History and Culture, De Montfort University, United Kingdom. He is the author of *Cricket, Literature and Culture* and co-editor of both *Sporting Sounds: Relationships Between Sport and Music* and the forthcoming *Cambridge Companion to Cricket*.

David Boulting is an independent scholar and Americanist. He has taught at the University of Salford, Manchester Metropolitan University, both in the United Kingdom, and at the University of Ljubljana in Slovenia. His research interests include war and representation in contemporary and historical American culture, the American gothic, the short story, and the frontier in American film and literature. His doctoral thesis was entitled *Garden of Evil: Images of the Enemy in American War Literature 1962–1990*. He is also currently the Production Editor of Cathedral Communications Limited, an independent publisher specializing in architecture and the built heritage.

Katharine Burkitt teaches at the University of Liege in Belgium. Her PhD was awarded in 2007 from University of Salford, UK, for a study of the correlation between epic form and the contemporary postcolonial verse-novel entitled *Epic Proportions: Post-Epic Verse-Novels and Postcolonial Critique*. In line with this, her research remains focused in the field of postcolonial studies, particularly on verse-novels, as well as other abstract formal engagements like the long poem and the poetic novel. She has recently published on texts by Derek Walcott, Les Murray, Anne Carson, Bernardine Evaristo, and Michael Ondaatje.

Rainer Emig is Chair of English Literature and Culture at Leibniz University in Hanover, Germany. He is especially interested in the link between literature and the media and in Literary, Critical, and Cultural Theory, especially theories of identity, power, gender, and sexuality. His publications include the monographs *Modernism in Poetry* (1995), *W. H. Auden* (1999) and *Krieg als Metapher im zwanzigsten Jahrhundert* (2001) as well as edited collections on *Stereotypes in Contemporary Anglo-German Relations* (2000), *Ulysses* (2004), and *Gender ↔ Religion* (2008).

He has recently completed a monograph entitled *Eccentricity: Culture from the Margins* and a co-edited collection on *Hybrid Humour: Comedy in Transcultural Perspectives*. He is one of the three editors of the *Journal for the Study of British Cultures*.

Wolfgang Funk studied English, German, History, and Transnational Competence at the University of Regensburg in Germany, and graduated with an MA and a Teacher's Diploma in 2005. From 2006 to 2008 he taught Gender Studies and English Literature at Regensburg. Since 2008 he has been a lecturer in English at Leibniz University Hanover, Germany, while at the same time working on his PhD thesis with the working title *Discourses of Authenticity in Contemporary Metafiction*. He has published articles on contemporary British drama and fiction, among others on Bryony Lavery (2007), Jasper Fforde and Matthew Kneale (2010).

Wendy Ho is Associate Professor and Chair in the Department of Asian American Studies at the University of California, Davis, USA. She also holds a joint appointment in the Women and Gender Studies Program. Her book *In Her Mother's House* examines the cultural politics of Asian American mother–daughter writing. She is currently writing on a range of topics: Asian American masculinities, the politics of food in Asian American literature and a book-length literary study on new Asian American understandings of self and community as they are etched into the land and environment. She directs the Asian Pacific American Cultural Politics Research Group and is on the Advisory Boards of the University of California Humanities Research Institute at UC Irvine and at UC Davis. Her research interests are in feminist and critical race theory; Asian American literatures and women; women's ethnic literatures in the Americas; US masculinities; politics of food; and environmental and cultural studies.

Lucia Krämer is Lecturer in English Literature and Culture at Leibniz Universität Hanover, Germany. She obtained her PhD in 2002 at the University of Regensburg in Germany with a study of the biofictional representation of *Oscar Wilde in Roman, Drama und Film* (2003) and continues to work on Wilde, for example as an associate editor of the electronic journal *THE OSCHOLARS*. Other research areas, on which she has published various articles, include British heritage culture, the theory and practice of adaptation, and animation film. Her current main research project concerns the reception of popular Indian cinema in Britain.

Jessica Malay is a senior lecturer at the University of Huddersfield in the United Kingdom. She has published a monograph entitled *Textual Constructions of Space in the Writing of Early Modern Women* (2006) and articles on gender and literature. She has recently completed a monograph on Sibylline imagery in the early modern period and is presently working on autobiography and abuse narratives in the seventeenth century.

Antony Rowland is Professor of English at the University of Salford in Greater Manchester, United Kingdom. His research interests include memory studies, Holocaust studies, contemporary poetry, and masculinity. His most recent book *Holocaust Poetry* (2005) is the first critical study of post-Holocaust poetry in Britain, and focuses on the work of Sylvia Plath, Tony Harrison, Geoffrey Hill, and Ted Hughes. Other critical works include *Signs of Masculinity* (eds, 1999) and *'Choosing Tough Words': the Poetry of Carol Ann Duffy* (eds, 2003). He has also written a monograph on Tony Harrison's Holocaust poetry (2001) and is a published poet himself, whose latest volume of poetry is *The Land of Green Ginger* (2008).

Diego Saglia is Associate Professor of English literature and culture at the University of Parma in Italy. His research focuses mainly on Romantic-period literature and culture, with a particular interest in the cross-cultural exchanges between the British and other European traditions. He has contributed essays to the *Encyclopedia of the Romantic Era, 1760-1850*, ed. Christopher John Murray (2004); *A Companion to European Romanticism*, ed. Michael Ferber (2005); *Jane Austen in Context* (The Cambridge Edition of the Works of Jane Austen), ed. Janet Todd (2005); and *A Companion to Jane Austen*, ed. Claudia Johnson and Clara Tuite (2009). His essays have appeared in *Textual Practice, Studies in Romanticism, La questione romantica, The Keats-Shelley Journal, Nineteenth-Century Contexts, ELH, Studies in the Novel, Philological Quarterly, ELN*, and other international journals. He is the author of *Poetic Castles in Spain: British Romanticism and Figurations of Iberia* (2000) and co-editor, with Laura Bandiera, of *British Romanticism and Italian Literature: Translating, Reviewing, Rewriting* (2005). He has recently published *Lord Byron e le maschere della scrittura* (2009) and is currently working on the first critical edition of Robert Southey's *Roderick, the Last of the Goths*.

Sven Schmalfuß studied English and Political Science at Regensburg University in Germany and the National University of Ireland, Galway. He graduated with a work on gender roles in the Alice-works of Lewis Carroll, the Walt Disney Company and in the Alice PC game designed by American McGee. Sven Schmalfuß currently works as a lecturer in Gender Studies at Regensburg University and is the head of the digital games studies workgroup in Regensburg. His main areas of interest are digital game journalism, gender and digital games, and games and politics.

Gerald Siegmund studied Theater Studies, English, and French Literature at the Johann-Wolfgang-Goethe University in Frankfurt/Main, Germany. His PhD thesis on *Theatre as Memory* was completed in 1994. In 1998, he joined the staff of the Department of Applied Theatre Studies at the University of Gießen, Germany. Between 2005 and 2008 he was Professor of Contemporary Theatre at the University of Berne, Switzerland. Currently he is Professor of Dance Studies and Head of the MA program 'Choreography and Performance' at the University of Gießen. Gerald Siegmund is editor of *William Forsythe – Denken in Bewegung* [*William Forsythe: Thought in Motion*], published in 2004. His most recent book *Abwesenheit: Eine performative Ästhetik des Tanzes* [*Absence: A Performative Aesthetics of Dance*] was published in 2006.

Introduction

Rainer Emig and Antony Rowland

Describing gender relations has become more complex since a man could confidently assert that women's hair grows longer because it waves and screens the delicate shoulders from injuries 'which might be sustained by free exposure to air' (Rowland 10). Yet the study of masculinity in the late twentieth century had a hard time when it came to finding critical acceptance. Initially it was frequently understood as an anti-feminist backlash, a typical joke being 'Why study masculinity now? We haven't been doing anything else for centuries!' For some, the concept of masculinity itself was an irrelevant joke: in 1994, *Private Eye* condemned one of the editors to 'Pseuds' Corner' for daring to instigate a conference on the topic, presumably because of the advertised desire to explore homoerotic triangles in Renaissance literature and yoghurt. Yet the common observation that what is pervasive in society and culture often remains invisible also holds true for masculinity. As John McLeod has argued, until recently, the cultural critic was faced with blankness 'when interrogating the abstractions of masculinity' (218). In this volume, Gerald Siegmund explores this paradox of masculinity being both everywhere and nowhere in relation to Romantic ballet: he focuses on the gradual uncovering of the semiotics of the male dancer on stage, and the contradiction between the requirement for male dancers in classical ballet and their relegation to the background. Since in the early nineteenth century masculinity was figured to be a kind of violent blundering, the invisibility of masculinity could be said to appertain particularly to the middle classes; this process continues apace today, since suspicious 'hoodies' and failing working-class children at school are the focus of media attention, rather than performances of masculinity in more authoritarian forms (such as the semiotic behavior of Gordon Brown and Angela Merkel).

When Harry Brod published his anthology *The Making of Masculinities* in 1987, he referred to the study of masculinity as invisible in the sense that it constituted a 'recent and ... relatively small' field (1). His point of comparison was, of course, Women's Studies, which, as a result of 1960s and 1970s feminism, had transformed itself from a partisan activity to a mainstream academic discipline. Yet feminism, somewhat ironically and partly against its own intentions, also triggered the development of Masculinity Studies. For traditional feminists, men were the Other, as was blatantly evident in the title of Simone de Beauvoir's famous treatise *The Second Sex* of 1949. Men were the dominant force against which women were defined, by which they were shaped and oppressed and against which they had to stand firm. Yet in the same way as later generations of feminists attacked both the notion of inferiority and sup-plementarity of women and the idea that 'woman' was a homogenous and universal entity, more and more people in – and outside – academia questioned the simple and uniform existence of 'man.' Traditional fem-inism had subsumed all men under the umbrella term 'patriarchy,' the traditional passing on and sharing of power between men. Yet not all men felt empowered by patriarchy; indeed lots of men, initially largely gay men, signalled that they perceived themselves as much oppressed by it as women, though usually in different ways.

Nonetheless, Men's Studies had to go through roughly the same phases that Feminism underwent before it transformed itself into Gen-der Studies. Initially, the inquiry followed quite traditional paths, namely by questing for an essence of manliness. This was, with tradi-tional Romantic fervour, usually found 'in nature,' which meant, away from civilization, and frequently in male bonding, that is, away from women and the family. In a section of an anthology called 'Approach to Wildness,' William Carlos Williams discovers his manliness in his shoul-ders, flanks, and buttocks when he dances naked before a mirror in his 'north room,' waving his shirt around his head; unsurprisingly, his wife, children, and Kathleen are sleeping downstairs when he engages in such activity (6). Diverse forms of therapy and experience tourism thrived on this search, which, it was easy to point out, was merely the traditional assumption of an essential (strong, autonomous) manhood in a new and fashionable disguise. Calvin Thomas argues that some feminists were justifiably critical of such 'bloated versions of "men's studies" – particu-larly those influenced by the mythopoetic school of Robert Bly', which were 'spectacularly uninformed by and/or hostile to feminism' (20).

Performance masquerades here as nature. Historically, however, the accomplishments of masculinity are usually the results of a process,

'typically one that involves some degree of physical or symbolic violence' (Forth 2). Sven Schmalfuß's chapter on masculinity in computer
games outlines this nexus of symbolism, violence, and gender very
clearly. Theodor Adorno criticizes such symbolic acts of violence in
his brief investigation of masculinity as masochism in *Minima Moralia*.
The 'hard-boiled' man performs a supposedly natural self by paradoxically inuring himself gradually to the cultural products of whisky and
cigars (45–46). As Christopher Forth argues in *Masculinity in the Modern West*, such masochistic practices require 'endless reinforcement and
repetition,' which may appear to present a 'natural' masculinity, but
actually 'underscore the constructed nature of the masculine self' (2).
The film *Raging Bull* highlights this instability: the elegiac shots of the
hooded boxer in the opening credits emphasize the finite ability of the
self to ascertain its masculinity through performances of violence. Jake's
demise illustrates that performances of masculinity interweaved with
athleticism and violent acts prove that 'masculinity...is a dynamic and
ultimately unachievable process' (2). Forth's statement is applied more
widely to *any* form of 'personal identity': 'the performance of gender is
also prone to failures, lapses and refusals...Attempts to ground gender
differences in the bedrock of "nature" must conceal the secret history of
becoming' (2). Lucia Krämer's chapter on rock star films highlights the
importance and inevitable failure of such posturing in an environment
that thrives on a gendered 'image.'

Such poststructuralist accounts of gender must avow the ultimate
impossibility of a simple identity politics. Yet for most men, the idea
that struggles for identity could be simply shrugged off would prove
hopelessly utopian in a Western world where the perils of masculine performance include the effects of 'mental illness, nervous disor-
ders and suicide' (6). Wolfgang Funk's chapter on Martin McDonagh's
plays demonstrates that contemporary drama has already taken these
issues on board. The latter offshoots of supposedly 'advanced' societies
will coexist with atavistic displays of masculinity in a 'future society
populated by well-fed and complacent people immersed in an ever-
expanding array of consumer pleasures and labor-saving devices' (201).

This paradox of civilization is illustrated in the film *Fight Club*: one of
the reasons for the protagonist's turn to bare-knuckle fighting comprises
his disgusted contemplation of his flat, which consists of the insipid uni-
formity of IKEA-style furniture. Civilized society itself becomes regarded
as a threat to masculinity (it is no accident in the film that the fighters'
organization culminates in fascistic activities); men reduced to soft-
ness by glossy furniture catalogues are contrasted with the 'benefits of

hardened and stoic bodies' (204). Forth argues that the phenomenon of Club Med comprises such an instance of performed atavism, 'a further packaging of the primitive as something capable of existing both within and against modernity' (218). The protagonist's failure in *Fight Club* is to recognize the fisticuffs as a form of 'packaging,' a carnivalesque activity easily subsumed within corporate modernity. For Forth, the advent of the New Lad comprises just another recent incarnation of the urban primitive (227). The New Lad's magazine *Maxim* offers another route to the performed naturalness of 'Iron John' by suggesting that men learn what it is like to be eaten by a shark, how to survive snakebites and how to spot a lesbian in a crowd (120–124, 114–118, 54).

It took Gender Studies to unravel the conundrum of identity, not by making things clearer, but by showing how entangled they were. Judith Butler's *Gender Trouble* is generally and rightly regarded as a foundational text, but not so much because it describes gender as a construction (this had been done by de Beauvoir and others before; if one looks closely, it had indeed frequently been done all through the history of Western thought). Butler's achievement was to show the hitherto so troublesome, because simultaneously related and distinct fields of biological sex, cultural gender, and sexuality as structurally connected, though not in the way essentialist thinkers, be they biologists or theologians, liked to propose. In her model, which inherited its structural foundation from Michel Foucault's theses on power, the compulsory pronunciation of heterosexuality as the natural, sane, and legal norm by society predetermined the existence of two complementary genders, masculine and feminine, as the expressions of human identities that guarantee and safeguard heterosexuality and with it the traditional family and procreation. Rainer Emig's chapter on Victorian comedy shows this ideal at the time of its assumed general currency – and argues that the norm already displayed cracks then. Even biological sex, Butler demonstrated, hinged upon such cultural definitions and did not, as had hitherto been naively assumed, simply determine masculine and feminine behavior as a natural consequence of the biological sex with which one is born.

Butler's model explained why it was so hard to escape the clichés and stereotypes of the binary oppositions 'masculine' and 'feminine,' even or precisely in manifestations of gender and sexuality that otherwise seemed to transgress or transcend the norm, such as male and female homosexuality. How come these also displayed clichés of 'butch' and 'femme,' if they were otherwise 'unnatural' according to the proponents of normative heterosexuality?

Like any constructivist model, Butler's explicitly refused to give answers as to the 'essence' or 'nature' of any of its constituent elements, be they homo- or heterosexuality or masculine and feminine identity or behavior. This enraged especially politically active feminists and gay and lesbian activists, since it seemed to deprive them of a ground from which to argue their case and defend their positions.

Instead, Butler proposed that gender was the result of performance, a performance that did not so much imitate a given essential model as create the idea of such a model and norm through incessant repetition in the first place: '*gender is a kind of imitation for which there is no original*; in fact, it is a kind of imitation that produces the very notion of the original as an *effect* and consequence of the imitation itself' (Butler 1997: 306). In doing so, Butler shifted the debate on gender from that of an essential (natural) quality to a set of performances inside the power structures of society.

Yet Butler's stress on performance contained its own snares, and it was none other than Butler herself who noticed and tried to remedy them when the world wide success of her treatise produced a fashion for performative notions of identity in many fields. The notion of performance is still not free from essentialism in that it can be misread as the playing of an already formulated role. Feminists such as Germaine Greer, for example, were often critical of Butler's favourite illustration, transvestites, because to them they only seemed to reproduce in exaggerated shapes traditional patriarchal gender idea(l)s. The second trap that the concept of performance contains is the notion of free choice: if I perform identity, then I might believe that I can put it on and off again as and when I want. Butler, however, wished to show that things were by no means up to a free and autonomous liberal humanist subject who picked its identities as it desired.

In order to draw a line, she introduced the term 'performativity' of gender and sexuality from the follow-up to *Gender Studies*, *Bodies That Matter*, onwards, to show that the performative is not within the grasp or control of the individual, but a societal and cultural *sine qua non*. Drawing on psychoanalytic concepts of the inaccessibility of the unconscious and expanding them into cultural processes, she describes the performativity of gender and sexuality as the equivalent of the Freudian repetition compulsion, whose real aim remains opaque to those who are subject to it, yet without which they could not exist: 'In other words, heterosexuality is always in the process of imitating and approximating its own phantasmatic idealization of itself – *and failing*. Precisely because it is bound to fail, and yet endeavours to succeed, the project of heterosexual identity is propelled into an endless repetition of itself' (Butler 307).

This is also the notion of performativity that the present volume upholds. This does not exclude poses and posture, imitations and caricatures. Yet it also addresses the many shapes in which masculinity manifests itself that do not immediately signal that they are performances, but strongly insist that they are 'the real thing.' As such a supposed 'real thing,' masculinity leads a contradictory life in Western culture. It may be the invisible constant in patriarchal discourses of power and knowledge, but its ubiquity does not mean that it is empowering for individual men participating in its structures. This becomes evident when masculinity turns into a problem (as it indeed frequently does). For Siegmund, the bodies of middle-class men were becoming problematic in the nineteenth century in that 'They had to define their physicality against both the old aristocracy and the labouring classes – and moreover against the bodies of women with their distinguishing feature, the womb, and the emotional and social codes in which the female body was conceptualised.' In his chapter on Lord Byron, Diego Saglia argues that the spectacle of the poet's body was so disturbing for some viewers because men were increasingly encouraged to measure themselves against supposedly genderless codes of reserve and stern morality in Evangelical and utilitarian notions of 'man.' Byron's body was therefore troubling to the point of 'fundamental ambiguity': it was 'fat and thin, covered yet in full view, elusive though spectacularized.' For men today, 'normative' masculinity still encompasses power, assertiveness, and invulnerability, yet, in the 1990s, men replaced women as the problem sex in public debates, since they appeared to be suffering from 'falling levels of confidence, "losing out" in schools, jobs, personal relationships, overall health and well-being' (Segal 18–19). Young men are increasingly encouraged by the media to work on and discipline their bodies, while being paradoxically required to disavow 'any (inappropriate) interest in their own appearance': such uneasy responses to male spectacle mirror the process in which male viewers of lithe dancers in the nineteenth century worried about becoming 'feminized,' Siegmund argues, and 'homosexual simply by watching men dance' (18). Even 'cock rock' today contains its own problematic contradictions, since, as Lucia Krämer argues in this volume, an 'extreme flaunting of heterosexuality' is offset with potentially feminizing attributes such as long hair, make-up, and theatrical clothing.

Australian media researcher Jim Macnamara goes as far as to state that masculinity is a 'problem' in so far as 75 per cent of reports on men in the media are unfavorable: men are categorized as rapists, harassers or 'deadbeat dads,' or are ridiculed as ineffectual in advertising and in TV programmes such as *Ally McBeal* and *Sex and the City* (Segal 19). Such instances of negative masculinity are frequently reflected in university courses, where the canonical cultural texts about masculinity highlight the machinations of serial murderers (Bret Easton Ellis's *American Psycho*), adolescents who engage in incest (Ian McEwan's *First Love, Last Rites*, and *The Cement Garden*) and repressed, violent, impotent, and homophobic instigators of domestic violence (Martin Scorsese's *Raging Bull*). As Malay demonstrates in this volume, the current and common association of masculinity with the problem of violence is not new: in the nineteenth century, Manchester was a place where 'man is turned back into a savage': six-year olds fought in the street until 'the blood streamed from the faces'; when a solicitor attempted to intervene in one such incident, 'he was assaulted himself by one of the men who boasted that since the child was his brother he had the right to train him as he liked.' Malay points out that in the Victorian era violence was not seen as a particular aspect of working-class masculinity, since 'manhood was conceived as an unstable equilibrium of barely controlled energy that may collapse back into the inchoate flood or fire that limns the innate energy of maleness.' In contrast, Siegmund points out in his chapter on ballet that the active male body was conceived as inherently working class in the early nineteenth century, since visible male dancers provoked horror in some viewers, who could only see the bloated calves of a parish beadle.

If, according to Judith Butler, the heterosexual matrix needs to maintain itself by the incessant performance of its binaries and their compulsory relation, this places an enormous burden on masculinity. Changing social and economic circumstances and altering self-perceptions and roles of women as well as men are among the pressures that make any understanding of masculinity as an essential quality highly dubious. When gay men started questioning traditional thinking – or rather not thinking – about masculinity, their motivation as disempowered members of an otherwise dominant group was easy to see. It was also equally easy to denounce their criticism as a minority problem. Now that the media urgently remind us that men die eight years earlier than women, are three times more likely to be murdered, more frequently die of heart attack, AIDS, and cancer, are more often homeless, are forced to go to war, become criminals and terrorists in much larger numbers, are expected to perform sexually, but also to repress emotions, suffer circumcision, have their pain trivialized, conform to rigid dress codes and commit suicide in much higher numbers than women (Yúdici 270),[1] we might slowly stop thinking of masculinity as a trivial or exotic subject. Indeed, *The Guardian* figured the potential nuclear conflict over Kashmir to be a clash of competing masculinities: in a 1998 cartoon, mushroom clouds replace penises as the two skeletal nations, India and Pakistan, face each other at the brink. The frequent failure of boys in the education system is also, for some, another source of anxiety, something that is noticeable even at university level.[2] Some US universities are now beginning to discriminate positively in favor of men.

Yet how are Literary and Cultural Studies supposed to deal with issues that, one might argue, are the domain of sociologists and psychologists? One argument could be that they ought to do their job properly. Masculinity as part of the constructions of power and knowledge has always been a crucial element in cultural texts, be they literary or otherwise. It should not take the popularity of pop fiction of the Nick Hornby or Tony Parsons type with titles such as *About a Boy* or *Man and Boy* to interest literary scholars in fictional constructions of masculinity. They have always been around – and even emphasized, from Medieval epics through Renaissance poetry and plays, Restoration Comedy, Enlightenment and Sentimental texts, Romanticism, Victorianism, Modernism, and Postmodernism.[3] They proliferate everywhere, often invisibly: as Antony Rowland argues in his chapter on camp poetics, classical control over poetic diction and form has – often unconsciously – been construed as a masculine pursuit, 'as opposed to effeminate dalliance with supposedly inferior forms such as the dramatic monologue.' In contrast, Mannerist poetics 'undercut (constructed) signs of normative masculinity, since the hyper-intensity of such writing eschews [Robert] Bly's notion of classical *gravitas.*' And as Anthony Bateman illustrates in his chapter on cricket, in the nineteenth century the game was quietly but successfully transplanted to Britain's colonies, 'where it was endowed with the ability to transform the identities of male imperial subjects in accordance with ideals of English bourgeois civility.' Katharine Burkitt's chapter on Les Murray and Michael Ondaatje in turn shows – from the perspective of Postcolonial Studies – how notions of cultural and national identity were negotiated in the literature of former colonies.

Following the expertise of the researchers writing in this volume, this study focuses on the various constructions of Western masculinity in the nineteenth, twentieth, and twenty-first centuries. Katharine Burkitt's chapter on an Australian and a Sri Lancan/Canadian writer and Wendy Ho's chapter on Asian-American masculinities introduce a transcultural perspective and – together with Anthony Bateman's chapter on the import and export of masculine values through the medium of sport – show that even the supposedly homogenous entity of 'Western culture' is traversed by the complicated negotiation of masculinity. This complex focus allows for various interdisciplinary approaches in a specific time frame as the semiotics of masculinity shift from the errant working-class males fighting in the street in Malay's chapter to the troubled, masculine 'Blair's babes' of the 1990s. As opposed to many recent texts on masculinity, this volume is genuinely interdisciplinary, with contributions from an international field of academics working in the areas of literature, Cultural Studies, Media Studies, Sports, and Performance Studies. Fictional constructions of masculinity are not a new subject of cultural study, but they need to be analyzed with a contemporary methodology – one that carefully abstains from essentialist clichés such as 'human nature' and refuses to accept supposedly 'typical' or 'natural' attitudes uncritically. By 2006, nearly 50 per cent of the books published on masculinity were in the areas of Literary and Cultural Studies, focusing on a plurality of masculinities rather than 'essential' attributes: alongside texts on the Masai people of Ngong, Masonic temples, and Islamic masculinities were studies of gay men in modern Southern literature, Irish women writers and anti-heroes in the American football novel. More recently, these pluralities have included analyses of masculinity and ethnicity in Britain, athletics, boys' education, and metrosexuality.[4] Statements about the matrices of variant masculinities are now critically commonplace, such as the assertion in *Representing Masculinity: Male Citizenship in Modern Western Culture* that masculinized citizenship 'was a site that represented intricate entwinements of masculinity with categories of difference such as class, race, and religion' (Dudnik, Hagemann, and Clark ix). Different generic interventions in, and engagements with, masculinity are also clearly key: this study's originality comprises its attempt to allow for various disciplinary angles within a single study, hence considering a 'range of experiences and representations that move beyond the usual preoccupation with penises, pecs and biceps' (Forth 17). Perhaps such studies are moving toward an endpoint in this particular development of men's studies. The next stage remains uncharted: the continued focus on pluralities of masculinity can only be continued finitely.

Nevertheless, when cultural critics do their current job properly, they will see that what is often called a 'crisis of masculinity' is not merely a contemporary experience as far as masculinity is concerned. Already the Old English poem 'The Wanderer' exclaims, 'That time is over, / Passed into night as it had never been' when it talks about its ideals of masculinity (Hamer 181). Leo Braudy's *From Chivalry to Terrorism: War and the Changing Nature of Masculinity* is illustrative of recent criticism in Men's Studies in its attempt to deconstruct this 'crisis,' to note its internal contradictions and paradoxes: 'Near the end of the twentieth-century the "crisis of masculinity" was seen in the chronic tunnel vision of the present as a phenomenon solely of our own time' (Braudy x). (Forth prefers 'the instabilities of Western masculinity' to the term 'crisis,' 6.) We might even learn to suspect that 'crisis' is perhaps a way in which patriarchy, like other ideologies, maintains and reproduces itself in spite of its contradictions. David Boulting's chapter on James Jones's novel *The Thin Red Line* uncovers this paradoxical process in a fictionalized account of the Second World War. Attention to constructions of masculinity also encourages us to be critical of commodification – not only of gender norms, but also of supposed resistance to them (cf. West 2000). Besides the already mentioned best-sellers from the new genre of 'lad lit,' the recent debate about so-called 'metrosexuality' is another indication that supposed subversion can be cleverly disguised marketing. This emphasizes once again that Gender Studies cannot exist in isolation from other critiques of ideology. Gender Studies also invite us to critically participate in the most fertile shifts in the Humanities in recent years: the visual turn, the performative turn and the corporeal turn – all of which are at the heart of its debates. The chapters in the present study have taken these shifts to heart, so to speak, in that they are concerned not merely with literary expressions of masculinity, but also with visual and performative forms, such as those of Romantic ballet, sports, film, and computer games.

Notes

1. In *Masculinities*, Raewyn W. Connell argues that these statistics are 'a product of the advantages men enjoy. Men remain overwhelmingly the sex in control of our business, political, cultural, and media worlds. They hold power in all the coercive institutions of society, earn, on average, twice as much as women and receive more social support and servicing from women in the home and elsewhere' (Segal 18).
2. Segal argues that 'there is nothing new in the educational failure of working-class and specific ethnic-minority boys, whose alienation in school has always accompanied the assertion of rebellious bravardo .... It is *particular* groups of men, especially unemployed, unskilled and unmarried, that have higher mortality and illness rates compared with other groups of men. Class, ethnicity

and race, not gender, are the major predictors of young men's educational underachievement, unemployment and resort to criminality' (18).
3. Cf. Rosen (1993). In a wider context, 'public fears over crises in masculinity ... worries that men are receiving the wrong cultural messages' have always been around (Segal 19).
4. *Gendering Migration*, ed. Louise Ryan and Wendy Webster; Michael Geerd, *Men Who Dance*; W. Martino, *The Problem With Boys*; David Coad, *The Metrosexual*.

Works Cited

Adorno, Theodor. *Minima Moralia*. Trans. E. F. N. Jephcott. London: Verso, 1951.

Beauvoir, Simone de. *The Second Sex*. 1949. Trans. and ed. Howard Madison Parshley. London: Vintage, 1997.

Braudy, Leo. *From Chivalry to Terrorism: War and the Changing Nature of Masculinity*. New York: Alfred A. Knopf, 2003.

Brod, Harry. 'Introduction: Themes and Theses of Men's Studies.' *The Making of Masculinities: The New Men's Studies*. Boston: Allen and Unwin, 1987. 1–17.

Butler, Judith. *Gender Trouble: Feminism and the Subversion of Identity*. London and New York: Routledge, 1990.

Butler, Judith. *Bodies That Matter: On The Discursive Limits of "Sex."* London and New York: Routledge, 1993.

Butler, Judith. 'Imitation and Gender Insubordination.' *The Second Wave: A Reader in Feminist Theory*. Ed. Linda Nicholson. London and New York: Routledge, 1997. 300–315.

Coad, David. *The Metrosexual: Gender, Sexuality and Sport*. Albany: New York UP, 2008.

Connell, Raewyn W. *Masculinities*. 2nd Edn. Cambridge: Polity, 2005.

Dudnik, Stefan, Karen Hagemann and Anna Clark, eds. *Representing Masculinity: Male Citizenship in Modern Western Culture*. New York/Basingstoke: Macmillan, 2007.

Forth, Christopher E. *Masculinity in the Modern West: Gender, Civilization and the Body*. London: Palgrave Macmillan, 2008.

Geerd, Michael. *Men Who Dance: Aesthetics, Athletics and the Art of Masculinity*. New York/Oxford: Peter Lang, 2006.

Hamer, Richard, ed. and trans. *A Choice of Anglo-Saxon Verse*. London and Boston: Faber & Faber, 1970.

Hornby, Nick. *About a Boy*. London: Gollancz, 1998.

Maxim: The Magazine for Men (July 1997).

Martino, Wayne. *The Problem With Boys: Beyond Recuperative Masculinity Politics in Boys' Education*. London: Routledge, 2008.

McLeod, John. 'Men Against Masculinity: The Fiction of Ian McEwan.' *Signs of Masculinity*. Eds Antony Rowland, Emma Liggins and Eriks Uskalis. Amsterdam: Rodopi, 1998. 218–245.

Parsons, Tony. *Man and Boy*. London: HarperCollins, 1999.

Raging Bull. Dir. Martin Scorsese. United Artists, 1980.

Rosen, David. *The Changing Fictions of Masculinity*. Urbana: U of Illinois P, 1993.

Rowland, Alexander. *The Human Hair: Popularly and Physiologically Considered*. London: Pipe Brothers, 1853.

Ryan, Louise, and Wendy Webster, eds. *Gendering Migration: Masculinity, Femininity and Ethnicity in Postwar Britain*. Aldershot: Ashgate, 2008.

Segal, Lynne. 'Being a man just ain't what it used to be.' *THES* 22 September 2006, 18–19.

Thomas, Calvin. *Masculinity, Psychoanalysis, Straight Queer Theory: Essays on Abjection in Literature, Mass Culture, and Film*. Basingstoke/New York: Palgrave Macmillan, 2008.

West, Russell. 'Men, the Market and Models of Masculinity in Contemporary Culture: Introduction.' *Subverting Masculinity: Hegemonic and Alternative Visions of Masculinity in Contemporary Culture*. Ed. Russell West and Frank Lay. Amsterdam and Atlanta: Rodopi, 2000. 7–26.

Williams, William Carlos. 'Danse Russe.' *The Rag and Bone Shop of the Heart: Poems for Men*. Ed. Robert Bly, James Hillman and Michael Meade. New York: HarperCollins, 1993. 6.

Yúdici, George. 'What's a Straight Man to Do?' *Constructing Masculinity*. Ed. Maurice Berger, Wallis Brian and Simon Watson. New York: Routledge, 1995. 267–283.

1
Touching Byron: Masculinity and the Celebrity Body in the Romantic Period

Diego Saglia

Abstract

If Byron's contemporaries were entranced by his poetry and personal myth, many of those who met him for the first time also invariably recorded their impressions of his body. 'That beautiful pale face is my fate,' said Lady Caroline Lamb. Contemporary accounts often contained depictions of Byron's physique, which sought to capture the peculiarities of his face, eyes, voice and gait. As these features stimulated the inquisitive gaze of onlookers and admirers, Byron became a body to observe and scrutinize; a spectacular body inspiring curiosity and fascination. However, Byron's was also a body that repeatedly eluded decodification and exceeded cultural norms at a time when conservative gender codes were increasingly linking masculinity to notions of productivity, domesticity, reserve and probity, an image promoted by such powerful advocates of Evangelical values as Hannah More and William Wilberforce. In contrast with this prescriptive discourse, Byron's body functions in Romantic culture as the opposite of, and an antidote to, this conventionally regulated male body and masculine identity. Specifically, the desire for the irregular, excessive body of Byron (and, indeed, that of his fictional heroes) emerges powerfully in a number of accounts which hint at the possibility of breaking verbal, visual and social barriers in order to touch Byron. Inviting scrutiny and attracting physical contact, Byron-as-body is a flagrantly non-normative object, a magnetic physique that, moreover, does not lose its cultural power after the poet's death in 1824. In fact, its persistent relevance may be gauged through its influence on the silver-fork and dandy novelists of the 1820s and 1830s, a generation of writers who looked back to Regency society as the moment of origination of dandyism and a time when aristocratic codes of behavior were still relatively unchallenged. Yet, for the silver-fork novelists the Byronic body proves too much. Their narratives, in particular Edward Bulwer-Lytton's Pelham *and Benjamin Disraeli's* Vivian Grey, *ultimately deflect its subversive potential, just as they neutralize the eccentricity of the dandy code and realign their dandy heroes with established conventions. If, in the earlier period, touching Byron's body implied a brush with disturbing celebrity, touching it in the silver-fork implies an initial recovery of its subversive value and the eventual neutralization of its disturbing potential. These narratives effect a move from the Byronic to the normative body which enables the dandy hero to be reintegrated as a fully-fledged and active member of society. Nonetheless, although the silver-fork novels reduce its eccentric and excessive import within their normalizing conclusions, the Byronic body remains tantalizingly enigmatic and unavailable to the desire to touch it, a differential mode of masculinity that stands its ground as an alternative to the influential conservative models emerging in the Romantic period.*

> ... when we think of Byron, the first thing that comes before our eyes is a physical presence, a profile.
>
> (Praz 147)

The centrality of Lord Byron's body to his personal image and legend was an undisputed fact for his contemporaries, whether men or women. More recently, in *Sexual Personae* (1990) Camille Paglia has summarized its cultural import for current critical debates by observing that 'Byron created the glamorous sexy youth of brash, defiant energy, *the new* embodied in a charismatic sexual persona' (357). If contemporaries were entranced by Byron, his poetry and his myth, what they also almost invariably recorded after meeting him, and not just for the first time, were the impressions made by his body. Letters, diaries and other accounts from the period are filled with sketches and portraits that seek to capture the moment of meeting Byron, the instant of contact with the celebrity personality through contact with the celebrity physique. Whether detailed or broad-brush, these accounts focus on Byron's eyes, voice, foot and gait; and, as these features stimulate the inquisitive gaze of onlookers and admirers, Byron's becomes a body to scrutinize and revere, a seductive object of curiosity. Edward Trelawny summed up this double status when he described Byron's body as 'the form and features of an Apollo, with the feet and legs of a sylvan satyr' (166). Since, as is well known, for the poet himself, his own body became a life-long obsession, especially because of its lameness and unbearable tendency to grow fat, his reactions to the observer's gaze were typically ambivalent. He studiously sought to hide his body and make it inconspicuous, for instance by not being seen walking into rooms or refusing to dance; at the same time, he constantly paraded it in the public and private spaces of Regency social and cultural life. Rooted in this context and crucial to the poet's complex personality and experience, Byron's body identifies a significantly conflictual model of masculine identity, the import of which continues to resonate well into the nineteenth and twentieth centuries.

One of the most arresting aspects of this male body is a fundamental ambiguity – it is both fat and thin, covered yet in full view, elusive though spectacularized – that invites speculation and contact, even as the body refuses to meet the observers' inquisitive eyes. Byron's is a spectacular physique that elicits curiosity and fascination, yet also constantly eludes interpretation. Indeed, Byron's body stands out in the Regency and Romantic-period cultural archive in that, as the object of multiple cross-currents of curiosity and desire, it has survived in countless inscriptions. In this respect, it may be linked to those other, 'eccentric' and 'abnormal,' bodies of eighteenth- and nineteenth-century culture, those of actors and actresses.[1] Moreover, because of this spectacular status, Byron's also recalls former 'irregular' bodies such as those of the 1770s *macaronis* described by Miles Ogborn as figures centered on a dress code that was fundamentally 'a matter of masculine fashion and display' at the core of 'a competitive and European world of men turning themselves into spectacles to impress other men' (448).

On the basis of these cultural precedents, Byron's body breaks boundaries, invites scrutiny, and, occasionally, even physical contact. Yet Byron capitalized on vision and self-display at a time when gender codes were increasingly removing masculinity from these dimensions and pushing it toward models of behavior centered on reserve and stern morality. Thus, his body was eccentric for contemporaries also in that it ran counter to notions of masculinity predicated on the 'domestication' of man, the growing importance of Evangelical values, and notions of virtue and productivity, promoted by conservative ideologues such as Hannah More and William Wilberforce (cf. Davidoff and Hall 81–95). This model of masculinity has recently been complicated by John Tosh, who has drawn attention to further aspects of 'resilient' or 'enduring masculinity' in the period from 1750 to 1850, those traits of an older code of virile identity, not exclusively the prerogative of aristocratic men, such as the bearing of arms, heroism, household authority, and sexual rites of passage into maturity (67).

The body of Byron was problematic because of its resistance to the new Evangelical and utilitarian notion of man, as well as because, owing to its perverse attractiveness, it assumed a disturbingly spectacular position that clashed with more unambiguously virile codes of masculinity. Male observers repeatedly called Byron 'beautiful' and 'handsome,' one of the most insistent being, perhaps unexpectedly, Samuel Taylor Coleridge (cf. Lovell 169). But, at the same time, because of its lameness, Byron's is a mysterious body, irregular and repulsive, contravening the norms of health, vigor, and shapeliness that were beginning to inform medical science and its pronouncements on the body (cf. Youngquist 3–27). Through its ambivalence and inexhaustibly productive signifying operations, the Byronic physique erects a barrier between itself and its observer, while at the same time inviting the same observer to access and explore its own carefully delimited and jealously protected space.

Researching his *Life of Byron*, Thomas Moore wrote to his friend Lord John Russell asking for any useful memories and recollections. The politician answered reporting the following remark, which dates back to Byron's period of fame after the publication of the first two cantos of *Childe Harold's Pilgrimage* in 1812: '[Samuel] Rogers says he used to be asked by ladies to get him [Byron] to sit next to them at supper, &c., &c., &c' (Russell 266; vol. 1). The fashionable ladies of the early 1810s insistently courted the presence of the beautiful young poet. And we may suppose that, with some notable exceptions, these ladies tended to keep a respectful and decorous distance between themselves and the noble bard. Unexpectedly, however, a number of contemporary accounts of Byron also hint at the possibility of breaking the verbal or visual barriers implied in Russell's and Rogers's pictures. Indeed, these accounts even evoke the possibility of touching Byron's body.

In an anecdote dating probably from the same period, Byron and the writer and wit James Smith (co-author, with his brother Horace, of *Rejected Addresses*, 1812) discuss the poet's 'parsimonious dinner,' his body, his constant fight against its tendency to run to fat and his attempt to control it through what he calls 'starvation' (Lovell 132–33). Of course, these are well-known topics, ubiquitous in Byron's letters and diaries, as well as in conversations with and reports about him. For instance, in 1811 Samuel Rogers invited Byron to dine and was surprised to find that the young man was satisfied with 'potatoes bruised down on his plate and drenched with vinegar' (Lovell 41). Sometimes these accounts use the word 'obesity' (Lovell 178) or remark that '[Byron] neither ate nor drank' (Lovell 179).[2] In 1816, in a letter to John Cam Hobhouse, Dr William Polidori observed that 'Exercise and peace of mind, [are] making great advances toward the amendment of his [Byron's] *corps délabré*' (Lovell 181), an image of his body in ruins that interestingly anticipates Byron's own presentation of himself as 'A ruin amidst ruins' in *Childe Harold's Pilgrimage* IV (25. 3).

Nonetheless, deviating from this rather unexceptional topic of conversation, James Smith's exchange with Byron concludes in an unexpected way. Smith reports Byron saying: 'I have told you how fat I was at Harrow: lend me your hand: what do you think of me now?'. To which Smith adds: 'Thus speaking, he passed my hand down his left side. "I can count every rib in your body." – "Indeed? I am delighted to hear you say so" ' (Lovell 133).

This brief dialogue reveals an instantaneous shift from the spectacle of the body to actual physical contact with it. In and through Smith's words, the celebrity physique is suddenly available to touch. In fact, some caveats are in order. There is something tentative, exploratory and almost medical about Smith's touch as he verifies Byron's thinness. Moreover, since Smith is invited to do so by the poet himself, his gesture evidently falls within the conventional code of early nineteenth-century homosociality, that form of male bonding based on close physical proximity that is socially acceptable yet also threaded through with desire. Between the eighteenth and nineteenth centuries, the homosocial sphere comprises such spaces as educational and military institutions (the reference to Harrow in the anecdote is a relevant hint), the world of the theater, coffee houses, and gentlemen's clubs, or such physical activities and professional sports as fencing, boxing, or hunting – all of which, except for the military, are relevant to Byron's experience.[3] Nonetheless, even within the scope of these social conventions, Byron and Smith's hand unexpectedly transgress a boundary. The poet is parading his body to a fellow writer, inviting him to touch it and then going on to discuss its merits. His passion for effect and his self-dramatizations – the deep-seated theatrical quality of Byron's masculinity – here acquire a decidedly physical form. Moreover, Smith's tone implies admiration mixed with the awareness that he is contravening codes of gender, sexuality, and class, and the fact that Byron generally avoided contact with his body according to what Roy Porter has termed his overall 'lofty disdain for the flesh' (453). The result of this verbal and physical exchange is a body in full sight, magnified through words and touch, and a body that does not follow conventional norms of behavior and self-management.

This episode may be compared further with another anecdote involving the young female writer Eliza S. Francis, author of the metrical tale in two volumes *The Rival Roses, or Wars of York and Lancaster* (1813) and the poem *Sir Wilbert de Waverley, or The Bridal Eve* (1815). On 24 October 1814 Miss Francis turns up on Byron's doorstep in Albany, Piccadilly, to seek his advice on one of her poetical compositions. This first encounter, and those that followed, had some quite unexpected consequences according to the young woman's account written some 49 years after the event in a series of letters addressed to an aged Teresa Guiccioli (cf. Origo 1–2).

Before her meeting with the celebrated writer, Francis is nervous and expectant. She explains why she has applied to Byron and yet feels embarrassed and tries to leave: 'I now made an effort to go away, but my tremor increased, and had he not promptly extended his arm, I should have fallen at his feet' (Lovell 92). But she does not faint, and, as she stands with her head bent down, Byron unexpectedly touches her: 'he lightly put aside some little curls which had escaped from my cap behind and kissed my neck'; and, while she struggles to break free, 'he then clasped me to his bosom with an ardour which terrified me' (92). Francis is completely transported by this contact with the celebrity body and, while absorbed in the thought that 'For a moment I clung to him – I loved for the first time,' she simultaneously realizes that the 'transcendent Being' (that is, the poet) 'had drawn me down upon his knee, his arms were round my waist, and I could not escape' (Lovell 93). Eventually, after many more such melodramatic antics, Francis manages to disengage herself and reach the door – her honor preserved by her own sensibility just in time.

This anecdote, one that is not unknown to Byron's biographers and scholars, paints a portrait of the author that is deeply indebted to the brand of eighteenth-century seducers of the Lovelace kind, a familiar model for the Byronic hero, combined with traits of the *maudit* Byronic aura and references to his sublime creative genius. But these precedents – all available to Francis from the scripts of amatory fiction, the Gothic, Byron's dark heroes and the budding Byronic myth – intersect with the image of a Byron bent on seeking physical contact through gestures ranging from the avuncular to the predatory. Importantly, this *vignette* also reveals the woman's desire to touch Byron, be electrified by his body and thus infused with his genius. This young woman's expectations transform the body of Byron into the body of the writer as point of access to the corpus of writing. More overtly than in Smith's anecdote, this micro-narrative points out the essential role played by the word as a mediating instrument to touch Byron.

In this perspective, Francis's account throws light on yet another contact with Byron's body – one established exclusively through the medium of memory, the imagination, and desire – recorded by Benjamin Disraeli who, as a young man, was an ardent worshipper of the Byron myth.[4] In a letter to his father from Geneva dated 1 August 1826, the young dandy and writer narrates how he went out to row on the lake with Maurice, Byron's one-time boatman, and the latter told him how, on the night of the famous storm described in *Childe Harold* III (13 June 1816), 'He told Lord Byron at first of the danger of such a night voyage, and the only answer which B. made was stripping quite naked and folding round him a great *robe de chambre*, so that in case of wreck he was ready prepared to swim immediately' (Lovell 183). An instance of the great man's aristocratic *insouciance*, indeed a kind of *sprezzatura* well attuned to Byron's persona, this anecdote presents strong voyeuristic overtones intensified by the sudden undressing of a celebrity body that, two years after the poet's death, was quickly assuming mythical status.

In depicting a 'heroic' body ready to plunge into the waters, a body that is suddenly and directly visible, without clothing but shrouded in the words of the boatman, Disraeli places his desire for Byron at center stage. In point of fact, underlying this anecdote is the notion that if one can see Byron's body – the next best thing to touching it as in the cases of Smith and Francis – one enjoys a more unmediated and effective access to the myth in its entirety. The boatman's narrative offers Disraeli the possibility of visualizing his own hero's body and lays claim to some 'direct' contact with its defiantly displayed flesh.

This intersection of language, skin, and desire finds a revealing echo in Roland Barthes's *Fragments of a Lover's Discourse* (1977), and particularly in the following remark: 'I am searching the other's body, as if I wanted to see what was inside it, as if the mechanical cause of my desire were in the adverse body' (71). With a further twist, this desire to search the other and adverse body translates into a linguistic operation, as Barthes observes that 'Language is a skin: I rub my language against the other. It is as if I had words instead of fingers, or fingers at the tip of my words. My language trembles with desire' (73). Language transmutes into touch and the conductor of desire, while the fragmented, disjointed body acts as an ineluctable magnet for language which, in turn, functions as a skin endowed with the sense of touch. Focusing on mechanisms of desire relevant to Disraeli's fantasy, Barthes's picture of an interconnection and a co-respondence between linguistic and bodily contacts goes some way toward explaining the young writer's use of language as a mediating instrument to gain access to the unavailable, seductive body of Byron.

Discussing Byron's fraught relationship with his physique, Roy Porter speaks of a fundamental 'irresolvability of the flesh' and thus stresses the deeply ambiguous status of the poet's body as a cultural construct (456). As a fragmented entity that escapes the constrictive boundary of a frame and invites, yet also rejects, scrutiny and contact, this body sets in train a variety of seductions and displacements of cultural norms. Evading classifications, Byron's physique and masculinity encode abnormality, eccentricity, and aberrance; by the same token, it becomes a body of promises tantalizingly (un)available to those who (seek to) touch it with their fingers or their language.

The persistent cultural relevance and mutations of this rebellious body may be assessed through its influence on the silver-fork and dandy novelists of the 1820s and 1830s, a generation of writers who looked back to Regency society as the original period of dandyism and a time when aristocratic codes of behavior were still relatively unchallenged. In this context, Byron represents a model of alternative masculinity which, in view of its opposition to moral, social, and economic norms, may warrant a type of aristocratic masculine self that successfully withstands the encroachment of bourgeois respectability and Evangelical morality.

The presence of Byron is manifest throughout the novelistic output of silver-fork authors. If it was a known fact that Byron practiced shooting at Manton's, the London gunmaker's and shooting gallery, Pelham does much the same in Edward Lytton Bulwer's eponymous novel of 1828 (cf. Adburgham 59). In addition, during his stay in Paris, Pelham reports that his new acquaintance, the fascinating Duchesse de Perpignan, 'could not be excessively enamoured of any thing but an oyster *pâté* and Lord Byron's Corsair' (Bulwer-Lytton 85). Later, three weeks before the publication of Disraeli's *Vivian Grey* (1826, 1827), the *New Monthly Magazine* ran a puff piece on the novel describing it as 'a sort of Don Juan in prose' (Stewart 113).[5] Again, Disraeli's *roman-à-clé Venetia* (1837) awards Byronic features to both the characters of Marmion Herbert (Shelley) and Plantagenet Cadurcis (Byron) (cf. Elfenbein 2000: 82–83). In a later example of the genre, Catherine Gore's *Cecil; or, The Adventures of a Coxcomb* (1841) – in Alison Adburgham's opinion 'the silver fork novel to end silver fork novels' (314) – the elderly protagonist remembers how, as a young man during the dissolute post-war Regency period, Byron himself introduced him to the decadent pleasures of Venice and Rome.[6]

As Disraeli's anecdote about Byron in Switzerland makes plain, the poet's body is a crucial icon for this generation of young dandy writers. As is well known, Disraeli's infatuation with Byron led him to imitate the older poet's poses, engage the latter's servant Tita and, in order to escape his creditors, live for a while with the Countess of Blessington and Count D'Orsay who had met Byron in Genoa in 1823 and had made much of the encounter (Ridley 25, 28, 46, 53). The young Disraeli also records a conversation with Tom Moore at one of John Murray's literary dinners in November 1822, when the Irish poet discussed Byron's ageing body, then moved on to consider his current way of dressing: 'He's very dandified, and yet not an English dandy. When I saw him he was dressed in a curious foreign cap, a frogged great coat, and had a gold chain round his neck... I asked him if he wore a glass and took it out, when I found fixed to it a set of trinkets. He had also another gold chain tight round his neck, something like a collar' (qtd. in Ridley 25). Moore's words, which Disraeli will rework in *Vivian Grey*, portray a Byronic body that is made 'other' by the poet's residence in Italy. Here, Byron the former associate of the London dandies and the friend of Beau Brummell is a mutated dandy, an outlandishly overdressed one.[7] On the whole, therefore, the young Disraeli's references to Byron's body disclose a deep-seated desire to 'touch' Byron, that is, to get in contact with the precedent, the model, the original. In addition, such references are invariably mediated by language, a Barthesian 'language as fingers' that seeks to bridge the temporal and cultural divide between novelist and poet, epigone, and celebrity.

Vivian Grey constantly rehearses the gesture of touching Byron's body through words. Indeed, critics have suggested that the Byronic 'touch' is also evident in the androgynous figure of the protagonist, since the homosocial intimations associated with Byron's body are essentially related to the fact that Disraeli ends both parts of the novel with an unmarried hero and thus contravenes the conventions of the silver-fork genre and of nineteenth-century fiction more generally.[8] Specifically, a variety of Byronic features emerge in the figure of Lord Alhambra, who in Book II, Chapter 12 appears at a fashionable gathering in Mameluke boots, is noted for his general 'ottomanization' and renowned for his exotic poetry. In addition, in Book IV, Chapter 1, Disraeli reproduces *verbatim* the conversation at John Murray's recorded above. Moore's words are given to Vivian Grey's friend Cleveland, who says: 'I met him in Italy. It was at Pisa, just before he left for Genoa. I was then very much struck at the alteration in his appearance.' This introduction is followed by a reprise of Moore's portrait of Byron's decaying body: 'his face was very much swollen, and he was getting fat. His hair was gray . . . His teeth were decaying; and he said, that if ever he came to England, it would be to consult Wayte about them' (Disraeli 144).[9] This picture of ill health recalls Polidori's definition of Byron's *corps délabré*, or 'body in ruins,' given in 1816. Yet, Disraeli's striking verbal portrait of Byron's decaying physique is also in conflict with the evident desire to establish contact with it, as language and the gaze cannot detach themselves from the magnetic body of Byron. Aptly, Cleveland sums up his picture of Byron by quoting from Goethe's *Götz von Berlichingen*: 'The sight of him touched my heart. It is a pleasure to have seen a great man' (145). Again, touching the celebrity body through words leaves a deep trace on, indeed 'touches,' the latter-day dandy in search of ancestors.

In *Pelham*, like *Vivian Grey* another of Henry Colburn's popular fashionable novels, Edward Lytton Bulwer (he changed his name to Bulwer-Lytton in 1844) produced his own riposte to the success of Disraeli's novel. Yet, if *Pelham* bears deep traces of *Vivian Grey*, it also takes the character of the dandy in new directions that fascinated Disraeli himself who, after reading the novel, wrote a letter to Bulwer and the two authors soon became friends (cf. Ridley 69–70). Taking the market for fashionable tales by storm, the novel imposed itself as the *vademecum* of dandyism, and was even held responsible for popularizing black and white evening dress for men. As with his forebear Vivian Grey, Pelham is a product of Regency society besotted with the figure of Byron, his myth and his poetry. Romantic icons are ubiquitous in the novel and the possibility of a contact with the Byronic and Byron-related body constantly haunts its narrative, especially through the figure of Reginald de Glanville, whose uncommon physical attractions repeatedly induce Pelham to linger over the contours of the attractive Byronic body through the medium of language – 'I had never seen so perfect a specimen of masculine beauty' (184).

Glanville is Byronic in very evidently mimetic ways, and Pelham's judgment on his physical attractions effectively re-echoes Coleridge's words on Byron's personal beauty. The actual contact with this surrogate Byronic body eventually takes place when Pelham and Glanville leave a fashionable *soiree*:

> I was descending the stairs in the last state of *ennui*,
> when Glanville laid his hand on my shoulder.
>
> 'Shall I take you home?' said he: 'my carriage has just drawn up'.
> I was too glad to answer in the affirmative. (187)

Here, it is the Byronic body that seeks and establishes contact with the younger dandy in a *vignette* endowed with strong homosocial suggestions. The protagonist courts the possibility of an encounter with the Byronic body, while also posing as the passive recipient of its electrifying touch.

A similar and even more revealing instance of physical contact with another stand-in for a previous generation of dandies takes place in Calais, where Pelham meets Mr Russelton, an *à clé* version of Beau Brummell, 'the contemporary and rival of Napoleon – the autocrat of the great world of fashion and cravats – the mighty genius before whom aristocracy hath been humbled and *ton* abashed – at whose nod the haughtiest *noblesse* of Europe had quailed – who had introduced, by a single example, starch into neck-cloths, and had fed the pampered appetites of his boot-tops on champagne' (125).[10] Both ironic and earnest, this description perfectly captures Brummell's achievement in overcoming class boundaries and being accepted into the aristocratic circles of the Regency era. What is even more interesting, however, is the expression of Pelham's veneration for this august predecessor: 'I recognised in him a congenial, though a superior spirit, and I bowed with a profundity of veneration, with which no other human being has ever inspired me' (125). With a tone often verging on the comical, Bulwer evokes the encounter as a minuet of homosocial conventions and fixes it as a pivotal moment in the development of his protagonist's dandy identity. Once the opening social niceties have been dealt with, physical contact may take place: 'Mr. Russelton seemed pleased with my evident respect, and returned my salutation with a mock dignity which enchanted me', and then 'He offered me his disengaged arm; I took it with transport' (125).

As Jerome McGann remarks, this encounter represents the climax in Pelham's preliminary phase of existential 'testing,' those early experiences and explorations that constitute the groundwork of his *Bildung*. During his meeting with Russelton, McGann adds, 'we realize that the dandy Pelham is not only the intellectual and moral superior of the king of fashionable life, but his equal in elegance and wit as well' (Bulwer-Lytton xvi). On closer inspection, however, there is more at stake in this bridging of the gap between two generations of dandies. The touch between Pelham and Russelton is electrifying for the young hero and laden with emotional intensity – 'transport' is indeed a clichéd term in sentimental fiction – and offers direct access to the past through the mediation of the dandy's body. Touching the latter – the body of an old associate of Byron and an 'aberrant' body of the Regency – is the next best thing to touching Byron for the younger dandy. Thus, that of Russelton/Brummell is yet another celebrity body through which the silver-fork epigone establishes a genealogy of dandyism that justifies his current non-normative mode of masculinity.

A further instance of touching a dandy body as a kind of retroactive contact with Byron was recorded in 1830 by the journalist (and future music critic and historian) Henry Fothergill Chorley in his impressions of Edward Lytton Bulwer as they left a party at Lady Blessington's: 'I had guessed pretty much of what I did see – an egotism – a vanity – *all* thrown up to the surface. Yes, he is a thoroughly *satin* character; but then it is the *richest* satin... There was something inconceivably strange to me in his dwelling, with a sort of hankering, upon the Count D'Orsay's physical advantages' (Chorley 194–95; vol.1). The sense of touch is evidently central to Chorley's description of Bulwer in terms of a costly and eminently sensual fabric, a description which links the journalist and the young dandy writer in a suggestively tactile bond. In addition, Chorley's words confirm Bulwer's emphatic and implicit desire to touch D'Orsay's celebrity body in order to become associated with it. And this desire is once more mediated through and realized in words – Bulwer's 'dwelling, with a sort of hankering tone.' Again, the body of the dandy and contact with it through this kind of 'language-turned-fingers' provides the material for the definition of an ambiguous masculine identity. And this identity finds its place in the present social and cultural dimension by repeatedly invoking contacts with the body of Byron and the bodies of Byron-related dandies such as Brummell and D'Orsay.

As Andrew Elfenbein observes, Byron provided Disraeli and Bulwer with 'a repertoire of poses for impersonating the success vital to the fashionable world that had so much power over literary and political careers in the 1820s and 1830s' (1995: 216). Nonetheless, despite their electrifying contacts with Byron's unruly body and its non-normative masculinity, the heroes of their silver-fork novels are usually brought back into line with acceptable social conventions. Indeed, with the partial exception of Vivian Grey who is unmarried at the conclusion of both parts of Disraeli's novel, the dandy heroes ultimately become responsible husbands and politicians, thus taking their appointed station in life and becoming respected members of their social *milieus*, both in private and in public.[11]

These narratives, and *Pelham* most visibly, invoke Byron's body as a prototype of aristocratic uniqueness and eccentricity against bourgeois norms; yet, as this body proves excessively troublesome, they limit its impact by eventually reintegrating the dandy into the sphere of accepted social conventions. If, on the one hand, silver-fork novels attest to a discourse of aristocratic critique and a subversion of bourgeois principles aimed at feeding the appetite of middle-class readers – as Elfenbein notes, 'the wives and daughters of wealthy northern manufacturers or London merchants and bankers' – on the other, they promote a critique of aristocratic norms and the celebration of a tamer, more conservative, family-centered and career-orientated world (2000: 79). Albeit keen to tap into the currents of desire released by Byron's body and its theatricalized masculinity, the bodies of silver-fork dandies are allowed to be rebellious within a rather limited narrative frame.

At length, Byron's masculinity as the epitome of the Regency revolt against bourgeois codes of regimented masculine identity, and the embodiment of a creative genius, a social lion, and cosmopolite, not to mention an exile, proves just slightly too rebellious to be perfectly comfortable. His body as an eccentric and destabilizing system of signs becomes productive of contradictory cultural meanings that defy the ideological structures of the silver-fork genre and its ultimate regimentation of the dandy, his lifestyle, and social sphere. If touching Byron's body generally implied a brush with the *maudit*, touching it in the silver-fork means both recapturing the value of that body and neutralizing its disturbing potential. Nonetheless, the lasting cultural impact of Byron's body lies in that, as Disraeli's and Bulwer's fictions testify, it remains tantalizingly unavailable to those who desire to touch it. For, even when silver-fork narratives create contact with it and then annul its fascination for the sake of a normalized and conventional masculinity, Byron's body maintains its elusive and enigmatic quality. With its differential value intact, it retains the power to inspire language to become tactile, 'language like fingers,' and produce endless re-tellings of the constantly deferred touch.

Notes

1. On eighteenth-century actors' bodies as non-normative, see Straub and on portraits of actors, see West.
2. For Byron and food, see Porter (447–61) and Jones (116–19).
3. On the concept of homosociality, see Sedgwick; and on eighteenth-century precedents of Regency homosocial codes, see Mulvey-Roberts. About homosexuality between the eighteenth and nineteenth centuries, see Crompton.
4. On the obsessive presence of Byron in Disraeli's life and early literary production, see Weintraub, Ridley, and Elfenbein (1995: 206–29).
5. For Disraeli's debt toward *Don Juan*, see Schwarz (20).

6. Elfenbein notes that silver-fork novels associate Byron 'with [the] glittering elegance and moral emptiness' of the Regency, but also tend to picture him as an incarnation of 'the inadequacy of Regency values and the need for their ultimate suppression by the supposedly better world of Victorian England' (2000: 78).
7. On Byron and Brummell, see Kelly (117–18, 306–07). About the later, more colorful attire of dandies, especially foreign ones such as Alfred d'Orsay, see Harvey (31).
8. His male protagonists are generally characterized by a 'homo-uncertainty' that goes hand in hand with their Byronic inspiration, as well as with the 'uncertainty' of Byron's sexuality. Cf. Kuhn (24).
9. This novel presents interesting connections with Oscar Wilde's *The Picture of Dorian Gray*. Indeed, Wilde was familiar with and appreciated Disraeli's fiction, and early reviewers of his novel were alert to the similarities between their productions. Thus, for instance, in his 1890 piece on *Dorian Gray* Julian Hawthorne remarked: 'The general aspect of the characters and the tenor of their conversation remind one a little of *Vivian Gray* [*sic*] and a little of *Pelham*' (80).
10. This description rehearses most of the clichés and myths associated with Brummell. On the comparison with Napoleon – once more, one mediated by the figure of Byron – see Kelly (211–12).
11. Interestingly, Vivian's fate is uncertain at the end of the volumes published in 1827: 'Here we leave Vivian! It was my wish to have detailed, in the present portion of this work, the singular adventures which befel him…' (528).

Works cited

Adburgham, Alison. *Silver-Fork Society: Fashionable Life and Literature from 1814 to 1840*. London: Constable, 1983.

Barthes, Roland. *A Lover's Discourse: Fragments*. Trans. Richard Howard. Harmondsworth: Penguin, 1990.

Bulwer-Lytton, Edward George. *Pelham or the Adventures of a Gentleman*. 1828. Ed. Jerome J. McGann. Lincoln: U of Nebraska P, 1972.

Chorley, Henry Fothergill. *Autobiography, Memoir, and Letters*. Comp. by Henry G. Lewett. London: Richard Bentley and Son, 1873.

Crompton, Louis. *Byron and Greek Love: Homophobia in 19th-century England*. Berkeley and Los Angeles: U of California P, 1985.

Davidoff, Leonore and Hall, Catherine. *Family Fortunes: Men and Women of the English Middle Class 1780–1850*. Rev. edn. London and New York: Routledge, 2002.

Disraeli, Benjamin. *Vivian Grey*. Ed. Michael Sanders. London: Pickering and Chatto, 2004.

Elfenbein, Andrew. *Byron and the Victorians*. Cambridge: Cambridge UP, 1995.

Elfenbein, Andrew. 'Silver-Fork Byron and the Image of Regency England.' *Byromania: Portraits of the Artist in Nineteenth- and Twentieth-Century Culture*. Ed. Frances Wilson. Basingstoke and New York: Palgrave, 2000. 77–92.

Harvey, John. *Men in Black*. London: Reaktion, 1995.

Hawthorne, Julian. 'Review of *The Picture of Dorian Gray*.' *Oscar Wilde: The Critical Heritage*. Ed. Karl Beckson. London: Routledge and Kegan Paul. 1970, 79–80.

Jones, Christine Kenyon. 'Fantasy and Transfiguration: Byron and his Portraits.' *Byromania: Portraits of the Artist in Nineteenth- and Twentieth-Century Culture*. Ed. Frances Wilson. Basingstoke and London: Macmillan, 1999. 109–37.

Kelly, Ian. *Beau Brummell: The Ultimate Dandy*. London: Hodder and Stoughton, 2005.

Kuhn, William M. 'Review of *The Early Novels of Benjamin Disraeli*.' *TLS 5304* 26 Nov. 2004: 24.

Lovell, Jr. Ernest J., ed. *His Very Self and Voice: Collected Conversations of Lord Byron*. New York: Macmillan, 1954.

Mulvey-Roberts, Marie. 'Pleasures Engendered by Gender: Homosociality and the Club.' *Pleasure in the Eighteenth Century*. Ed. Porter, Roy and Mulvey-Roberts, Marie. Basingstoke and London: Macmillan, 1996. 47–76.

Ogborn, Miles. 'Locating the Macaroni: Luxury, Sexuality and Vision in Vauxhall Gardens.' *Textual Practice* 11 (1997): 445–61.

Origo, Iris. 'The Innocent Miss Francis and the Truly Noble Lord Byron.' *Keats-Shelley Journal* 1 (1952): 1–10.

Paglia, Camille. *Sexual Personae: Art and Decadence from Nefertiti to Emily Dickinson*. Harmondsworth: Penguin, 1992.

Porter, Roy. *Flesh in the Age of Reason*. Preface by Simon Schama. London: Allen Lane, 2003.

Praz, Mario. *The House of Life*. 1958. Trans. Angus Davidson. London: Methuen, 1964.

Ridley, Jane. *The Young Disraeli*. London: Sinclair-Stevenson, 1995.

Russell, Rollo, ed. *Early Correspondence of Lord John Russell 1805–40*. London: T. Fisher Unwin, 1913.

Schwarz, Daniel R. *Disraeli's Fiction*. Basingstoke and London: Macmillan, 1979.

Sedgwick, Eve Kosofsky. *Between Men: English Literature and Male Homosocial Desire*. New York: Columbia University Press, 1985.

Stewart, R. W., ed. *Disraeli's Novels Reviewed, 1826–1968*. Metuchen: The Scarecrow Press, 1975.

Straub, Kristina. *Sexual Suspects: Eighteenth-Century Players and Sexual Ideology*. Princeton: Princeton UP, 1992.

Tosh, John. *Manliness and Masculinities in Nineteenth-Century Britain*. Harlow: Pearson Longman, 2005.

Trelawny, E. J. *The Last Days of Byron and Shelley, Being the Complete Text of Trelawny's 'Recollections.'* Ed. Morpurgo, J. E. Westminster: The Folio Society, 1952.

Weintraub, Stanley. *Disraeli: A Biography*. London: Hamish Hamilton, 1993.

West, Shearer. *The Image of the Actor: Verbal and Visual Representation in the Age of Garrick and Kemble*. London: Pinter, 1991.

Youngquist, Paul. *Monstrosities: Bodies and British Romanticism*. Minneapolis: U of Minnesota P, 2003.

2
Turning into Subjects: The Male Dancer in Romantic Ballet

Gerald Siegmund

Abstract

This essay starts from the observation that in the course of the nineteenth century male dancers were, at least in the Paris Opera, gradually removed from ballets. As becomes apparent in Théophile Gautier's writings on ballet, men had to define their physicality against both the old aristocracy and the laboring classes – and moreover against the bodies of women with their distinguishing feature, the womb, and the emotional and social codes in which the female body was conceptualized. Masculinity in nineteenth-century ballet is not an essence but relational. This chapter argues that, as in La Sylphide (1832), the male dancer is the representation of the male gaze lurking in the shadows and yet organizing the whole field of vision according to its principles. While the male body in the Romantic ballet phantasmatically becomes one with the detached gaze, it nonetheless remains an abstract entity that is inscribed in the geometrical ordering of the dancing bodies in space. In order to be the dominant structure, any claim to a positively defined masculine identity must be abandoned. With Vaslav Nijinsky's Le spectre de la rose *(1911) the male dancer enters the frame of representation, thus becoming a subject by being an object of female desire. Like the sylph he acquires a body only in the process of becoming a disembodied thing that is always on the verge of turning into an image. Thus, unlike the male gaze in* La Sylphide, *once the male dancer has entered the picture, his modern gaze is split. There is something he can no longer control from his newly gained position: the gaze of the other that gives him a body.*

Not all was fair in the fairy land of ballet in the Romantic period. This was even noticed by Théophile Gautier, the eminent French poet and, from 1838 to 1871, author of a whole range of reviews on ballet in general and Romantic ballet in particular. In fact, it was Gautier who helped to establish the new form on the stage of the Paris Opera in the first half of the nineteenth century – not least by writing the libretto for the genres most prominent example: *Giselle*.[1] In one of his reviews, he complains: 'Nothing is more distasteful than a man who shows his red neck, his big muscular arms, his legs with the calves of a parish beadle, and all his strong massive frame shaken by leaps and pirouettes' (Gautier 60, own translation).[2] In the context of Gautier's review of *La Volière*, staged at the Opera in 1838, his remark was intended as praise for the choreographer Mademoiselle Thérèse Elssler's wisdom *not* to have given any solo dances to the male dancers of the production. Gautier's comment sums up the general attitude toward male dancers on stage in the nineteenth century. From 1831 onward their function on stage was considerably reduced in scope. Gone were the days of male stars like Gaétan Vestris, Pierre and Maximilian Gardel, or Jean Dauberval who had dominated the French stage during the late eighteenth century with their virtuoso performances. The choreographers simply did not give male dancers anything to do any more. In the second half of the nineteenth century the male *corps de ballet* disappeared completely, and often male roles would be taken on by female dancers in drag.

Undoubtedly male dancing had fallen out of taste with the audience. Ballet had become the realm of women, of ethereal creatures like the *wilis*, the sylphs or the little *péris* who conquered the air with their daring arabesques that elongated the body into space and their dancing on *pointe* that tried to defy gravity and lift the body off the ground. And yet the stories that Romantic ballets like *La Sylphide* of 1832 or *Giselle* of 1841 told could not do without men. Men were a necessary ingredient of their tales of erotic desire, which could not function without them on the conventional heterosexual matrix that was and is the norm in narrative ballet. The desire they speak off consequently casts men and women alike in specific gender roles that play off one against the other.

In the present essay I would like to concentrate on the contradiction that men in classical ballet are needed on the one hand, but are relegated into the background on the other. First I would like to offer some explanations for the male dancers' fall from grace during the nineteenth century. What happened to masculinity or a specific kind of masculinity that turned it into something nobody was allowed to see anymore? I shall then continue with a brief discussion of the representation of masculinity in *La Sylphide*, the first full-length Romantic ballet. In my last section I will jump to the beginning of the twentieth century. In 1911, for the third season of the *Ballets Russes* in Monte Carlo and Paris, Mikhail Fokine choreographed a *pas de deux* for Vaslav Nijinsky and Tamara Karsavina: *Le spectre de la rose*. The ballet has become famous for Nijinsky's giant leap out of the window at the end of the short ten-minute piece. What has gone widely unnoticed so far is that Fokine's story is an exact reversal of the first scene of *La Sylphide*. What Fokine reverses is precisely the role of the male dancer, who now appears simultaneously as a ghost and as an object of desire. Before I explore this, however, let us return to Gautier's quotation above.

Masculinity under siege

The quotation is typical of Gautier. His critical eye is very quick in discerning individual body parts, literally cutting up the body in his verbal description of the dance. There is a parallel quotation describing a woman, Fanny Elssler:

> Mlle. Fanny Elssler is tall, supple, and well-formed, she has delicate wrists and slim ankles; her legs, elegant and well-turned, recall the slender but muscular legs of Diana; the virgin huntress ... they are not the calves of a parish beadle or of a jack of the clubs which arouse the enthusiasm of the old roué in the stalls and make them continuously polish the lenses of their Opéra-glasses. (Gautier 49, own translation)[3]

Whereas the female body parts are eagerly fetishized, the male ones are regarded with disgust.

Masculinity in the first quotation, and by implication also in the second, is threatened from two sides simultaneously. The unfortunate parish beadle whose calves cause so much horror to Gautier exudes a certain physicality that must be avoided at all costs. The emphasis on the physical presence of the male body is met with criticism because the male physique in general cannot be ideal. It is not the imperfections of one particular dancer that are criticized, but male dancing in general. With men, it seems, physicality is always associated with manual labor and the lower classes. The working-class bodies are bodies not properly cleansed or washed and therefore not properly civilized and kept under control. If the working classes are the enemy on the one side, the old aristocracy is the enemy on the other. The 'pirouettes and leaps' do not only speak of the body; they also put physical prowess on display. They are reminiscent of aristocratic values, such as ostentatious representation of power and pleasure hunting for the sake of itself, as personified in the old *roués* in the stalls, rather than for some higher, spiritual cause. The male dancer triggers a fear of the body and a fear of showing the body. It was the spectacle of a man, as Ramsay Burt has argued, that was forbidden in the new social climate of the early nineteenth century, which redefined masculinity in specific middle-class terms (Burt 10–30).

In the context of emerging middle-class values it is important to realize that the Paris Opera was governed by a middle-class board of directors after the bourgeois revolution of 1830 that overthrew Charles X and established a constitutional monarchy under Louis-Philippe. Susan Leigh Foster remarks on the link between politics, economy, and aesthetics:

> Once an institution that received funding in order to make manifest the aesthetic standards of an absolutist government, the Opéra transformed during the 1830s into an institution whose responsibilities divided between an authorizing state and a consuming public. (Foster 209)

What the consuming public wanted to manifest as its own aesthetic standard was a new relationship between men and women that redefined gender roles and the respective fields of activity deemed suitable or unsuitable for them.

Dancing was eminently suitable for women, so much so that ballet became an almost exclusive realm for the representation of women. How does that reflect back on the problem of masculinity? The second quotation by Gautier stresses the whiteness and the purity of Fanny Elssler's body by comparing her to the mythological figure of Diana, the virgin huntress. Even for Gautier's contemporaries this must have seemed a strange projection, given that the ballerina was sleeping her way around European high society at the time. By fetishizing the female, ballet strives toward pure spirituality, a spirituality that is made manifest in the *body* of the female dancer. All her body parts fit together perfectly because they are all in the right proportional relation to one another. This perfection can only be achieved by ballet training, which under the auspices of Charles Blasis and his writings from 1820 onward was undergoing a similarly gendered revolution at the time. Ballet training teaches you how to align your body parts. The perfect alignment then represents the perfect harmony, which in turn transcends the dancing body and turns its physicality into spirituality. When a woman dances, it is never her body that dances, but only her soul. In the Christian tradition that forbade dancing as part of the liturgy in the sixth century, the dancer overcomes the sinful flesh of the Original Sin by transforming the body into the soul worthy of seeing God.

From what I have just said it follows that not only are men too ugly to dance, they are too ugly because they are never pure and graceful enough. Their bodies can never acquire the spirituality of a female body. The body of the male dancer will, according to nineteenth-century gender ideology, forever remain a fallen body unfit for dancing in front of God. This is precisely why he needs women to perfect him and lift him up, while he must beware of her fallen nature at the same time. At the core of this argument there are, of course, more general implications concerning the social roles of men and women. According to Thomas Laqueur (1990), women in the nineteenth century were thought to be more animal in nature than men because of their monthly periods. They were, however, perfectly able to cope with those, which was taken as a proof of their moral superiority. Since this anatomical specificity of the female body, the womb, took up so much of her physical and mental energy, however, a woman was also deemed unfit for professional life. Her realm was, as the immortal poem by Coventry Patmore 'The Angel in the House' suggests, the house where she had to play the role of the angel.

To sum up: Romantic ballet with its ideal of weightlessness and a spirituality that strives to transcend the flesh seems to be particularly suited to represent this new idea of both the female and, in its absence, the male body. For the middle-class men of the first half of the nineteenth century, their bodies were becoming a problem. They had to define their physicality against both the old aristocracy and the laboring classes – and moreover against the bodies of women with their distinguishing feature, the womb, and the emotional and social codes in which the female body was conceptualized. Masculinity, at least when it is viewed from the perspective of nineteenth-century ballet, is not an essence but relational. It defines itself by what it is not, rather than gaining any positive discerning features. Masculinity, therefore, does not exist without the various enemies at the gates that form the focal points of its identity: the lower classes, the aristocracy and, most important, women. Underlying all this was, of course, the fear of becoming feminized by dancing and, what is more, to become feminized and, by implication, homosexual simply by watching men dance. This becomes apparent in another quote by Gautier. In his review of the opera *Zingaro* in 1840,

Gautier for the first time describes the dancer and choreographer Jules Perrot:[4]

> Perrot is not beautiful, he is even extremely ugly. Down to his waist he has the physique of a tenor, which says it all. But from there onward he is charming. It is hardly in keeping with modern morals to occupy oneself with the perfection of a man's shape; nonetheless, we cannot pass over Perrot's legs in silence. (Gautier 110, own translation)[5]

Further on in his review he remarks:

> These eulogies on our part are the less suspect since of all the things in the world we like men dancing the least. A male dancer executing anything else than *pas de caractère* or pantomime has always appeared to us to be some kind of monster (Gautier 111, own translation)[6]

Although Gautier does not like to watch men dancing, he likes Perrot. But in order to be allowed to enjoy watching him dance, he invokes as an excuse the well-known fact that he abhors the spectacle of men on stage. So much so, in fact, that he is even tempted to support the popular opinion that (with the exception of Mabille and Petipa) men ought to be entirely excluded from the *corps de ballet* in favor of an all-female *corps*. The underlying suspicion is, of course, the threat of becoming or appearing to be a homosexual. Therefore, male dancers are not entirely human. They are monstrous beings. They defy the rules and regulations of proper physical shape and behavior. Their bodies are not normal, because their monstrosity infringes on the bodies of other men who come into contact with them, even if it is only by sight.

The argument can, of course, be extended to contact with women. Spending too much time in the company of women may turn men into effeminate creatures. It is not fit for a man to have a graceful body like a ballerina because then he loses his manhood, which is, however, based on nothing substantial. Because men can never overcome their natural drives, their realm is the homosocial milieu of sports, in which men, among themselves, apparently are under less pressure to be perfect, graceful, beautiful, and pure. There, as Eve Kosofsky Sedgwick has shown, the thin line between the homosocial and the homoerotic has already been transgressed (Sedgwick 1).

La Sylphide

In his review of the rerun of *La Sylphide* in 1838, the ballet that started the Romantic craze in 1832, Gautier praised the piece as a great achievement, not least because, as we might have guessed by now, 'it does not contain any dances for men, which is very agreeable' (Gautier 79, own translation).[7] This is, of course, slightly exaggerated, for there is at least one man central to the story who is also involved in some dancing. The story is set in rural Scotland and the narrative revolves around James, a young peasant, who wakes up on his wedding day to find an enchanting sylph lying at his feet. Intrigued, he follows her around the room, but she teases him and escapes through the chimney. Needless to say, he cannot get her out of his head and in the end his fiancée marries his friend Gurn, while James is left with nothing. Women are the touchstone of his masculinity. They are his doing and undoing.

La Sylphide tells the story of a man led to a tragic end by two women. The women in the ballet come in three categories. First there are the mother and the fiancée, Effie, about whom nothing much can be said. They are as nondescript as they are part of everyday mundane reality. The second and third categories of women are associated with nature, night, and life on the emotional and spiritual edge. They therefore stand in binary opposition to the norms and values of society, and the regularity of daytime and life in the village. All these women taken together represent the above-mentioned dichotomy of angel and whore, of women as animal spirits that are nonetheless morally superior to men. The sylphs in this set-up are not living human beings, but belong to the realm of fantasy. There are good elemental spirits. On the other end of the spectrum of undomesticated femininity is the cunning witch Madge and her infernal fellow witches. They gather at the start of Act 2 to create a magic shawl designed to turn James's fairy lover into a human being and thus kill her. James is in love with a dangerous ideal that can never become reality, because once the sylph is reduced from ideal spiritualized femininity to non-spiritual corporeality, she dies. James's masculine identity is striving to manifest itself in the destructive force-field between these complementary yet also mutually exclusive conceptions of femininity: Effie, whom he is supposed to marry, the spurious ideal of the sylph and the scheming witch Madge who claims she will help him to fulfil his dream but only ends up disillusioning him. That it is reality that presents the greatest disillusionment is both a typically Romantic feature of the ballet and already a hint at the proto-modernism of the piece.

The male dancing in Act 1 is largely pantomime, propelling the narrative forward, or ornamental as part of group sequences. There is only a short solo dance for James in Act 1, designed to attract the initial attention of the sylph. The only extended spectacle of men dancing together is tellingly provided by a lively *pas de deux* between the young Scotsmen in Act 1. Characteristically, it emphasizes physical prowess rather than spiritualized transcendence.

In all other configurations, the male dancer supports the woman in her aerial exploits by resting firmly on the ground, his torso stiff on the hips. There are three ways of doing this: both of his hands hold the torso of his partner, he holds the hands of the woman or he puts his lower arm around her waist. All this is to be done from behind, so that all attention is focused on the female dancer. The male dancer in *La Sylphide* is thus literally eclipsed by his female partner. He is there to support her presentation to the audience, who receive her from his hands. While she is the center of attention, he is the magician who pulls the strings. Although he is the protagonist of the story, he is completely upstaged in the actual dancing.

But pulling him out of the action without really doing so is a telling strategy. On the one hand, he is physically removed, thus countering the male anxiety of being turned into a spectacle. On the other hand, he does remain involved despite the reduction of his physical presence. He remains on stage as an explicit gaze directed toward the female body, which thereby becomes an object of its *scopophilia*, its voyeuristic desire.[8] He can do so by becoming a kind of blurred presence in the picture, a blind spot that establishes the possibility of a perspective without which the picture could not exist in the first place. The male dancer is the representation of the male gaze lurking in the shadows and yet organizing the whole field of vision according to its principles. While the male body in the Romantic ballet phantasmatically becomes one with the detached gaze, it nonetheless remains an abstract entity that is inscribed in the geometrical ordering of the dancing bodies in space. In order to be the dominant structure, any claim to a positively defined masculine identity must be abandoned.

In Lacanian terms we could say that (the gaze of) the male dancer is the locus in the picture. There the picture as a symbolic structure gains an insight into its own mechanisms. It is the spot where the symbolic order of the theater may gain a glimpse of itself as the place where bodies are presented to be seen. Ever since the advent of the Italian perspectival constructions of the Renaissance stages all over Europe, this exposure of bodies has taken place in a theater separating the stage from the auditorium by a proscenium arch that functions as a picture frame. The bodies on stage are framed; the stage designers and choreographers paint, as Jean-Georges Noverre would have it, pictures with the bodies of their dancers (Noverre 9). The visual apparatus of the architectural theater space directs the gaze toward the stage where bodies appear framed and thereby cut off from living and lived exchanges of gazes. This gaze embodied in the architecture is the symbolic order of the visual regime of the theater. The symbolic gaze is therefore independent of any actual gaze any member of the audience could throw toward the stage. It is then doubled by the male dancer on stage exposing or giving his female partner to the audiences to see. The male dancer's body therefore functions as a frame within the frame.

This also means that both male dancer and his voyeuristic yet controlling gaze lack ontological grounding, since both are relational rather than foundational. The male dancer is a stand-in, a literal emptiness, which in order to come into being needs an imaginary and necessarily distorted reflection of itself in the image of an Other, here of the women. Since he is both inside the picture, as part of the performance and the images it creates, and outside the picture as an extension of the male viewer's gaze, he occupies an impossible position. We can imagine this paradoxical position of masculinity in Romantic ballet as the equivalent of a fold in an image or a blind spot within representation. The body becomes the locus of this constitutive contradiction.

As a consequence, men are not subjects in Romantic ballet, because being a subject implies that there is a distance between you and the symbolic, a gap between yourself as a signifying subject and your desire, which remains outside your signifying powers. The body is both the locus of desire and offers the means of signification. Yet the two cannot be brought together. In order to become subjects (and acquire a body that means more than sheer physicality), the men would logically have to be subjected to the gaze, too. They would have to become objects first. Yet this is not yet possible, since the gaze inscribed in the ballet (and in its projected audience) is itself a male gaze whose heterosexual orientation precludes any desiring glances at the men in the piece. This changes at the beginning of the twentieth century. Evidence of this shift can be found in Vaslav Nijinsky in *Le Spectre de la rose*.

Le spectre de la rose

The plot of *La Sylphide* is based on a story by Charles Nodier from the year 1822, 'Trilby, or the Imp of Argyll.' In this short story, a male spirit seduces the wife of a fisherman. Adolphe Nourrit, in his adaptation of the story for the libretto of *La Sylphide*, reversed the roles and made the woman the object of desire. Mikhail Fokine's version from 1911, *Le spectre de la rose*, reversed the roles again. The ballet was inspired by two lines from a poem called 'Le spectre de la rose' by Théophile Gautier, 'Je suis le spectre d'une rose/Que tu portais hier au bal,' thereby acknowledging the Romantic spirit on which the ballet is based (Buckle 127).

In Fokine's ballet, a beautiful young woman returns from a ball to her room and dreams of love. She clutches a rose to her bosom that, depending on the version you like to believe, she has either plucked from a vase or from her dress.[9] She sinks into an armchair placed in front of an open window and falls asleep. It is the same set-up as in *La Sylphide*. The spirit of the rose appears in the window, framed like an image, his body elongated into phallic shape by a series of *pas de bourrées sur place*. With a giant leap the spirit jumps into the room, dances around the armchair, touches the woman gently, and asks her to dance. During the ten-minute waltz that follows, the longest dance ever conceived at the time, she averts her gaze, never once looking at him, thus implying that she is sleepwalking and dreaming the entire incident. After the dance, he leads her back to her chair and leaps out of the window while she awakes.

Fokine and Nijinsky, who is said to have altered most of Fokine's hastily arranged and insipid steps according to his taste, clearly focus on the male dancer as an object of desire. Now it is not the woman who is a disembodied spirit, but the man. He is the fantasy of the girl, who, by implication, is now granted a desire and a body of her own that is more than a symbol of the spiritual. From the very beginning it is clear that the rose the girl is holding functions as a fetish for the absent male dancer. When Nijinsky appears, he is dressed as a rose. He, too, is presented as a fetish, a stand-in for female desire both onstage and in the audience. Nijinsky's two jumps that frame the ballet can be read as leaps of desire into representation and out again. They weave the obscene, that which lies behind the scenes, *ob-scena*, into the scene and seen, the forbidden into the permitted.

With his low-cut rose costume that accentuated his naked shoulders, his behind and the genital area, Nijinsky clearly made a spectacle of himself. In order for the male body to be allowed to present itself as an obscene object of desire, various precautions had to be taken. First, Nijinsky would not have been allowed to dance what he danced had he portrayed a man. The role of the spirit appearing in a dream was considered to be a ruse to prevent this interpretation and to protect

Nijinsky from accusations of unmanliness. Secondly, in a similar vein, his dancing had to be strong, muscular, and vigorous in order to present it as an athletic and therefore manly activity. Despite the fact that he was the object of desire and the women the desiring subject, Nijinsky still led and guided her protectively around the stage. He ruled the stage, circling it, cutting across its diagonals with jumps, pirouettes, and *entrechats*.

What does this analysis mean for the above argument about the gaze? The male dancer, Nijinsky, presents himself as a sexualized object of desire in *Le spectre de la rose* while at the same time retaining control over the woman. Yet, for the first time in a hundred years, he actually appears in the picture of somebody else's desire (a female character introduced in the story as a woman and not as a fantasy) and thus gains an imaginary body that permits him to be an object and a subject simultaneously. The woman on stage may not be allowed to look at him the way James could look at the sylph in *La Sylphide*; but the audience certainly could. In the case of the *Ballets Russes* there consisted a large proportion of women and gay men (Burt 76). Like the sylph 80 years before, the male dancer is now subject and object at the same time, actively guiding the phantasm and being exposed to it. Neither women nor men are victims in this game. It has repeatedly been pointed out that, although the sylph is a disembodied male projection hovering on the brink of death and relegated to the realm of fantasy, it is precisely her status as a fantasy that serves as a protection for her to express her desire and actively advance it (cf. Garafola 1997). The same holds true for Nijinsky. He is made surreal in order to be allowed to promote himself as an object of desire. His androgynous look, which defied easy categorization of any particular desire, surely helped to attract the gazes of both women and homosexual men.

Like the sylph, he acquires a body only in the process of becoming a disembodied thing that is always on the verge of turning into an image. He only acquires an image of and a body for himself by means of being looked at. Thus, unlike the male gaze in *La Sylphide*, once the male dancer has entered the picture, his modern gaze is split. There is something he can no longer control from his newly gained position: the gaze of the other giving him a body. The gap that opens up between looking and being looked at is the gap the subject emerges from. It is also the position inside which a modern notion of masculinity finds its unstable locus.

As an outlook I would suggest that what we are experiencing in our societies today is the continuation of this 'subjectivation' of men. Men are becoming subjects of and subjected to the rules they have made for a long time. Once, as an image and representation of God and his all-seeing eye or I, they were identical with the structure they had imposed on society and culture. Now, like Nijinsky's spirit, they are (also) part of the structure. The gap that opens up in this complicated set-up is the space where identities are now negotiated – and not simply posited any longer. Like women long before them, men now have to meet the demands of others. This, in turn, leads to a splendid spectralization of masculinity in many realms of modern life.

Notes

1. The year of the birth of the Romantic period in ballet is now generally considered to be 1831. The Paris Opera production of Giacomo Meyerbeer's opera *Robert le diable* featured a nocturnal scene where deceased nuns rose from their graves to dance in the cloister.
2. 'rien n'est plus abominable qu'un homme qui montre son cou rouge, ses grands bras musculeux, ses jambes aux mollets de suisse de paroisse; et toutes sa lourde charpente virile ébranlée par les sauts et les pirouettes.'
3. 'Mlle Fanny Elsler est grande, supple et bien decouplée; elle a les poignets minces et les chevilles fines; ses jambes d'un tour elegant et pur, rappellent la sveltesse vigoureuse de jambes de Diance, la chasseresse virginale...ce ne sont pas ces mollets de suisse de paroisse ou de valet de trèfle qui exitent l'admiration des vieillards anacréontiques de l'orchestre et leur font récurer activement les verres de leur telescope.'
4. 'I am grateful to Ramsay Burt for drawing my attention to this passage.'
5. 'Perrot n'est pas beau, il est meme extrèmement laid; jusqu'à la ceinture il a un physique de tenor, c'est tout dire, mais à partir de là il est charmant. Il n'est guerre dans les moeurs modernes de s'occuper de la perfection des formes d'un home; cependant nous ne pouvons passer sous silence les jambes de Perrot.'
6. 'Ces éloges sont d'autant moins suspects de notre part que nous n'aimons pas le moins du monde la danse des homes: un danseur exècutant autrechose que des pas de caractère ou de la pantomime nous a toujours paru une espèce de monstre....'
7. 'il n'y a presque pas de dances d'hommes, ce qui est un grand agreement.'
8. Susan Leigh Foster speaks of the male dancer as 'a prosthetic extension of the viewer's gaze,' but she does not pursue this line of thought (220).
9. The description of the ballet in Buckle (127) differs from the re-staging of the ballet in the video by the Paris Opera.

Works cited

Buckle, Richard. *Nijinsky*. Herford: Busse Seewald, 1987.

Burt, Ramsay. 'The Male Dancer.' *Bodies, Spectacle, Sexualities*. London: Routledge, 1995.

Foster, Susan Leigh. 'Choreography & Narrative.' *Ballet's Staging of Story and Desire*. Bloomington/Indianapolis: Indiana U P, 1996.

Garafola, Lynn, ed. 'Rethinking the Sylph.' *New Perspectives on Romantic Ballet*. Middletown: Wesleyan U P, 1997.

Gautier, Théophile. *Écrits sur la danse*. Paris: Actes Sud, 1995.

Laqueur, Thomas. *Making Sex: Bodies and Gender from the Greeks to Freud*. Cambridge. Mass: Harvard UP, 1990.

Noverre, Jean-Georges. *Letters on Dancing and Ballets*. Trans. Cyril W. Beaumont. Alton: Dance Books, 2004.

Sedgwick, Eve Kosofsky. 'Between Men.' *English Literature and Male Homosocial Desire*. New York: Columbia U P, 1985.

3
Industrial Heroes: Elizabeth Gaskell and Charlotte Brontë's Constructions of the Masculine

Jessica L. Malay

Abstract

The associations of masculinity with industrialization are explored in Charlotte Brontë's Shirley *and Elizabeth Gaskell's* North and South *in the present essay. It demonstrates that control of the self and of others is essential to the Victorian understanding of masculinity and class structure. Yet the frequent use of violence in connection with this (self-)control simultaneously props up and undermines mastery – by making it morally and socially dubious. Masculinity is therefore most unstable when it is most physically present. Hard and unyielding men, furthermore, need tempering by feminine influence to turn pure mercantile thinking into socially acceptable care. This also turns them from newfangled captains of industry into the recognizable equivalent of the traditional paternalistic squire. Masculinity in Victorian industrial novels is therefore a project, a goal, a case of redemption of a degraded and contradictory structure rather than the simple assertion of an unproblematic norm.*

Charlotte Brontë's *Shirley* and Elizabeth Gaskell's *North and South* are primarily concerned with the social implications of an increasingly industrialized North in the middle of the nineteenth century. However, within the framework of these novels emerges a dialogue concerning representations of the 'industrial male.' Within each novel a variety of masculinities are performed through which the novelists attempt to define and identify a masculinity suited to emerging social realities. In order to accomplish this, the novels present performances of several possible 'masculinities' reflecting what Herbert Sussman terms the 'instability of manhood' arising from rapid societal changes in the late eighteenth and nineteenth centuries (10). The performances of manhood constructed and explored by Gaskell and Brontë reflect their own perceptions, prejudices, and concerns and should not be taken to represent actual men engaged in the industrial project. Indeed, an anonymous reviewer in the *Leader* criticized Gaskell's *North and South* complaining that she failed in this novel to 'throw a light on the vexed questions of masters and men.' This review goes on to criticize her for idealizing her hero Thornton, stating contemptuously 'Your grand ideal manufacturer...is utterly false.' Indeed, this anonymous critic condemned the dialogue of Gaskell and Brontë on questions of industrial manhood quite roundly by insisting that 'if there are two classes that should give trade and masters-and-men questions a wide berth, those classes are clergymen and women' (Easson 336). By this measure both women were doubly damned, one being the daughter of a clergyman, and the other the wife. And yet, this critic, could he have looked beyond the idealized portrait of Gaskell's great Captain of Industry, Thornton, would have realized that his own sense of the actual character of the industrial male, both master and man, shares much with Gaskell's as well as Brontë's explorations of the industrial male depicted in the novels. These novels wrestle with shared contemporary estimations of the characteristics possessed by men engaged in industry in the North of England, while attempting to construct an ideal performance of industrial masculinity.

The discussion of 'industrial manhood' in the novels of Brontë and Gaskell can be usefully interrogated first through the anxieties surrounding male violence and its correlative, male control. Sussman notes that for Browning and Carlyle the 'central issue within masculinity is the management of male energy' (73). Thus, according to Carlyle the challenge to industrial men was to restrain the 'potentially destructive energy in one's self and in others' (31), or as the anonymous *Leader* reviewer instructs, the problems connected to unrestrained male energy could only be managed by 'sound, strong, masculine, practical insight' (Easson 336). The underlying tension grounding both Brontë's and Gaskell's novels is the ability of the masters to control themselves and thus exert authority over their violent and unruly men. Both were keen to identify the social forces, along with what was increasingly being seen as a masculinity of interiority, through which violence could be controlled, if not completely eradicated (Tosh 231). This was a concern both Gaskell and Brontë shared with many reformers. The Manchester visitor Alexis De Tocqueville described Manchester as a place where 'Humanity attains its most...brutish...and man is turned back into a

savage' (108). This general condemnation had its roots in many incidents reported in the newspapers of the time. The *Manchester Guardian*
from 5 March, 1851 reported on a disturbing incident where children
were being trained to fight:

> Mr. Edward Bennett Solicitor... observed a great crowd of probably
> 200 persons and went to the spot to ascertain what had happened.
> There he found [two men] encouraging a young child, some six or
> seven years of age, to buffet his opponent, until the blood streamed
> from the faces of both.
>
> ('Training Children' 5)

Mr Bennett attempted to stop the contest, but was assaulted himself
by one of the men who boasted that, since the child was his brother,
he had the right to train him as he liked. Another incident, this time
from a first-person account, also serves as an illustration of the sort of
violence that so frightened the middle classes. Here a youth remembers
outside a public house, 'two men stripped to their naked waists who
began to fight and they fought until their naked bodies were stream-
ing with blood. I thought, when I am a man I would like to be able to
fight like that' (Davies 353). In another act of violence, reported by the
Manchester Guardian in 1851, a 'labouring man' attacked first a bystander
and then a policeman with lethal results. On the 29 May during the
arrest of 'a man named Bailey' a 'mob' came to Bailey's rescue. At this
point, the arresting officer, a John Allsop, called for the help of a fellow
officer, Enoch Masters, age 21. Allsop described what followed during
the inquiry into Masters's death:

> The mob assailed them with stones and every species of missile.
> A labouring man knocked down the deceased [Masters] with a blow
> on his mouth. A body of police arrived at this juncture, when
> the deceased [Masters] and witness [Allsop] attempted to arrest the
> labouring man, whom the mob defended, [the labouring man] strik-
> ing the deceased [Masters] a blow on the back of his neck which felled
> him to the ground and quite stunned him.

Masters later died as a result of the blows which exacerbated a pre-
existing condition ('Alleged Murder' 7). Again the disturbing combination of a crowd or mob and the unruly and dangerous 'labouring
man' brought home the point to Victorian newspaper readers that
the world of the working-class male was a place where violence was

commonplace, spontaneous, and sometimes lethal. The individuals in these incidents certainly portray the most salient models of violent behavior in society: the unruly 'labouring man' who actively seeks violent encounters, or at least is quick to respond according to what was assumed to be his violent nature. But what the *Manchester Guardian* readers would find even more disturbing was the level of violence reported from working men described as 'steady, well-conducted men' as in the case of John Wilkinson and his cousin, John Batterley, 'a goods porter on the Manchester, Sheffield, and Lincolnshire Railway.' One evening, Wilkinson was apparently engaged in violence against his wife who, according to her testimony, made her 'escape from the alleged violence of her husband...through a window.' After Mrs Wilkinson's escape, Batterley, who was lodging with the Wilkinsons, admitted to murdering Mr Wilkinson. The article provides a vivid and visceral description of the murder scene for the benefit of the readers: 'The body of deceased was then found in a prostate position, in a pool of blood; the furniture, walls, and ceilings were besprinkled with it. Wounds were found on the head and throat, and a pocket-knife was discovered under a chair at the feet of the deceased' ('Murder in Sheffield' 5). That even 'well-conducted' men could erupt into such violence would have been intensely disturbing.

Of course, individual incidents such as these, while certainly dramatic, were not in and of themselves particularly threatening. However, it was the fear that the 'hands' or working men of Manchester and other industrial cities would join together, unleashing a maelstrom of carnage that caused the most anxiety. It is this anxiety that Brontë capitalizes on in *Shirley*, written in 1848. The novel is set during the Luddite disturbances of 1811 and 1812 finally ending with the arrest and execution of 14 men. In the intervening months, properties were raided and textile mills were attacked by large bodies of men who destroyed machinery and other property. A handbill printed by the rioters and thrown into a Huddersfield mill makes clear their purpose:

> We give Notice when the Shers is all broken the Spinners shall be next if they be not taken down Bickerman taylor mill...has had his garded but we will pull all down som night and kill him that Nave and Roag.
>
> (qtd. in Briggs 76)

In one of the most violent attacks, Rawfolds Mill in Liversedge near Leeds was set upon by a large crowd of armed men. The owner, William

Cartwright, put up a spirited defence which resulted in the death of two of the rioters and many others being injured. With the failure of this enterprise the Luddites, led by George Mellor, decided a change in strategy was needed. Instead of targeting the mills, they decided to target the mill owners themselves. William Horsfall, the owner of Otti-well's Mill in Marsden, became a victim of this new policy. He was shot dead as he traveled home from Huddersfield on the night of 28 April 1812.

Records of these threats and the violence of the rioters can be found in a collection of documents once owned by the Radcliffe family (cf. Briggs 73–74).[1] Joseph Radcliffe, a Huddersfield Magistrate, petitioned the government for troops and was thus a target of Luddite wrath. Radcliffe was threatened in a letter from a 'Friend' who warned, 'there is dreadful preparation going forward for great destruction... you must side with the Luds if you Live' (Radcliffe 28). Another letter threatens the lives of two mill owners, Thomas Atkinson and William Horsfall: 'Mr. Th. Atkinson & Mr. Wm. Horsfall, who will soon be number'd with the dead' (38). The threat was made good in the case of Horsfall, as noted above. The real anxiety caused by the Luddite threat is recorded in a letter from 3 May 1812 written by Joseph Scott to Radcliffe contend-ing that the reinforcements of the militia had ceased to be a 'sufficient defence' and that 'law abiding citizens' would willingly surrender their firearms to a militia in order to protect them from Luddite violence (59). While on 7 May 1812 the Secretary of State, Robert Jenkinson, 2nd Earl of Liverpool, wrote to Radcliffe that extraordinary mea-sures were needed 'to prevent the farther spreading of this destructive flame' (57).

The raw violence of these months remained a salient reminder of the potential for large-scale destruction from groups of laboring men. The fear aroused during the Luddite riots continued to profoundly influ-ence attitudes toward unrestrained groups of hands whose working relationship with the masters improved very little in the interven-ing decades. Brontë's novel makes it quite clear that memories of the Luddite riots were still vivid more than 30 years later. Elizabeth Gaskell in her *Life of Charlotte Brontë* claimed that the recollections of Miss Wooler, whose school at Roe Head Brontë attended as student and later as a teacher, was only a few miles from the gathering place of the Luddites on the night they attacked Rawfolds Mill. Patrick Brontë would also have recollections of the event which both inspired and colored the depiction of the mob attack on Robert Moore's mill in *Shirley*, as Patrick Brontë was then living at Hartshead, just three miles from the attacked mill.[2] Gaskell's vivid account of the incident garnered from Patrick Brontë's recollections is recorded in her biography of Brontë (1966):

> Mr. Cartwright was a very remarkable man, having, as I have been told, some foreign blood in him, the traces of which were very apparent in his tall figure, dark eyes and complexion, and singular, though gentlemanly bearing. At any rate, he had been much abroad, and spoke French well, of itself a suspicious circumstance to the bigoted nationality of those days. Altogether he was an unpopular man, even before he took the last step of employing shears, instead of hands, to dress his wool. He was quite aware of his unpopularity, and of the probable consequences. He had his mill prepared for an assault. He took up his lodgings in it; and the doors were strongly barricaded at night...On the night of Saturday the 11th of April, 1812, the assault was made. Some hundreds of starving cloth-dressers assembled in the very field near Kirklees that sloped down from the house which Miss Wooler afterwards inhabited, and were armed by their leaders with pistols, hatchets, and bludgeons, many of which had been extorted by the nightly bands that prowled about the country...The silent sullen multitude marched in the dead of that spring night to Rawfolds, and giving tongue with a great shout, roused Mr. Cartwright up to the knowledge that the long-expected attack was come. He was within walls, it is true; but against the fury of hundreds he had only four of his own workmen and five soldiers to assist him...His dwelling was near the factory. Some of the rioters vowed that, if he did not give in, they would leave this, and go to his house, and murder his wife and children. (85–86)

Gaskell's novelistic tendency may have dramatized the event which had already received a similar treatment in its rendition in *Shirley*, yet it does reveal Gaskell's attitude toward the potential for indiscriminate violence among laboring men. Their base passions, she believed, had the potential to make them bay for the blood of even women and children. Gaskell's belief in the working class' propensity for brutality is perhaps most emblematically portrayed in this passage by her description of their choice of weapons, 'pistols, hatchets, and bludgeons,' all of which are representations of personal, not martial violence.[3] The words used to describe the men, 'silent,' 'sullen,' 'rioters,' are enough to deface what appears to be a weak early attempt at assigning motives – the description of the men as starving. Also, it is clear that Gaskell here infers that immoral leaders incited the working men, already prone to violent outbursts, to their murderous ends.

Gaskell, of course, had already portrayed these elements of the mob in her novel *North and South* set in the 1850s and begun during the Preston Strike of 1853–1854. While in this instance the Preston strike was peaceable, fears born of the violence of earlier labor actions created tension. In *North and South* Gaskell vividly represents this fear of the threatening violence of the mob when she describes the riot during the strike which is a central feature of the novel: '[Margaret] looked round and heard the first long far-off roll of the tempest; – saw the first slow-surging wave of the dark crowd come, with its threatening crest, tumble over, and retreat, at the far end of the street' (170). A few pages later she describes the rioters as 'mere boys; cruel and thoughtless, – cruel because they were thoughtless; some were men, gaunt as wolves, and mad for prey' (176).

Yet this propensity for masculine violence was not seen in the Victorian period as a particular quality of the working men only, but of masculinity itself. Herbert Sussman contends that '[f]or nineteenth-century men, manhood was conceived as an unstable equilibrium of barely controlled energy that may collapse back into the inchoate flood or fire that limns the innate energy of maleness' (13). This instability of male energy was described by John Sterling in a letter to Thomas Carlyle as 'the Titanic heaving of mountain on mountain; the storm-like rushing over land and sea' full of 'confusions' (qtd. in Sussman 25). The antidote to this instability Sterling identifies as 'duty' which promises to still the metaphorically tumultuous waves of uncontrolled male energy into 'an icy fixedness and grandeur which will reduce all confusions to shape and clearness' (25). Sterling's comments represent a definition of manliness 'as a form of sanity characterized by restraint of the potentially destructive energy in one self and in others' (31). It was just such men of steely control that John James Tayler, minister at the Unitarian Mosley Street Chapel in Manchester 1821–1853, described as 'stewards' of the 'destabilized social environment' of the industrial urban North (qtd. in Wach 426).[4]

It is also this ideal man of 'icy fixedness' that features so saliently in the characters of Brontë's Robert Gérard Moore and Gaskell's John Thornton. Moore is described as a resolute, acute, and hard man by his neighbor Yorke (51), while Thornton is described as a man who 'has been called upon to exercise judgment and self-control' from a very early age (165). Both masters are presented at the beginning of the novel as a type of industrial male Catherine Barnes Stevenson describes as '[h]ard, unyielding, sharp-tongued to their "hands"...inflexible in the face of their workers' demands, and...determined to employ outside force when enraged hands attack their mills' (11). However, neither Brontë nor Gaskell was simply content with this portrayal of the necessarily harsh master in the face of intransigent and often violent hands. Instead both women were interested in taking such men as their starting point and molding from these caricatures ideal stewards, who with the help of their female guides, place stewardship ahead of purely mercantile gain.

Both women recognized that in the unstable and rapidly changing environment of nineteenth-century industrial England, manhood was not fixed, but as Sussman notes, 'an ongoing process, a plot, a narrative over time' (45–46), what Foucault describes as 'the construction of male consciousness' which is 'specific to individuals and to groups or classes of men at any given historical moment' (qtd. in Sussman 11). As her starting point in this construction, each woman took into consideration the generally held view of this class of men that tended on the unflattering. For example, Charles Dickens in a letter to Gaskell complained of the 'monstrous claims at domination made by a certain class of manufacturers, and the extent to which the way is made easy for working men to slide down into discontent under such hands' leading often to violence among the working classes (21 April 1854). Again the anonymous critic in the *Leader* complained that many of these men 'with capacities little removed above that of swine...make fortunes in trade' by endeavoring to keep 'the operative's wages as low as they can' (Easson 334).

Thornton and Moore are never quite so negatively portrayed. However, in each novel their narrative of masculinity begins by exposing the characteristics each man has in common with contemporary portrayals of manufacturers. Most especially at the beginning of the novels money is the fundamental motivator for both men.

However, if money is the motivator for Thornton and Moore, a secure masculine identity is the goal. As Stevenson points out at the beginning of the novel, both men are shown to have entered industry in order to 'redeem a "compromised masculinity".' Each does this by transforming himself into a self-made man, 'thrifty, self-denying, entrepreneurial, and contemptuous of others who haven't made it' (11). Thus, Brontë describes Moore as a man who does not 'deliberate much as to whether his advance was or was not prejudicial to others...he never asked himself where those to whom he no longer paid weekly wages found daily bread; and in this negligence he only resembled thousands besides' (29). Gaskell's Thornton is no more solicitous at the opening of the novel when he is shown arguing with Margaret Hale: 'We won't advance a penny. We tell them we may have to lower wages; but can't afford to raise...We, the owners of capital have a right to choose what we will do with it' (117). And indeed, if both women were simply interested in acknowledging generally accepted definitions of manhood, they could easily have stopped within these first few pages, for 'bourgeois industrial manhood' often defined 'manliness as success within the male sphere, the new arena of commerce and technology' (Sussman 4). In this view, 'The masculine persona...was organized around a man's determination and skill in manipulating the economic environment' (81).

Yet, neither woman was prepared to stop there, indeed their very purpose, taking their lead and perhaps some inspiration from Thomas Carlyle, was to model Thornton and Moore, at least in part, on Carlyle's 'Captain of Industry,' a phrase he coined in *Past and Present*, published in 1843 (cf. Dixon 198). In this work Carlyle insisted that these men, these 'warriors,' would transform the working classes by 'just subordination; noble loyalty in return for noble guidance' calming the violence and chaos of the hands into 'a firm regimented mass, with real captains over them' (247). For, as Carlyle (1888) explains, '[i]n all European countries, especially in England, Captains of Industry' are needed, otherwise '[c]aptainless, uncommanded, these wretched outcast "soldiers" since they cannot starve, must needs become banditti, street-barricaders, – destroyers of every government that *cannot* put them under captains, and send them upon enterprises, and in short render life human to them' (31).

It is in this sense that we can begin to approach Gaskell and Brontë's construction of characters who could perform the role of the ideal industrial male. Certainly both go to some length to establish the warrior credentials of their Captains of Industry. In the opening pages of *Shirley*, Moore guards his mill with his musket. Shirley Kildare teasingly refers to Moore as 'Captain Gérard Moore, who trusts much to the prowess of his own right arm,' (248) and later he does indeed become a 'Captain' leading the defence of his mill with military fortitude: 'Moore had expected this attack for days...he had fortified and garrisoned his mill...he was a cool, brave man: He stood to the defence with unflinching firmness; those who were with him caught his spirit, and copied his demeanour' (345). Thornton is also figured as a captain in the first half of *North and South*. He is open in his admiration of Oliver Cromwell stating that 'Cromwell would have made a capital mill-owner' (123), he continues, 'I maintain that despotism is the best kind of government for them, so that in the hours in which I come in contact with them I must necessarily be an autocrat' (120). Mr Hale also recognizes Thornton's martial qualities during a discussion of the type of man needed in the industrial North, 'we have many among us who...could spring into the breach and carry on the war' (81). Thornton's comment here elicits a quotation from Hale, 'I've a hundred captains in England' (82). Thornton is also shown facing a crowd, attempting with the sheer strength of his presence, to quell the disturbance. And yet while each author initially presents her industrial male as possessing warrior qualities, these are shown to be insufficient for the task of quelling the violent male energy both within themselves and certainly within the men they oppose. Instead, Gaskell and Brontë place these moments of martial activity within their narrative of industrial masculinity, using them to inform the development of each character rather than define him.

In this again, they share perhaps more of their definition of desirable masculine qualities with Carlyle than might initially be expected. In a letter to James Garth Marshall in 1841, Carlyle discusses his ideal industrial male with less vitriol than in previous essays. He contends: 'we must have industrial barons, of a quite new suitable sort; workers loyally related to their taskmasters, related in God...not related in Mammon alone! This will be the real aristocracy' (De Ryals and Fielding 317). Carlyle's use of the words 'related' and 'aristocracy' are telling. Ideas of relational reciprocity point to stewardship rather than military authoritarianism. By terming this relationship 'aristocratic' Carlyle inserts the idealized concept of an unspecified past, where a strict hierarchical structure maintained an orderly society through reciprocity. He returns to this theme in *Past and Present*: 'To be a noble Master, among noble Workers, will again be the first ambition with some few.' Should such men proliferate, Carlyle asserts, 'By degrees, we shall again have a society with something of Heroism in it, something of Heaven's Blessing on it; we shall have...instead of mammon-Feudalism...noble just Industrialism' (243). Both Brontë and Gaskell rely heavily on this model of the noble steward master in the construction of their ideal industrial male. Moreover, as this narrative of masculinity develops in both novels, it becomes apparent that the women deeply distrust contemporary constructs of the industrial manhood, characterized by what Carlyle (1921) terms the 'Profit-and-Loss Philosophy and Life-theory, which we hear jangled on all hands of us' (169). In their novels, both women, like Carlyle and many others, come to question the fundamental effect of the industrial environment on men of all classes.

In this we see Gaskell and Brontë finally reject a masculinity that Øystein Gullvåg Holter describes as the 'masculinate' power of the industrial nineteenth century with its emphasis on entrepreneurial success, for a '[p]aternalistic or paternate' masculinity rooted in an idealized representation of prior ages (19). This paternate masculinity was, according to David Leverenz, 'grounded in property ownership, ideas of decorum and commitment to institutionalized social structures' (74). Both Carlyle in *Past and Present* and Ruskin in 'The Nature of Gothic' promoted a hierarchical social arrangement imagined from the past which they believed could remedy present social problems (cf. Zlotnick 283). Gaskell and Brontë engage with this idea in their construction of Thornton and Moore, who guided by their female mentors and their own experiences, develop beyond 'Captains of Industry' instead becoming Lords of a beneficent social hierarchy.

To effect this change Gaskell and Brontë draw upon plot devices often borrowed from novels of sentiment. Both Moore and Thornton have to suffer physical and mental affliction in order to emerge transformed from a self-involved industrialist into an aristocrat of industry. In eighteenth- and nineteenth-century novels of sentimentality the hero has to undergo the 'refiguration of the male body' in order for a 'desirable romantic hero' who is 'real, strong and great' to emerge (Wagner 477). Brontë conducts this 'refiguration of the male body' through actual bodily illness. Moore, in his role as a Captain of Industry, hunts down those involved in the attack of his mill, wreaking all the legal vengeance allowed him before he is shot down both figuratively and literally. First he is humiliated in his proposal to Shirley Kildare, who ascertains rightly the mercenary motivations of her suitor:

'I did respect – I did admire – I did like you,' she said: 'yes – as much as if you were my brother; and you – you want to make a speculation of me. You would immolate me to that mill – your Moloch!' (535)[5]

This outburst certainly bears traces of attitudes expressed by Dickens, Carlyle and the *Leader* critic, who attributed to the industrial male a single-mindedness capable of destroying others to achieve his own ends. This assessment is brutally laid before Moore in a powerful scene of verbal chastisement. Shortly after Moore recounts, and thus acknowledges and internalizes, this humiliation to the Yorkshire gentleman Mr Yorke, Moore is shot by the crazed weaver, Michael Hartley. This physical wound following on from his moral humiliation results in Moore being, by his own description, 'unmanned' (584). Moore describes his humiliations, wounds, and long convalescence as a journey where he was transformed from 'a proud, angry, disappointed man'

into a man who fears nothing and who has emerged from 'slavish ter-
rors.' He ends his narrative of transformation by turning to his sister
and telling her 'I am pleased to come home.' He, whom the narrator
informs us, had never called that place home before (596). Moore's reformation into a patrinate male is completed through his marriage to
Caroline Helstone, whose guidance, her role as 'David' to his 'Solomon,'
presages the transformation of Hollow's Mills from a strictly industrial
or hollow enterprise to a hierarchical social community where Moore
figures as a patrinate male, a Lord of his industrial manor which Brontë
describes as

> a manufacturer's day-dreams embodied in substantial stone and
> brick [where the] unemployed shall come to Hollow's mill from far
> and near; and Joe Scott [Moore's foreman] shall give them work,
> and Louis Moore [Moore's brother] shall let them a tenement, and
> Mrs. Gill [Shirley's Cook] shall mete them a portion till the first pay-
> day ... Such a Sunday school as you will have, Cary! Such collections
> as you will get! Such a day-school as you and Shirley, and Miss Ainley,
> will have to manage between you! The mill shall find salaries for a
> master and mistress, and the Squire or the Clothier shall give them a
> treat once a quarter. (644)

This passage conflates the terms Squire and Clothier and in so doing
echoes Carlyle's call for the 'Industrial Baron' of the new aristocracy.
It is a patrinate scene of reciprocity where the 'Squire' provides for the
physical and spiritual needs of the worker, thus avoiding periods of starvation and want which reduce men to uncontrollable violence, making
them easy prey for the leaders of anarchy. It is an idealized portrait set
in the future tense and one which, as will be discussed, Brontë found
ultimately unconvincing.

The reformation of Gaskell's John Thornton is more complex, though
it also requires that he go on a journey of pain and humiliation in
order to emerge refigured as a more robust industrial or patrinate male.
His journey also begins with the humiliations of rejected suits: one he
receives and one he metes out. His proposal to Margaret Hale receives
a forthright rejection. She rebukes his advances in the harshest terms:
'Your way of speaking shocks me. It is blasphemous ... your whole manner offends me' (193). As with Shirley, the words Margaret uses to answer
Thornton's proposal are designed to inflict immense emotional pain. Yet
the pain this rejection awakens in him results in a nascent sympathy
for the suffering of others. This development of Thornton's character is

shown as a result of his own brusque rejection of the laboring Higgins's request for work:

> I say No! to your question. I'll not give you work. I won't say, I don't believe your pretext for coming and asking for work; I know nothing about it. It may be true, or it may not. It's a very unlikely story, at any rate. Let me pass. I'll not give you work. There's your answer. (313)

Like Margaret Hale's response to him, Thornton deals out verbal blow after verbal blow with little compassion for the recipient of his disdain.

Yet, after this incident, Thornton, newly educated through his own humiliation, quickly regrets the harsh behavior he would have been proud of at the beginning of the novel. Instead, while he 'dreaded exposure of his tenderness, he was equally desirous that all men should recognize his justice; and he felt that he had been unjust' (317). This incident moves Thornton to seek out Higgins and thus go into the homes of his workers. This allows him to develop a greater appreciation of his responsibility and moves him to reject entrepreneurial success characterized by financial gain, as he shows soon after in his declaration to Mr Bell that 'money is not what I strive for' (325). Later in this conversation Mr Bell playfully accuses Thornton of wishing to set up again an independent kingdom like the Anglo-Saxon kingdoms of the Heptarchy (326), inferring again this idealized patrinate past. Certainly, Thornton's desires are more modest. Rather than building a kingdom, he instead installs a kitchen for his hands, fulfilling a role where he describes himself as 'something like a steward' (353), inferring that he has begun to recognize his moral responsibility to not only lead, but also to protect his hands. When he loses his fortune and sees the imminent loss of the mill, he refuses to take into partnership the disreputable son of a fellow industrialist, Mr Hamper, and instead seeks employment in a position where he can continue to develop a relationship with the workers beyond what he describes as the 'cash nexus' (420). At this point in the novel, Thornton's understanding of the relationship between master and man is completely transformed:

> He had never recognized how much and how deep was the interest he had grown of late to feel in his position as manufacturer, simply because it led him into such close contact, and gave him the opportunity of so much power, among a race of people strange, shrewd, ignorant; but above all, full of character and strong human feeling. (409)

While, unlike Moore, Thornton's journey does not 'unman' him, it certainly un'masters' him for a time (420). Yet this refiguration of his masculinity results in a character which Gaskell described as 'consistent with itself, and large and strong and tender, and yet a master' (*Letters* 321).[6]

This conceit of the refiguration of the male character through physical and mental affliction borrowed from eighteenth- and nineteenth-century novels of sentimentality certainly serves to allow the development of the Captain of Industry into the Lord of an industrial manor. However, this transformation is not as uncomplicated as it initially appears, revealing a pervasive anxiety about the industrial project in the minds of Gaskell and Brontë. Instead, these authors look to the patrinate past as the preferred model of masculinity, where their heroes are placed at the top of a hierarchical yet reciprocal community that encompasses both work and home life. Both writers also subtly distance their ideal manufacture and his community from the taint which comes from other industrial projects present on the peripheries of their narratives. They do this by not only presenting their manufacturers as morally superior to the other manufacturers that people their novel, but also through the very cash that finances their concerns. In the end, the social hierarchies of Moore's Hollow's Mill and Thornton's Marlborough Mill are not financed through the sort of immoral speculation practiced by Thornton's brother-in-law, Mr Watson, who, as Gaskell makes clear, 'increased his own fortune, but risked the pain of many' (416). Instead Thornton's and Moore's money is channelled through the pre-industrial economic model of tenant rents paid to resident lords of the manor. The 'old' money that saves and funds Thornton's new social project comes from the Oxford gentleman Mr Bell, through Margaret Hale, whom Thornton ultimately succeeds in marrying. Moore's enterprise is saved through loans from Shirley Keeldar, heir and titular lord of the manor of Fieldhead. It is also interesting to note that the conduit through which financial stability is achieved is female, doubly separating the cash flow from the contemned 'cash-nexus' of exploitation and speculation that was seen to contaminate many industrial projects.[7]

This returns us to the complaints of the anonymous *Leader* critic, who certainly realized that, at least in the case of Gaskell's *North and South*, Thornton had much more in common with the Merchant of Venice than the Merchant of Manchester. This critic emphatically announces that the fundamental principal of the industrial male is 'making money' and refuses to accept Gaskell's creation of an aristocrat of industry, when all he sees around him are weak and greedy men (Easson 334).

Indeed, in many ways Gaskell seems to implicitly agree with the *Leader* critic. Throughout *North and South* these weak and greedy men, who fuel the violence and lack the means to restrain the energies of their men, abound to the point of overwhelming the object lesson of Thornton's conversion. Gaskell peoples her novel with mill owners like Slickson and Hamper who are too timid or self-interested to use the legal means to constrain their hands to work, while both Slickson and another mill-owner, Henderson, use the strike as a 'dodge' to further their business interests. Thornton's brother-in-law, Mr Watson, as noted earlier, speculates with his creditor's money, while Mr Hamper's son is described as 'half-educated as regarded information, and wholly uneducated as regarded any other responsibility than that of getting money, and brutalized by both as to his pleasures and his pains' (415).

Gaskell has been here before, when in *Mary Barton* the philandering son of the wealthy mill owner Mr Carson attempts to seduce the working-class girl Mary, while mocking the desperate requests of the working men for money to feed their families. Charlotte Brontë is no more charitable about Moore's fellow mill owners in *Shirley*. They are depicted as cowardly and weak, and through this weakness are responsible for the violence of the men they refuse to restrain. Moore comments on Mr Sykes reaction to the sacking of Sykes's mill complaining: 'he gave up as tamely as a rabbit under the jaws of a ferret' (24). Brontë is no kinder to Sykes's son than Gaskell is to Hamper's or Carson's – the next generation of 'industrial male' is shown to be even more degenerate than their fathers.

However, Gaskell, while acknowledging such men exist, appears to be more sympathetic to the industrial male, who, leavened with learning and a connection to the patrinate past, can become Carlyle's 'real aristocracy.' In a letter written in 1850, before the composition of *North and South*, Gaskell wrote, 'I can not imagine a nobler scope for a thoughtful energetic man, desirous of doing good to his kind, than that presented to his powers as the master of a factory' (*Letters* 119). In her novel, the purely patrinate men do not possess the 'iron' of the manufacturers. Mr Bell is content to hide away in an anachronistic Oxford, while Mr Hale is shown throughout the novel to be a good, but weak and inward looking man. Her portrayal of Thornton is particular, but in this portrayal is a confidence that a type of masculinity could emerge which fosters men who are 'large and strong and tender, and yet a master.'

Brontë's work shows that, despite the many similarities of thought expressed in both works, she fundamentally rejects the idea that the emerging industrial masculinity could be transformed into something less brutish and more sublime. This attitude is subtly present in *Shirley*, advertised by the disdain with which Moore's fellow manufacturers are described, and the profoundly ambivalent passage at the end of the novel:

> I suppose Robert Moore's prophecies were, partially, at least, fulfilled. The other day I passed up the Hollow, which tradition says was once green, and lone, and wild; and there I saw the manufacturer's day-dreams embodied in substantial stone and brick and ashes – the cinder-black highway, the cottages, and the cottage gardens; there I saw a mighty mill, and a chimney, ambitious as the tower of Babel. (645)

Here Brontë undermines any belief in the ability of an aristocrat of industry to develop out of the industrial project. Moore's dream is only partially fulfilled and set against the unpleasant back drop of 'cinder-black highways' and Babel's tower, representative of man's pride and arrogance. These images are contrasted with memories of an idealized past when there was neither 'mill, nor cot, nor hall' but a 'bonnie-spot – full of oak trees and nut trees' (646). The criticism of man's destruction of nature is thinly veiled. Instead, it is the patrinate males in the novel, especially Hiram Yorke, whom the reader is led to admire the most. While Brontë goes to some lengths to criticize Yorke for his failings, these are followed by such glowing descriptions of his virtues that the effect is to leave the reader with a positive attitude of this gentleman, which does not diminish throughout the novel. Yorke, like his counterpart Hunsden Yorke Hunsden in *The Professor*, comes from the Yorkshire yeoman or gentry stock who may participate in manufacturing, but are not defined, or more to the point, defiled by it. Shirley Keeldar herself is often described in patrinate terms as the lord of the manor where she makes a point of playing her role of beneficent aristocrat. The Moores themselves are termed 'gentlemen' despite the pecuniary circumstances that require they earn a living, one through manufacturing and the other as a private tutor. Indeed, it can even be argued that Robert Moore's refiguration from a wolfish industrialist into a patrinate male is more a reversion than a transformation.

Yet it is in Charlotte Brontë's novel *The Professor* that perhaps the most critical commentary on the effects of industrialism upon the development of masculinity can be seen. This novel, written initially before *Jane Eyre*, but subsequently revised and published after the writing of *Shirley*, features the frightening spectacle of Edward Crimsworth who calls learning 'useless trash' (19) and is initially described as an 'animal' (17). When his young brother William arrives in the manufacturing district Bigben Close in order to train to be a manufacturer under the tutelage of Edward, he is greeted with disdain and arrogance. Edward violently rejects his own patrinate lineage on his mother's side, even going so far as to sell his mother's portrait. His relationship with his genteel brother William, raised by the funds of aristocratic maternal uncles, ends in a violent quarrel. Edward also quarrels with Hunsden Yorke Hunsden – a man who shares several similarities with Hiram Yorke in *Shirley*, as noted above, and whose home at the end of the novel was most likely based on Oakwell Hall, the same model Brontë used for Shirley Keeldar's home Fieldhead. Thus, Edward Crimsworth is portrayed as having severed all connections with a patrinate masculinity. Brontë characterizes him as a man depraved and distorted by industry. He is described as a 'proud, harsh master' (21), having 'no god but mammon' (23), who tries to whip not only his horse, a beast controlled only by brutish force, but also his own brother. Early in the novel, Hunsden predicts that Edward will prove a tyrant even to his wife, and this is later proven to be the case when his wife is reported to have left Edward because 'he used her ill' (199).

Ironically this 'monster' (42) does not suffer in the least for his behavior but makes so much money through speculation that even his wife returns to him. Brontë also distances her yeoman and gentleman Hunsden from manufacturing, having him give up his manufacturing concerns and eventually settling into the estate he inherits through his father, Hunsden Wood with its large woodland and timber 'old and of huge growth' (248). Both Hunsden and William Crimsworth become the models of masculinity Brontë finds most attractive. Her removal of both men from the industrial environment reveals her cynicism about the possibility of a 'new aristocracy' born of a socially aware industrial male, and echoes Carlyle's own lament (1829):

> It has come to pass, that in the management of external things we excel all other ages; while in whatever respects the pure moral nature, in true dignity of soul and character, we are perhaps inferior to most civilised ages … only the material, the immediately practical … is important to us. (452–53)

Gaskell and Brontë in their novels *North and South* and *Shirley* set out to explore performances of masculinity in the emerging industrial environment. The anxiety caused by what appeared to be an unrestrained male energy that could spontaneously or surreptitiously erupt into violence, encouraged these women to explore the ways in which the narrative of masculinity itself could be rewritten. The *Leader* critic denounces their intervention in the 'vexed questions... of masters and men' (Easson 333), and yet ultimately this critic missed the point. Neither Gaskell nor Brontë were intent on simply describing the industrial male as he existed, but rather to participate in the developing narrative of industrial masculinity. Their ambiguities and their particularities, rather than serving to fix this narrative in a particular moment, intervene momentarily, allowing the imagined performance of a 'grand ideal manufacturer' (334) amidst the extremes of wealth and poverty, violence and control that characterized much of the discourse surrounding masculinity within the Victorian industrial project.

Notes

1. The Radcliffe papers referred to by Briggs are now stored at the West Yorkshire Records Office, Leeds UK, in the Radcliffe of Rudding Park Papers, WYL5018.
2. Charlotte Brontë is also recorded as sending to Leeds for copies of the *Leeds Mercury* of 1812, 1813, and 1814, though Asa Briggs (84) contends this documentary evidence was for the purpose of informing and confirming her own knowledge of the Luddite disturbances.
3. The Radcliffe papers reveal that the rioters actually broke into homes to secure firearms, not the more savage instruments Gaskell lists.
4. Tayler was well known to Elizabeth Gaskell, as her husband William Gaskell was also a Unitarian ministers in Manchester and thus had many dealings with Tayler.
5. Moloch was, according to biblical tradition, a Phoenician deity to whom human sacrifices were supposedly made.
6. The letter which contains this quotation was written to Lea Hurst, October 1854.
7. Carlyle, in *Past and Present*, rages against the sole pursuit of financial gain asserting: 'Supply-and-demand is not the one Law of Nature; Cash-payment is not the sole nexus of man with man' (168).

Works cited:

'Alleged Murder of a Police Constable.' *Manchester Guardian* 25 June 1851: 7.

Briggs, Asa. 'Private and Social Themes in *Shirley*.' 1958. *The Collected Essays of Asa Briggs. Vol. 2: Image, Problems, Standpoints, Forecasts*. Urbana: U of Illinois P, 1985. 68–88.

Brontë, Charlotte. *Shirley*. 1849. Eds. Herbert Rosengarten and Margaret Smith. Oxford: Oxford UP, 1998.

——. *The Professor*. 1857. London: Penguin, 1995.

Carlyle, Thomas. *Past and Present*. 1843. Ed. Hughes A.M.D. Oxford: Claredon, 1921.
——. 'The Present Time.' 1850. *Latter-Day Pamphlets*. London: Chapman and Hall, 1888. 3–46.
——. 'Signs of the Times.' *Edinburgh Review* 49.98 (1829): 438–59.
Davies, Andrew. 'Youth Gangs, Masculinity and Violence in Late Victorian Manchester and Salford.' *Journal of Social History* 32.2 (Winter 1998): 349–69.
De Ryals, Clyde L. and Kenneth Fielding, eds. *Collected Letters of Thomas and Jane Welsh Carlyle*. Durham: Duke U P, 1985.
De Tocqueville, Alexis. *Journeys to England and Ireland*. Trans. George Lawrence. Ed. Mayer J. P. New Haven: Yale U P, 1958.
Dickens, Charles. *Letters of Charles Dickens*. Ed. Graham Storey, Kathleen Tillotson, et al. Oxford: Claredon, 1993.
Dixon, Robert. 'Captains of Industry.' *Journal of Economic Perspectives* 16.2 (2002): 197–206.
Easson, Angus. ed. *Elizabeth Gaskell: The Critical Heritage*. London: Routledge, 1991.
Gaskell, Elizabeth. *North and South*. 1854–1855. Ed. Patricia Ingram. London: Penguin, 1995.
——. *Life of Charlotte Brontë*. 1857. Oxford: Oxford U P, 1966.
——. *Letters*. Ed. Chapple J. A. V. and Pollard A. Manchester: Manchester U P, 1966.
Holter, Øystein Gullvåg. 'Social Theories for Research Men and Masculinities: Direct Gender Hierarchy and Structural Inequality.' *Handbook of Studies on Men and Masculinities*. Ed. Michael S. Kimmel, Jeff Hearn and Connell R.W. London: Sage Publications, 2005. 15–34.
Leverenz, David. *Manhood and the American Renaissance*. Ithaca: Cornell U P, 1989.
Luddite Papers of Sir Joseph Radcliffe, Bart., c 1812–1813, MM [microfilm] 53, U of Huddersfield, Huddersfield, West Yorkshire UK, April 1812: 126/28.
'Murder in Sheffield.' *Manchester Guardian* 10 May 1851: 5.
Stevenson, Catherine Barnes. 'Romance and the Self-Mad Man: Gaskell Rewrites Brontë.' *Victorian Newsletter* 91 (1997): 10–16.
Sussman, Herbert. *Victorian Masculinities: Manhood and Masculine Poetics in Early Victorian Literature and Art*. Cambridge: Cambridge U P, 1995.
Tosh, John. 'The Old Adam and the New Man: Emerging Themes in the History of English Masculinities, 1750–1850.' *English Masculinities 1660–1800*. Ed. Tim Hitchcock and Michèle Cohen. London: Longman, 1999. 217–38.
'Training Children to Fight.' *Manchester Guardian* 5 Mar. 1851: 5.
Wach, Howard M. ' "A Still Small Voice" from the Pulpit: Religion and the Creation of Social Morality in Manchester, 1820–1850.' *Journal of Modern History* 63.3 (1991): 425–45.
Wagner, Tamara. ' "Overpowering Vitality": Nostalgia and Men of Sensibility in the Fiction of Wilkie Collins.' *MLQ* 63.4 (2002): 471–500.
Zlotnick, Susan. 'Luddism, Medievalism and Women's History in Shirley: Charlotte Brontë's Revisionist Tactics.' *Novel: A Forum on Fiction* 24.3 (1991): 282–95.

4

Low on Assurance: The Troubled Masculinity of Victorian Comedy

Rainer Emig

Abstract

Victorianism is often associated with a monolithic patriarchy that oppresses women but gives men almost unlimited power. The present essay challenges this assumption and shows that men and the masculinity that is supposed to shape them are also subjected to the great ideologies that rule the nineteenth century: class and wealth. Men have price-tags on the marriage market, rise or fall according to their changing market value and are ultimately as hollow as that which supposedly gives them an identity: money. The discussed plays by the successful Victorian playwrights Dion Boucicault and Edward Bulwer-Lytton display this nexus between their supposed display of the gentleman ideal and their underlying materialism even in their titles. In them, assurances and money come to dominate any trace of what might be a 'natural,' 'normal,' or 'ideal' masculinity and replace it by a vacuous and often comical, though nonetheless seductive, blueprint.

> What can be funnier than other people's anguish? Why do we enjoy Mr Maddison Morton's farces, and laugh till the tears run down our cheeks at the comedian who enacts them? Because there is scarcely a farce upon the British stage which is not, from the rising to the dropping of the curtain, a record of human anguish and undeserved misery.
>
> (Braddon 67)

What is the anguish and misery that Mary Elizabeth Braddon, the author of several successful sensation novels, talks about? Comedies and farces generally deal with personal relationships, and the tradition of the happy end usually involves an engagement or marriage. Braddon, who explores deception, adultery, and bigamy in her novels, clearly mistrusts the veneer of harmony of the conclusion of such plays and probes into their so-called complications. There, the present essay will argue, contradictions emerge that challenge not only the notion of comedy as an ultimately conciliatory genre, but also the gender ideals commonly associated with the Victorian period in which Braddon wrote. Masculinity will be shown to have an uneasy position in Victorian comedies. The so-called 'gentleman ideal,' a concept that emerged with the Restoration (and has its roots in the Renaissance courtier and idealized Medieval notions of chivalry) is usually taken to define Victorian middle- and upper-class men, even by Victorian writers and critics themselves (cf. Waters). Yet, in the subsequent analysis of two comedies from the nineteenth century, idealized Victorian masculinity will rather emerge as an area of tension, scepticism – and even ridicule – long before the so-called Decadents of the late nineteenth century tried to expose its contradictions and hypocrisy.

Victorianism has become largely, and somewhat uncritically, associated with the idea of patriarchy. Popularized in feminist discourse by Kate Millett in the late 1960s, its basic definition runs: 'the principles of patriarchy appear to be twofold: male shall dominate female, elder male shall dominate younger' (Millett 25). Even there, the second half of the definition is often conveniently ignored and its message, that men are both perpetrators and subjects of patriarchy, forgotten. Millett herself indeed continues with yet another qualification: 'However, just as with any human institution, there is frequently a distance between the real and the ideal; contradictions and exceptions do exist within the system' (25). What do these look like and how do they make masculinity appear on the stage in the context of the popular comedies of the Victorian era? Much work has been done on masculinity in Victorian prose and poetry. Yet surprisingly enough, the genre in which the performativity of gender, described by Judith Butler as the incessant compulsory repetition of an elusive ideal, literally meets performance, has been rather neglected, perhaps because there things appear to be too obvious.[1] This perception is wrong.

Let us start to unravel the issue from its end, the happy end of the comedy that kick-started the career of the most successful Victorian playwright, Dion Boucicault (ca. 1820–1890), *London Assurance* of 1841.[2] Its final lines belong to the aristocratic father who has just had to acknowledge that not he but his son will marry the rich heiress, an outcome that already reverses the traditional power structures of patriarchy. He admonishes his offspring as follows:

> And these are the deeds which attest your title to the name of gentleman? I perceive that you have caught the infection of the present age. Charles, permit me, as your father, and you, sir, as his friend, to correct you on one point. Barefaced assurance is the vulgar substitute for gentlemanly ease; and there are many who, by aping the *vices* of the great, imagine that they elevate themselves to the rank of those whose faults alone they copy. No, sir. The title of gentleman is the only one *out* of any monarch's gift, yet within the reach of every peasant. It should be engrossed by *Truth*, stamped with *Honour*, sealed with *good-feeling*, signed *Man* and enrolled in every true young English heart.
>
> (Boucicault 143)

Sir Harcourt Courtly, who is 63 but passes himself off as 40, is a bad loser. But his statements also completely contradict his own behavior, since he had himself intended to marry the 18-year-old Grace Harkaway merely for her land and wealth:

> SIR HARCOURT Having been, as you know, on the Continent for the last seven years, I have not had the opportunity of paying my *devoirs*. Our connection and betrothal was a very extraordinary one. Her father's estates were contiguous to mine. Being a penurious, miserly, ugly old scoundrel, he made a market of my indiscretion and supplied my extravagance with large sums of money on mortgages, his great desire being to unite the two properties. About seven years ago he died, leaving Grace, a girl, to the guardianship of her uncle, with this will: If on attaining the age of nineteen she would consent to marry me, I should receive those deeds and all his property as her dowry; if she refused to comply with this condition, they should revert to my heir presumptive or apparent. She consents.
> COOL: Who would not?
> SIR HARCOURT: I consent to receive her fifteen thousand pounds a year.
> COOL: (*aside*) Who would not? (85)

His argument also takes the patriarchal transfer of privilege from father to son out of his own hands by declaring gentlemanliness a virtue rather than a privilege, the traditional emulation of paternal ideals the aping of vice and aristocracy ripe for replacement by meritocracy, and a very nationalistic one to boot.

These are, of course, popular sentiments in a drama that would largely be watched by a middle-class audience, and they had been popular since the Restoration, to whose tradition of debauched older men Sir Harcourt belongs in name and actions – together with other characters of the play. Yet Restoration comedies would have countered this anti-ideal with a truthful witty loving young counterpart. Indeed at the start of the play Sir Harcourt views his son in such a way: 'Poor child! A perfect child in heart; a sober placid mind; the simplicity and verdure of boyhood kept fresh and unsullied by any contact with society' (85). It is a pity that the audience have just overheard the servants complaining that the perfect child has been out drinking all night and is in danger of being arrested for his debts. Sir Harcourt's typically patriarchal statement, 'In fact, he is my son and became a gentleman by right of paternity. He inherited my manners' (85), turns out to be uncannily accurate, only that it does not refer to the successful functioning of patriarchy, but rather to its threatening collapse due to its internal contradictions. Its central contradiction is the replacement of the traditional idea of honor with money and the attendant subscription of men to an ideology of commodification, consumption, and excess. This highlights an aspect of Victorian materialism that is frequently viewed one-sidedly. As Brent Shannon states:

> Recent scholarship has dismantled 'separate spheres' ideology that imagines men as producers and women as consumers and has challenged the notion of a 'Great Masculine Renunciation', in which nineteenth-century middle-class men adopted sober, unadorned business-oriented dress in an attempt to gain sociopolitical legitimacy.
>
> (Shannon 597)

In fact, Sir Harcourt already has a history of unwise actions, which traditional patriarchal views would call dishonorable, yet he simply considers profitable:

MAX Excuse the insinuation; I had thought the first Lady Courtly had surfeited you with beauty.

SIR HARCOURT No; she lived fourteen months with me, and then eloped with an intimate friend. Etiquette compelled me to challenge the seducer. So I received satisfaction – and a bullet in my shoulder at the same time. However, I had the consolation of knowing that

he was the handsomest man of the age. She did not insult me by
running away with a damned ill-looking scoundrel.

Max That certainly was flattering.

Sir Harcourt I felt so, as I pocketed the ten thousand pounds'
damages.

Max That must have been a great balm to your sore honour.

Sir Harcourt It was. Max, my honour would have died without it;
for on that year the wrong horse won the Derby – by some mistake.
It was one of the luckiest chances, a thing that does not happen
twice in a man's life; the opportunity of getting rid of his wife and
his debts at the same time.

Max Tell the truth, Courtly! Did you not feel a little frayed in your
delicacy? Your honour, now? Eh?

Sir Harcourt Not a whit. Why should I? I married *money* and
I received it, virgin gold! (86)

The shocking coupling of virginity and gold evokes the traditional value
of chastity in a wife – and instantly commodifies it. Marriage, the central motif in comedy and the most important life choice for both men
and women at the time, becomes an investment. Indeed, the play is saturated with economic terminology, starting with the 'assurance' of its
title. It refers to the self-confidence of the new generation, shaped by
the cosmopolitan mores of London. It of course also means securing a
title to property, insuring property in the event of loss, but also in a now
obsolete meaning a marriage engagement or betrothal. And it is by no
means only the men who view marriage as an investment. These are the
opinions of the young heiress:

> Marriage matters are conducted nowadays in a most mercantile man-
> ner; consequently a previous acquaintance is by no means indispens-
> able. Besides my *prescribed* husband has been upon the Continent for
> the benefit of his – property! They say a southern climate is a great
> restorer of consumptive estates. (94)

To which her maid replies: 'Well, Miss, for my own part I should like to
have a good look at my bargain before I paid for it; 'specially when one's
life is the price of the article' (94). Yet Grace counters her with the claim,
'A young husband might expect affection and nonsense, which 'twould
be deceit in me to render; nor would he permit me to remain with my
uncle. Sir Harcourt takes me with the encumbrances on his estate, and
I shall beg to be left among the rest of the live-stock' (94).

Even in her first exchange with her future husband, Grace insists on these pragmatic and deeply unromantic views, while he, otherwise a typical rake figure, suddenly starts spouting traditionalist romantic and nationalist notions:

> GRACE ... every London ball-room is a marriage mart. Young ladies are trotted out, while the mother, father, or chaperone plays auctioneer, and knocks them down to the highest bidder. Young men are ticketed up with their fortunes on their backs, and love, turned into a dapper shopman, descants on the excellent qualities of the material.
>
> COURTLY Oh! That such a custom could have ever emanated from the healthy soil of an English heart!
>
> GRACE It never did, like most of our literary dandyisms and dandy literature, it was borrowed from the French. (99)

What is easily overlooked in this exchange is that is not only women who are the commodities on the marriage market. Men, too, carry price-tags. In fact their identity is so tied up with their wealth that young master Courtly even manages to pretend to be someone else when he encounters his father in Grace's country home – and Courtly grudgingly accepts that he has made a mistake. The pillar of patriarchy, the transfer of power from father to son, is once again disrupted and ridiculed. But things get worse. If women are like horses at an auction (Grace is at one point described as almost as beautiful as a thoroughbred![3]), men are the gullible buyers. And those who lead them by the nose are women.

Besides Grace, another woman with ideas of her own dominates the play. The tellingly named Lady Gay Spanker, who appears *'fully equipped in riding habit'* (108), soon takes matters into her own hands and brings about the conventional happy end. One should not get overexcited about her name: the *Oxford English Dictionary* cites 1935 as the first recorded use of 'gay' for 'homosexual,' though it shows earlier associations with 'forward' and 'impertinent' and even 'immoral,' but also horses. 'Spanker' also has associations besides 'slapping,' namely again a fast horse, a sailing ship, or something precious. Nonetheless, compared to the male characters in the play, whose names smack of the fops of Restoration Comedy, Lady Gay is a thoroughly modern character. When asked about the whereabouts of her husband Adolphus, she replies:

> LADY GAY (*coming down*) Bless me, where is my Dolly?
> SIR HARCOURT You are married, then?

LADY GAY I have a husband somewhere, though I can't find him just now. *(Calls)* Dolly, dear! *(Aside to* Max) Governor, at home I always whistle when I want him. (110–11)

Although the Spankers's marriage is subsequently shown to be a happy one, Lady Gay clearly feminizes her husband and turns him into a childlike servile character, in short: she reverses traditional gender roles. When Grace adopts a similar attitude to her uncle, Lady Gay explicitly asserts female dominance:

GRACE You shall be king, and I'll be your prime minister. That is, I will rule and you shall have the honour of taking the consequences.
    Exit Grace Harkaway, L.
LADY GAY Well said, Grace. Have your own way. It is the only thing we women ought to be allowed. (111)

Lady Gay had earlier addressed her husband with 'bless his stupid face' (111). Even when Grace is about to accept young Courtley's stammering proposal, she cannot help but state in an aside to the audience 'How stupid he is!' (116). When Lady Gay is asked by young Courtley to make his father fall in love with her in order to estrange him from Grace, she replies once again in typically brutal terms, which, nonetheless, are those in which the play regards the manipulation and abuse of men by dominant women: 'Ha! ha! I see my cue. I'll cross his scent; I'll draw him after me. Ho! ho! Won't I make love to him? Ha!' (117). When Grace complains that women are traditionally banned from the company of men when these smoke their cigars after dinner, Lady Gay puts her right:

LADY GAY (R.) We are turned out just when the fun begins. How happy the poor wretches look at the contemplation of being rid of us.
GRACE The conventional signal for the ladies to withdraw, is anxiously and deliberately waited for.
LADY GAY Then I begin to wish I were a man.
GRACE The instant the door is closed upon us, there rises a roar!
LADY GAY In celebration of their short-lived liberty, my love; rejoicing over their emancipation. (119)

Not only does she confirm Germaine Greer's provocative thesis of a deep-seated hatred of men against women,[4] she partly subscribes to it as well – and reverses the common idea that women are in need of emancipating themselves. Here men are the subjects of patriarchy, but also most noticeably subjected by it. Lady Gay is in fact dissatisfied with her husband 'Dolly''s submissive attitude, but only a little: 'Poor Dolly, I'm sorry I must continue to deceive him. If he would but kindle up a little' (129). His verdict on himself – and by extension all married men – is: 'now I am defenceless! Is this the fate of husbands?' (134). Even the advocate Meddle and the trickster Dazzle, who are the other cogs in the machine of this drama, mistakenly spell his name 'Dolly' on the legal document they obligingly provide (135). His only attempt to assume control lies in the traditionally feminine threat of suicide: 'Farewell, base, heartless, unfeeling woman!' (135). Yet when a duel is threatened, Lady Gay intervenes, though again in telling terms: 'I would sooner lose my bridle hand than he should be hurt on my account' (138).

Her imagined renunciation of power is merely the replica of the traditional masculine resignation, which does not imply an actual loss of dominance, since it can only be made from a position of superiority. Her husband is very aware of this when he concludes the short-lived matrimonial quarrel with the declaration: 'No, no. Do what you like, say what you like, for the future! I find the head of a family has less ease and more responsibility than I, as a member, could have anticipated. I abdicate!' (140).

Gender relations are a question of investment, with risks and potential losses, and they are governed by legal as much as social constraints. In fact, as part of the supposedly happy end, Grace declares that her chosen lover, 'Mr. Charles Courtly is under age. Ask his father' (141). And when this father refuses to bail out his debt-ridden son, she takes over: 'Then, I will. You may retire' (141). Her last words are addressed to Isaacs, the Jewish money-lender, yet they might just as well be addressed to Sir Harcourt and to patriarchy in general.

Masculinity is reduced to the figure of Dazzle, who is suddenly revealed to be no one's acquaintance, in the same way that the heir to Sir Harcourt's name and depleted fortune had temporarily lost his identity. When asked who he is, Dazzle indeed boldly replies:

I have not the remotest idea! . . .

Simple question as you may think it, it would puzzle half the world to answer. One thing I can vouch: Nature made me a gentleman, that is, I live on the best that can be procured for credit. I never spend my own money when I can oblige a friend. I'm always thick on the winning horse. I'm an epidemic on the trade of tailor. For further particulars enquire of any sitting magistrate. (143)

The question that would puzzle half the world, its male half presumably, is that of the identity of the gentleman, the masculine ideal of the period. After an unconvincing claim to an essentialist identity (the old notion of privilege), however, we are soon in the realm of economy again, and it is an economy of debt and expenditure, indeed of waste and excess, to the degree that the final definition of the gentleman rests with the courts.

That this wasteful performativity, and not any idealist conception, is the other face of masculinity in Victorian culture is demonstrated by its humorous performance in comedy. It does more than reiterate the old clichés of henpecked husbands and deceived would-wits. It shows that commodification and commercialization are not merely powers wielded by men, but forces that affect their self-definition – all the way to the erstwhile core, but now merely sad veneer of their gender. When Sir Courtley swears to Grace that he was certain that the young man he had just encountered was his son, he once again exposes being a gentleman as empty performativity,[5] since he swears by his artificial hair! Grace, like the women in Boucicault's play in general, is not taken in by such recourse to traditional notions of masculine honor. Instead she translates it into the economic terms that the play employs for gender, marriage, family, and society in general: 'If that security would be called for, I suspect the answer would be "no effects"!' (104).

The bankruptcy of traditional notions of masculinity – as embodied in the established notion of the gentleman – can also be seen in another popular play from the 1840s, half a century before the better known subversions of gender in so-called *fin-de-siècle* writing take place. Edward Bulwer-Lytton's comedy from November 1840 even bears as its title that which has replaced traditional gender and moral values: *Money*.[6] Its opening shows the audience exactly such a dismantling of a gentleman, Sir John Vesey. It tellingly happens in front of a woman, his equally materialistic daughter Georgina. When she inquires whether he is really a rich man, she and the audience are in for a surprise:

> SIR JOHN Not a bit of it; all humbug, child, all humbug, upon my soul.... There are two rules in life: *First*, men are valued not for what they *are*, but what they *seem* to be. *Secondly*, if you have no merit or money of your own, you must trade on the merits and money of other people. My father got the title by services in the army and

died penniless. On the strength of his services I got a pension of four hundred pounds a year; on the strength of four hundred pounds a year I took credit for eight hundred pounds; on the strength of eight hundred pounds a year I married your mother with ten thousand pounds; on the strength of ten thousand pounds I took credit for forty thousand pounds and paid Dicky Gossip three guineas a week to go about everywhere calling me 'Stingy Jack.' (6)

Sir John freely concedes that a man's position in society does not depend on either essence or merits, but on performance. In a manner that would strike the audience as blasphemous (when he makes these statements upon his soul), he also describes this performance as a series of trans- actions, none of them based on a solid financial basis, but all of them speculative, if not indeed fraudulent. The most important of these trans- actions is marriage. It permits him to raise his annual income from 400 pounds (roughly the equivalent of 35,080 pounds today and thus a moderate income) to 40,000 pounds (approximately 3,508,000 pounds today, a millionaire's budget).[7] Performance (of non-existent wealth) indeed shades over into performativity, the obligation to perform that which gives a basis to the performed identity. This is shown in the strange strategy of paying someone to spread rumors of one's stinginess. Yet Sir John explains that this is 'a valuable reputation':

When a man is called stingy, it is as much as calling him rich; and when a man's called rich, why he's a man universally respected. On the strength of my respectability I wheedled a constituency, changed my politics, resigned my seat to a minister, who, to a man of such stake in the country, could offer nothing less than a patent office of two thousand pounds a year. That's the way to succeed in life. Humbug, my dear, all humbug, upon my soul! (6)

Empty promises and false surfaces can be used to gain credit, win a wife and even a seat in parliament. In short, the whole social system of Vic- torian Britain can be mastered by a performativity that subverts the traditional ideals connected with its central patriarchal tenet of mas- culinity: honor, integrity, and truthfulness. The crucial term used by Sir John for his strategy is 'respectability.' It has an interesting pedigree: the *Oxford English Dictionary* lists its first recorded occurrence as late as 1785 in John Trusler's novel *Modern Times*. It derives from the much older term 'respect,' which in turn has its roots in the Latin 'respicere,' which means seeing and observing and is also linked with 'spectacle.'

The modern masculine value of respectability is thus clearly performative and not substantial or essential. That Sir John's daughter Georgina has learned this lesson instantly becomes evident when she comments on her father's suggestion that Sir Frederick Blount might be a potential husband for her: 'Ah, Papa, he is charming' (6). Charm is not a respectable quality in a Victorian man, much less in a husband.

Unfortunately, the encounter of two empty performativities sees one cancel out the other. As soon as Sir John suspects that his daughter might inherit a fortune, Sir Frederick's charms evaporate for him: 'He *was* so, my dear, before we knew your poor uncle was dead; but an heiress such as you will be should look out for a duke' (7). This effect is reminiscent of Roland Barthes's description of the functioning of myths. For Barthes, myths are secondary sign systems that mimic 'natural,' that is, motivated forms of signification, and thereby make historical developments appear natural (129, 131, 142–43). If one broadens Barthes's semiotic model to include performative structures (since myth only becomes naturalized as a repeated utterance), one arrives at the mechanisms of Butler's performativity – and also at ways of exposing this performativity. In the same way as for Barthes myth can be exposed only through myth itself, through a highlighting of its patterns, masculinity, as depicted in plays like *London Assurance* and *Money*, uncovering its fictional ideological status itself – through the repetition and performance of the structures that establish it in the first place. As Judith Butler puts it:

> Performativity cannot be understood outside of a process of iterability, a regularized and constrained repetition of norms. And this repetition is not performed *by* a subject; this repetition is what enables a subject and constitutes the temporal condition for the subject. This iterability implies that 'performance' is not a singular 'act' or event, but a ritualized production, a ritual reiterated under and through constraint, under and through the force of prohibition and taboo, with the threat of ostracism and even death controlling and compelling the shape of the production, but not, I will insist, determining it fully in advance.
>
> (1993: 95)

We shall see in the subsequent section that, in doing so, masculinity is the structural equivalent of another large-scale structure in the nineteenth century and afterward: capitalism.

Bulwer-Lytton's play *Money* comes across as more conventional than Boucicault's *London Assurance* in that it contrasts the decadent characters of Sir John, his daughter Georgina and her lover Sir Frederick with two solid characters. Evelyn and Clara, his cousin, are poor relatives in the households of Sir John and Lady Franklin, Sir John's half-sister. They represent the good and earnest counterpart to the superficiality that surrounds them, but do so rather as an intertextual echo of the way in which Restoration comedy used such positive figures to signal emerging middle-class values. Evelyn indeed summarizes his typical middle-class background as follows: 'And thus must I grind out my life forever! I am ambitious, and poverty drags me down! I have learning, and poverty makes me the drudge of fools! I love, and poverty stands like a spectre before the altar!' (10).

Yet the simple opposition between upper-class surface respectability and middle-class honest labor fails in the play. Once Evelyn discovers that it is not Georgina but he who is the heir of the wealthy Mr Mordaunt, he instantly reverts to the same upper-class attitudes that he has hitherto found so despicable. Indeed the play is at pains to draw his new status as a consumer as vividly as possibly by parading in front of the audience, besides newly acquired servants, a whole range of stereotypical tradesmen: Frantz, the tailor; Tabouret, the upholsterer; Macfinch, the jeweller; Macstucco, the architect; Kite, the horsedealer; Crimson, the portrait-painter; Grab, the publisher; and Patent, the coach-builder.

What makes a man, more precisely, what makes a gentleman, are by no means the innate and interior qualities (such as honesty, integrity, and moral strength) that essentialist views of the nineteenth century and our present age so readily invoke. What matters are external and acquired status symbols, commodified forms of social respectability, which also function as symbols of a successfully acquired gender position. The underlying currency, this is made clear by the play's title, is money, material wealth. This is not a new phenomenon, but can be traced back to the Renaissance courtier via the Regency dandy and the Restoration fop. Yet in the nineteenth century, an era that wishes to connect material wealth with moral and social responsibility, this creates problems. These can be described in traditional Marxist ways, but they will also ultimately prove to be compatible with the notions of twentieth- and twenty-first-century Gender Studies. When Karl Marx describes the paradoxes inherent in the capitalist relationship of money and commodities, he also pinpoints the commodified structures of masculinity that form the core of Bulwer-Lytton's play *Money*:

> Capital is money: Capital is commodities. In truth, however, value is here the active factor in a process, in which, while, constantly assuming the form in turn of money and commodities, it at the same time changes in magnitude, differentiates itself by throwing off surplus-value from itself; the original value, in other words, expands spontaneously. For the movement, in the course of which it adds surplus value, is its own movement, its expansion, therefore, is automatic expansion. Because it is value, it has acquired the occult quality of being able to add value to itself. It brings forth living offspring, or, at the least, lays golden eggs.
>
> (Marx 20; vol. 1, pt. 2, ch. 4)

In the concrete terms of Bulwer-Lytton's play, Marx's abstract ideas relate to the spontaneous generation and expansion of the main protagonist Evelyn as a man, a rich man, a gentleman, and a capitalist fully immersed in the workings of capital, commodities, and their exchange and increase. Yet the paradoxical and empty process at the heart of the operation leaves both its mechanisms and its effects (here: the perfect Victorian gentleman) with the taint of a sham – in the same way that the gentleman Dazzle was exposed and exposed himself at the end of Boucicault's *London Assurance*. Marx pinpoints this paradox in the universal value of money as a means of exchange, which contrasts with the fact that money possesses no intrinsic value. First, Marx describes the privileging of money in capitalism in terms that would also apply to the privileging of the gentleman in a patriarchal society dominated by capitalist middle-class values:

> But a particular commodity cannot become the universal equivalent except by a social act. The social action therefore of all other commodities, sets apart the particular commodity in which they all represent their values. Thereby the bodily form of this commodity becomes the form of the socially recognised universal equivalent. To be the universal equivalent, becomes, by this social process, the specific function of the commodity thus excluded by the rest. Thus it becomes – money.
>
> (5; vol. 1, pt. 1, ch. 2)

This universality, however, goes hand in hand with a loss of definition. In semiotic terms, one would speak of a signifier that has lost its signified in the tautology of its creation: 'But money itself has no price. In order to put it on an equal footing with all other commodities in this respect, we should be obliged to equate it to itself as its own equivalent' (4; vol. 1, pt. 1, ch.3). The process is the equivalent of the way in which Barthes envisions the self-creation of myths. This tautological circle of significatory production that creates reality as a mere effect is moreover the equivalent of what Judith Butler describes as the heterosexual matrix. It produces gender as an effect of translating libidinal impulses into the hegemonic form of compulsory heterosexuality.[8]

One can take Marx's, Barthes's, and Butler's ideas together and see them in conjunction with another important theory of masculinity, Eve Kosofsky Sedgwick's concept of the homosocial. It describes the triangular relationship that connects competing masculinities through a desired third element. This is frequently a woman, but can also be status, wealth, and so on. If we do so, we are back in the world of our two Victorian comedies (cf. Kosofsky Sedgwick 21). There, the measure that indicates a successfully achieved, that is, performed, masculinity is the approval of other men and women. Despite their inferior status in patriarchal ideology, women – as the object of competition – play an important part in the constant challenges and tests to which men are subjected. Once can see this, for example, in their attitudes toward ostensibly expressed social status, without which Victorian society would lose its hierarchies and structuring mechanisms.

In *Money* masculine approval of the now wealthy Evelyn is signalled when he speaks of 'all my new friends – and their name is legion' (21). It becomes explicit when Lord Glossmore, who embodies the superficiality of rank already in his name, pays Evelyn a visit immediately after Evelyn's inheritance has become public knowledge and even tries to persuade him to stand for parliament.

In terms of feminine recognition Bulwer-Lytton's comedy plays a double game. On the one hand, as was pointed out above, it appears to be traditional when it sets the seemingly noble Clara against the mercenary Georgina. Clara is initially as poor as Evelyn before his inheritance, and the two are in love. Yet Clara rejects Evelyn as a suitor, since she is realistic about the chances in life of a couple on a low income: 'A marriage of privation, of penury, of days that dread the morrow! I have seen such a lot!' (12). Evelyn, though more in tune with romantic idealism, has previously made the interesting declaration:

> I am poor, penniless, a beggar for bread to a dying servant. True! But I have a heart of iron! I have knowledge, patience, health, and my love for you gives me at last ambition. I have trifled with my own energies till now, for I despised all things till I loved thee! With you to toil for, your step to support, your path to smooth, and I, I, poor Alfred Evelyn, promise at last to win for you even fame and fortune! (12)

Its terms are telling: inside the romantic vocabulary lurks a thoroughly Victorian middle-class terminology of knowledge, patience, and energies, even the iron that was so important for Victorian feats of engineering. Yet it takes the desired goal of a loved woman to harness Evelyn's potential. Once this goal is in sight, he becomes suitably competitive and willing to embrace fame and fortune, exactly the values he has hitherto despised. In line with Sedgwick's triangle of homosocial bonding, desire, and competition, it takes the ostensible passion for a desired object to trigger and legitimate the mechanisms of patriarchal masculinity, which are here as elsewhere not merely compatible with the structures of capitalism, but turn out to be identical with them.[9]

Thus nothing would be further from the truth than to misread Evelyn's and Clara's tricky love-affair (which is sorely tested by the rejected Evelyn's proposal of marriage to Georgina) as the idealist counterplot to the materialism that is so obvious in all other characters. Their true wit is here also the true expression of middle-class values. These demand a much more faithful adherence to patriarchal gender norms than those of the other characters, who have or pretend to have aristocratic notions of relationships, marriage, and so on. It is this emphasis on gender that forces Evelyn to undergo several (rather unrealistic) changes, if not of heart, then of attitude: from cynical observer of the consumer world that surrounds him to an ardent participant in this commodity culture, and then back to honest and true lover. These contortions show, once again in line with Structuralist and Marxist concepts and those of Gender Studies, that gender is by no means an essential quality, but a flexible performativity on the marketplace of a capitalism that is already in full swing. The play's central irony is encapsulated in Sir John's words of congratulation when Evelyn learns of his new fortune: 'You are a great man now, a very great man!' (17). It is underlined when Evelyn's only reaction to this (other than his aside for the audience that remarks on Clara's silence) consists of 'Lend me ten pounds for my old nurse!' (17).

Masculine greatness is a hollow affair in the two plays discussed in the present essay, and this is obvious to the plays themselves – where this irony forms a pervasive dramatic layer and produces a comedy that possesses much of the tragedy implied in Braddon's contemporaneous verdict. Yet the two plays differ in that Boucicault's leaves the paradox of self-generating performative masculinity exposed and unresolved, while Bulwer-Lytton's struggles to re-frame it in a more conventional happy end. It is achieved with the help of further plot complications. When Evelyn is still poor and wishes to support his ailing nurse, he is denied assistance by all around him. Yet Clara secretly donates the little money she has been able to save, but preserves her anonymity by making a servant-girl write the accompanying letter. When Evelyn professes to be touched by the gesture, Georgina is persuaded by her father to pretend to be the donor. Eventually, however, the true origin of the donation is revealed. Evelyn's reaction is telling: 'I am free! I am released! You forgive me? You love me? You are mine! We are rich, rich!' (61). In keeping with the play's unashamed materialism the evidence that brings about this turn-around is a banker's letter.

Clara does not respond to Evelyn's enthusiastic declarations. But nowhere does the play signal that she opposes Evelyn's plans. Rather than an oppositional pair, Clara and Evelyn now form one that is fully integrated in the commodified routines of the plot that encompass politics, class, the family, and marriage, and at whose hollow core rests a paradoxical notion of middle-class masculinity as the universal measure of exchange value.[10] This is emphasized one last time when the play's finale mocks traditional well-wishing and, as part of it, the traditional essentialist values associated with honest English manliness:

> GRAVES But for the truth and the love, when found, to make us tolerably happy, we should not be without –
> LADY FRANKLIN Good health –
> GRAVES Good spirits –
> CLARA A good heart –
> SMOOTH An innocent rubber –
> GEORGINA Congenial tempers –
> BLOUNT A pwoper degwee of pwudence – [Blount has a speech impediment.]
> STOUT Enlightened opinions –
> GLOSSMORE Constitutional principles –

Sir John Knowledge of the world –
Evelyn And – plenty of Money!
[Curtain]

Notes

1. What Butler claims for heterosexuality is also true for its crucial component, traditional masculinity: 'In other words, heterosexuality is always in the process of imitating and approximating its own phantasmatic idealization of itself – *and failing*. Precisely because it is bound to fail, and yet endeavors to succeed, the project of heterosexual identity is propelled into an endless repetition of itself' (Butler 1997: 306–07).
2. Boucicault's life and career are notoriously difficult to trace. The real name of the Dublin-born actor and playwright of probably French descent appears to have been Dionysius Lardner Boursiquot, and *London Assurance* is sometimes seen as the result of a collaboration with Charles Mathews (cf. Fawkes; Johnson).
3. Compare Gina M. Dorré, *Victorian Fiction and the Cult of the Horse* (Aldershot: Ashgate, 2006).
4. 'Women have very little idea of how much men hate them' is the famous opening of the discussion in Germaine Greer, *The Female Eunuch* (London: Paladin, 1971), 263.
5. Performativity, in the sense in which Butler uses it, is always empty, since its products (and ultimately also its origins) are effects. Thus she writes in *Bodies That Matter: On the Discursive Limits of "Sex"*: 'For discourse to materialize a set of effects, "discourse" itself must be understood as complex and convergent chains in which 'effects' are vectors of power. In this sense, what is constituted in discourse is not fixed in or by discourse, but becomes the condition and occasion for further action. This does not mean that any action is possible on the basis of a discursive effect. On the contrary, certain reiterative chains of discursive production are barely legible as reiterations, for the effects they have materialized are those without which no bearing in discourse can be taken' (Butler 1993: 187).
6. Edward Bulwer-Lytton's biography is very much a Victorian success story: from a rather impoverished military background, he simultaneously worked his way up in politics and in the public appreciation as a popular writer. However, and this might be of relevance for his cynical view of gender relations, his career was blighted by an unhappy marriage to a wife from whom he was legally separated after nine years of marriage. She later denounced him publicly at political events (and was duly thrown into a mental asylum, if only temporarily) (cf. Campbell).
7. The calculation is based on Robert Twigger, 'Inflation: The Value of the Pound 1750–1998,' *House of Commons Library Research Paper*, 99:20 23 Feb 1998: 11. The modern point of comparison is the year 1998. <http://www.parliament.uk/commons/lib/ research/rp99/ rp99-020.pdf>.
8. 'I use the term heterosexual matrix throughout the text to designate that grid of cultural intelligibility through which bodies, genders, and desires are naturalized' (Butler 1990: 151, n. 6).

9. See also Fisher.
10. "Masculine identity in this sense was very much a middle-class possession, available to the 'improving' echelons of the lower orders" (Tosh 236).

Works cited

Barthes, Roland. *Mythologies*. Trans. Annette Lavers. London: Vintage, 1993.

Braddon, Mary Elizabeth. *Aurora Floyd*. 1862–63. Ed. Edwards P.D. Oxford and New York: Oxford UP, 1996.

Boucicault, Dion. 'London Assurance.' *London Assurance and Other Victorian Comedies*. Ed. Klaus Stierstorfer. Oxford and New York: Oxford UP, 2001. 75–143.

Bulwer-Lytton, Edward. *Money*. *London Assurance and Other Victorian Comedies*. Ed. Klaus Stierstorfer. Oxford and New York: Oxford UP, 2001. 1–73.

Butler, Judith. *Gender Trouble: Feminism and the Subversion of Identity*. New York: Routledge, 1990.

——. *Bodies That Matter: On the Discursive Limits of 'Sex.'* New York: Routledge, 1993.

——. 'Imitation and Gender Insubordination.' *The Second Wave: A Reader in Feminist Theory*. Ed. Linda Nicholson. London and New York: Routledge, 1997. 300–15.

Campbell, James L. *Edward Bulwer-Lytton*. Boston: Twayne, 1986.

Dorré, Gina M. *Victorian Fiction and the Cult of the Horse*. Aldershot: Ashgate, 2006.

Fawkes, Richard. *Dion Boucicault: A Biography*. London: Quartet, 1979.

Fisher, James. ' "The Arithmetic and Logic of Life": The Forces of Commerce and Capital in a Revival of Edward Bulwer-Lytton's *Money*.' *Journal of Dramatic Theory and Criticism* 15.2 (Spring 2001): 115–32.

Greer, Germaine. *The Female Eunuch*. London: Paladin, 1971.

Johnson, Albert E. 'The Birth of Dion Boucicault.' *Modern Drama* 11 (1968): 157–63.

Kosofsky Sedgwick, Eve. *Between Men: English Literature and Male Homosocial Desire*. New York: Columbia UP, 1985.

Marx, Karl. *Capital: A Critique of Political Economy*. Trans. Samuel Moore and Edward Aveling. Ed. Friedrich Engels. Chicago: Charles H. Kerr & Co., 1906.

Millett, Kate. *Sexual Politics*. London: Abacus, 1972.

Shannon, Brent. 'ReFashioning Men: Fashion, Masculinity, and the Cultivation of the Male Consumer in Britain, 1860–1914.' *Victorian Studies* 46.4 (Summer 2004): 597–630.

Tosh, John. 'The Old Adam and the New Man: Emerging Themes in the History of English Masculinities.' *English Masculinities 1660–1800*. Ed. Tim Hitchcock and Michèle Cohen. London and New York: Routledge, 1999. 217–38.

Twigger, Robert. 'Inflation: The Value of the Pound 1750–1998.' *House of Commons Library Research Paper* 99.20 23 Feb. 1998): 3–22.

Waters, Karen Volland. *The Perfect Gentleman: Masculine Control in Victorian Men's Fiction, 1870–1901*. New York: Peter Lang, 1997.

5

Performing Imperial Masculinities: The Discourse and Practice of Cricket

Anthony Bateman

Abstract

Cricket is one of the mainstays of Englishness. The present essay shows that it is also crucial in defining a kind of national masculinity in performance. This is all the more important as cricket is a nostalgic celebration of 'white' rural Englishness, yet has from its beginnings also been used to educate young males for service in the colonies. Moreover, it has been instrumental in integrating players and teams from the former British colonies in British national culture. Inside the discourse of sports, issues of masculinity, race, ethnicity, and nationality are therefore enacted, all of which have an impact on and are projected onto the bodies of the players. The ideal elegance of the proficient player is, in keeping with the ideal of a healthy mind inside a healthy body, meant to represent both moral virtue and race and class superiority. The West Indies cricketer Learie Constantine and his style of play provided a first historic challenge to such established thinking.

The Author hopes that every reader will derive some pleasure from studying the pages of *The Cricketer's Companion*, and that it will help lay the foundation for a successful career in the game, and develop those qualities which build up the manhood of the Empire.

(Currie 3)

the principles they taught we absorbed through the pores and practised instinctively. The books we read in class meant little to most of us.

(James 35)

By the end of the nineteenth century the English game of cricket had come to assume enormous material and symbolic significance within Britain and its empire. Reflecting the agrarian rhythms of the pre-industrial society in which it originated, and played by men in white flannels suggestive of its lily-white moral values, this highly ritualistic and etiquette-bound sport had become nothing less than a national fetish due in large part to the literary endeavors of its zealous cultural gatekeepers and evangelicals. Institutionalized with religious devotion in the elite public schools, and structured around rigid class distinctions at its highest competitive levels, cricket was nevertheless represented as the symbol of a cohesive national community in which men of all social classes could come together in the spirit of 'fair play' under the benevolent authority of its laws. A potent symbol of the strength and unity of empire, cricket had been successfully transplanted to Britain's colonies where it was endowed with the ability to transform the identities of male imperial subjects in accordance with ideals of English bourgeois civility.

The two quotations cited above succinctly testify to the hegemonic status of cricket as both discourse and practice. The first, taken from an instructional manual published in 1918, expresses the hope that cricket and its discourses will continue as agencies in the production of imperial masculinity within the traumatic context of the immediate post-war period. The second, written by the Trinidadian Marxist and anti-colonial nationalist, C. L. R. James, apparently confirms such an aspiration by retrospectively emphasizing the extent to which cricket discourse informed the bodily practices of young male colonial subjects. James suggests that for the sons of the colonial middle class who, like him, attended British-style public schools, the discourse of cricket literally imprinted itself on their bodies to produce forms of performativity inevitably expressive of the disciplinary and identity-forming procedures of empire. However, the performance of cricket in Britain's colonies could destabilize the discourse of empire to produce alternative masculinities around which the political aspirations of the colonized could be mobilized.

This chapter intends to contribute to current debates on sport and masculinity by focusing on this important historical relationship between the discourse and embodied practice of cricket. By providing a broad, yet by no means comprehensive, historical overview of cricket, it suggests that the relationship between cricket as discourse and practice became increasingly unstable as Britain and its empire entered a phase of decline. To do so the analysis begins by tracing the emergence and development of cricket discourse, suggesting that the sport's literature (in its many forms) was an active agent in the production of particular modes of masculine performance and in inscribing upon cricket a series of moral ideals supposedly constitutive of hegemonic Anglo-British masculinity. While the Victorian cricket field was marked by a relative stability between discourse and practice, the second section suggests that destabilizing re-workings of its performative grammar during the inter-war years yielded a discourse that mediated the perceived crisis of Anglo-British masculinity during that period. Within this discourse the issue of gender consistently intersected with that of social class. The third section provides an important racial dimension to the analysis of cricket and masculinity through an examination of discourse surrounding the great West Indies cricketer, Learie Constantine. Here it is argued that Constantine's unique cricketing style provided English commentators with a model of how the engendering practice of cricket could be reinvigorated from the peripheries of empire.

The emergence and development of cricket discourse

Despite a historiography that has attempted to prove its ancient patrimony, organized cricket is a quintessentially modern cultural practice. The sport's national and imperial standardization and dissemination relied on the development of various forms of technology, notably print culture. Having been codified in the middle of the eighteenth century, from 1800 a technical discourse of cricket emerged that was instrumental in standardizing its laws and bodily practices. Such texts were crucial in increasing mass understanding of cricket's cultural codes, language, and performative grammar, and this disciplinary discourse was projected onto the bodily practices of vast numbers of young British, and subsequently colonial, males. As the following quotation from an instructional book published in 1816 suggests, cricket was emerging as a regulatory practice in which masculinity could be constantly reproduced at the level of performance: 'The object of this Work is to reduce Cricket Playing to a system, with as little variation as possible. It is intended as a help to young beginners, and also as a guide to older players who have accustomed themselves to habits inconsistent with good playing' (Lambert 6). Not only did such texts regulate the way cricket was played nationally and imperially (this particular book was later exported to Australia), to play cricket correctly according to the technical example of these books was to adopt certain bodily postures and enact particular economies of movement which were then becoming characteristic of an emerging bourgeois stylization of the masculine body.

In addition to its technical discourse, a prose literature of cricket appeared in the 1830s which exemplified the new literary and artistic sensibility emerging in the early modern period that according to George Mosse was 'crucial in defining the beauty of manliness' (7). This is evident in the first substantial work of reflective cricket prose, John Nyren and Charles Cowden-Clarke's *The Cricketers of My Time* (1832), a work that during the nineteenth and twentieth centuries came to form the cornerstone of a clearly defined canon of cricket literature. Consistent with Mosse's argument, in this text cricketers are presented as exemplary images of English masculinity in which 'body and soul, outward appearance and inner virtue were supposed to form one harmonious whole' (Mosse 5). In this sense Nyren and Cowden-Clarke's book shows that a series of aesthetic and ethical ideals were already being inscribed upon cricket and the bodies of its players before the Victorian period, and that the subsequent construction of moral manliness involved an adaptation of already existing discourses. Another important feature of the text as a canonical blueprint for future representations of cricket is that contrasting corporeal stylizations of the masculine body act as markers of social distinction, with the aristocratic and yeoman players described as displaying a more stylistically elegant economy of bodily movement than their social inferiors. For example, whereas the Duke of Dorset and Lord Tankerville are portrayed as 'pretty players,' Tankerville's gardener 'was not an elegant player, his position and general style were both awkward and uncouth,' a stylistic deficiency that supposedly indicates flaws in his character: 'he was,' we are told, 'as conceited as a wagtail' (Nyren 73). The bodily performance of the yeoman players denotes the possession of inner virtues that are defined as constitutive of a distinctively English form of normative masculinity. 'Silver Billy' Beldham, for example, is presented as 'the beau ideal of grace, animation, and concentrated energy' (91), and this mode of performance signifies 'sterling qualities of integrity, plain dealing and good english independence' (116).

As these examples suggest, the printed word was an important agent in promoting the bodily practice of cricket and in inscribing upon the sport a series of moral attributes. As such discourse gradually mutated into the ideal of moral manliness, particular modes of performativity in cricket took on a more urgent task as stylistic signifiers of inner virtue. For example, in 1851 the Reverend James Pycroft (one of a number of Anglican clerics who acted as cricket's cultural gatekeepers) published a canonized and much reprinted book, *The Cricket Field*. The text's obsessive preoccupation with matters of bodily style defines cricket as a non-instrumental practice, utterly uncontaminated by any taint of utility value. It states that a 'manly, graceful style of play is worth something independently of effect on the score' and that 'without elegance nothing counts.' The logic of this gendered discourse is to allocate a circumscribed, non-participatory role to women who should 'quiz, banter, tease, lecture, never-leave-alone, and otherwise plague and worry all such brothers or husbands as they shall see enacting these anatomical contortions which too often disgrace the game of cricket' (Arlott 127). The passage is an important reminder of the engendering function of modern sports. As women were increasingly interpellated into domestic roles, discourse increasingly placed emphasis on sports such as cricket as fields of specifically masculine performativity.

As has been well documented, from the middle of the nineteenth century cricket became an integral element in the middle-class reform and expansion of the public schools and in the ability of those institutions to discipline hegemonic representations of Anglo-British masculinity (Baucom 138). One text, Thomas Hughes's *Tom Brown's Schooldays*, was particularly significant in this process. According to James the novel's impact on the middle-class reading public was so significant that it was nothing less than 'the sacred text of Victorianism' (165). To some extent the novel is an autobiographical account of Hughes's schooldays at Rugby School under the headmastership of the pioneering educationalist Thomas Arnold, and a glowing testament to the reforms he had put in place. As well as exorcizing Rugby of the often anarchic behavior typical of the unreformed public schools, Arnold was concerned that the education of the sons of the ruling class should be a moral and spiritual, rather than a merely intellectual, process. Though Arnold had little interest in sport (indeed, in the novel the headmaster is not even present at Tom's valedictory 'Last Match'), Hughes's text became something of a blueprint for the later elevation of cricket to the head of a curriculum designed to foster moral and spiritual qualities in inextricable conjunction with the strengthening of sinew on the playing field. If the novel traces the rites of passage of its main characters, Tom, Arthur, and East to moral maturity and manhood, and if Arnold's pedagogic ideals were inscribed upon their bodies, here cricket itself underwent a process of re-inscription crucial to evolving hegemonies of Anglo-British masculine identity.

Tom Brown's Schooldays has often been misunderstood as a text that celebrates games-playing philistinism over intellectual achievement. However, as James has noted (162), it was the Victorian middle class who replaced Thomas Arnold's emphasis on learning and the cultivation of the intellect with an obsession for organized sports, and particularly cricket. Nevertheless, the novel was a seminal text in the emergence of the Victorian cult of Athleticism. While Tom's friendship with the physically fragile and scholarly Arthur is crucial in his passage to manhood, the latter is first presented as needing 'some Rugby air, and cricket' (Hughes 221). By the end of the novel Arthur is thoroughly assimilated into the cricket code, and as he, Tom and a young classics master watch the match between the school and a visiting team, they discuss the meaning of the game:

> 'Come, none of your irony, Brown,' answers the master. 'I'm beginning to understand the game scientifically. What a noble game it is, too!'
>
> 'Isn't it? But it's more than a game. It's an institution,' said Tom.
>
> 'Yes,' said Arthur, 'the birthright of British boys old and young, as *habeus corpus* and trial by jury are of British men.'
>
> 'The discipline and reliance on one another which it teaches is so valuable, I think,' went on the master, 'it ought to be such an unselfish game. It merges the individual in the eleven; he doesn't play so that he might win, but that his side may.' (354–55)

Played in a tranquil and elegiac atmosphere, the cricket match episode of *Tom Brown's Schooldays* indicates a sense of moral maturity lacking in earlier descriptions of sport in the narrative, and is the newly inscribed quality, not only of the boys, but also of the game of cricket itself. In the second half of the nineteenth century such discourse, with its metaphorical message of self-sacrifice in the cause of the greater national and imperial collectives, became nothing short of ubiquitous. Although this discourse was an integral element of the pedagogical philosophy of British and colonial public schools, the intention was that it diffused through all strata of late Victorian society. Instructional books, histories, cricketing biographies, essays, novels, and poetry were instrumental in its diffusion to an increasingly literate populace.

By the 1890s this discourse had been successfully inscribed upon the bodies of a significant number of famous cricketers, particularly the iconic W. G. Grace (see figure 5.1). With his imposing bulk and characteristically fulsome beard, Grace was identified as the embodiment of normative English masculinity in the press, in numerous poetic tributes, and in a string of 'ghosted' books attributed to Grace himself. Although

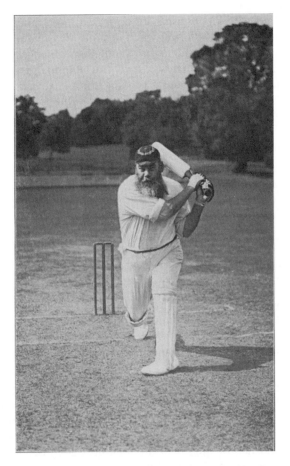

Figure 5.1   W. G. Grace (photograph from George W. Beldham and C. B. Fry, *Great Batsmen, Their Methods at a Glance.* London: Macmillan, 1905. 18.)

Grace was an amateur who amassed a fortune through cricket, and a player who frequently bent the laws to gain an advantage over an opponent, his literary image was the embodiment of the spirit of 'fair play' and moral manliness. An anonymous rhymester, employing one of the many moral metaphors now frequently being drawn from cricketing terminology, described him as 'The straightest bat that England ever saw' (Frewin 248). In 1895, the year in which Oscar Wilde's *The Importance of Being Earnest* was first produced and its author imprisoned for same-sex activities, Grace's unsurpassed achievements in the legitimate field of cricket were represented as the embodiment of solid Victorian respectability and sexual orthodoxy over and against the decadence of those intractable opponents of Athleticism, Wilde and the avant-garde. Grace's innovative mastery of the practice of cricket acted as a symbolic bulwark against the contemporary forces apparently threatening the edifice of hegemonic masculinity such as the New Women's movement and homosexuality. At the height of Britain's imperial power cricket was at once a symbol of the strength and unity of the British Empire and a privileged field in which the form of masculinity which supposedly underpinned it was repeatedly reproduced.

Cricket as discourse and practice 1918–1939

The death of Grace from a stroke in 1916 was felt by many as symbolic of the passing of an old order. A number of scholars have noted that the period following the First World War witnessed a significant reconfiguration of gender relations and a concomitant re-figuration of Anglo-British masculinity (cf. Light; Stevenson). Though war losses had been lower than those of France and Germany, the deaths of nearly three-quarters of a million British men and one-and-a-half million serious casualties led to the emergence of the idea of a 'lost generation,' an idea strengthened by the disproportionate loss of middle- and upper-class males (Stevenson 93–95). The many obituaries of former public school cricketers in the emaciated copies of cricket's annual yearbook, *Wisden*, in the war years and afterward testified to the frailties of an entire cultural system. In addition, employment opportunities for women had increased significantly during the conflict with the effect of liberating many from the domestic restrictions of their pre-war lives. As Jonathan Rutherford has argued, overall there was a 'sense of male disorientation given [the] changing nature of gender relations' (72). At the political level a parallel sense of dislocation was manifest in the decline of the Liberal party and the election of the first Labor government in 1923. Furthermore, the example of the 1917 Bolshevik revolution had to some extent mobilized working-class militancy, a trend seen by many in the establishment to have culminated in the 1926 general strike. In the international context, by the early 1920s the British Empire was beset by crisis. The 1916 Easter Uprising in Ireland was one of a number of events that seriously challenged the stability of the empire, while murderous British conduct during the 1919 Amritsar Massacre in India led to increasing doubts regarding its moral authority (Judd 277). Although much inter-war cricket discourse denied and attempted to transcend these contemporary conditions by reinforcing a sense of pre-war class and gender relations and by stressing the strength and unity of empire, the following sections suggest that the relationship between the discourse and practice of cricket became increasingly tense during the period. Cricket thus mediated many of the socio-economic and political factors outlined above.

In his book *English Cricket*, the most resoundingly canonical and influential cricket belletrist, Neville Cardus, retrospectively registered a sense of aesthetic decline in the cricket of the early 1920s. He suggested that it mediated nothing less than (in the words of Raymond Williams) a new 'structure of feeling' (cf. Williams 128–35):

> It was an age of some disillusionment and cynicism; the romantic gesture was distrusted. 'Safety First' was the persistent warning. We saw at once on the cricket field the effect of a dismal philosophy and a debilitated state of national health. Beautiful and brave stroke-play gave way to a sort of trench warfare, conducted behind the sandbag of broad pads.
>
> (Cardus 1945: 81)

In this discourse of national decline Cardus was specifically referring to an emergent re-working of cricket's performative grammar known as the 'two-eyed' or 'two-shouldered stance' (see figure 5.2). Utilitarian rather than aesthetically pleasing, the stance was adopted by many of the professional batsmen then beginning to challenge the amateur dominance of cricket. This technique was disapprovingly described in a coaching manual of the 1920s as:

> When the batsman stands 'wide open,' as it is called, i.e. with his left foot so far to 'leg' and so far out of line with his right, that he is standing almost square to the bowler. Now this cannot be sound policy, because it is practically an impossibility, when you are in this position, to put your left leg to the off side, maintain your balance, and drive the ball with your left shoulder well over it. Try it and see. You can't get their quickly enough can you?
>
> (Henley 8–9)

The stance was regarded as precluding the execution of the off-drive – the hallmark stroke of the pre-war gentlemen amateurs – and thus its emergence became a technical and aesthetic issue that mediated issues of political and socio-economic change. It led, its critics believed, to

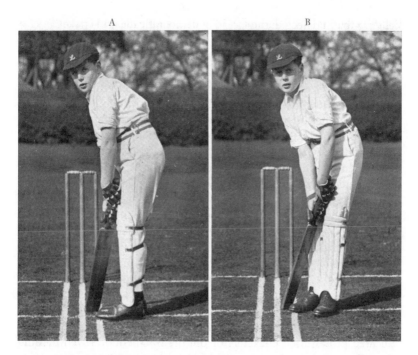

Figure 5.2 The orthodox and two-shouldered stances (A) If you study the positions of batsmen who play what may be termed "old-fashioned" cricket, *i.e.* those who still use the off drive, you will see that nearly all of them adopt a stance somewhat similar to that shown in A. Notice particularly the positions of the *left shoulder and the left leg.* Both are instantly ready to move into the correct place in order to make an off drive. *Both* eyes, too, are watching the bowler, so that the expression "the two-eyed" stance is incorrect, since everyone who is blest with the sight of two eyes invariably makes use of *both* of them. (B) The difference between the positions of the left shoulder and left leg in this picture and those in A is at once apparent. Here the bowler has a good view of *both shoulders* of the player as well as of both his eyes. Also the position in which the *feet – and more particularly the right one –* have been placed makes it *impossible to plant the left leg quickly across, get the left shoulder well over the ball,* keep the bat straight, and yet maintain perfect balance. Since many more balls are bowled on the *off* stump than on the *leg,* it follows that scoring must necessarily be slow and cricket unattractive to watch if this two-shouldered stance is adopted. (illustration and text from F. A. H. Henley, *The Boy's Book of Cricket.* London: G. Bell & Son, 1924. 10).

batsmen scoring runs (points) on the leg side (the side to the left of a right handed batsman) rather than stylishly scoring them on the off side (still occasionally referred to in cricket discourse as the 'posh side'). The political logic of this discourse was made explicit by Cardus who believed that it reflected 'the spread of democratic ideas in cricket' (1922: 85). As was shown in the previous section, in producing models of performative grammar, the technical discourse of cricket had facilitated the standardization and regulation of bodily practice in the sport since the early nineteenth century. However, in response to these apparently politically resonant re-workings of this grammar, a discourse emerged in which a number of cricket's cultural gatekeepers attempted to regulate and control the bodily practice of cricket in a more consciously corrective manner. Many of the critics of the two-eyed stance were pre-war amateurs now active as cricket writers such as A. C. 'Archie' MacLaren. In MacLaren's writings political and aesthetic judgments were always inextricably intertwined: the 'modern style' of 'getting in front and *facing* the bowler' may gain 'the applause of the vulgar,' but is 'against the spirit of cricket' (MacLaren 30–32). One remedy for the stylistic malaise in cricket proffered by MacLaren was for cricketers to immerse themselves in Pycroft's *The Cricket Field*, which, in an adoring essay, he canonized as a stable literary receptacle of timeless technical and aesthetic truths (MacLaren 39–50). But the writer who most obviously implicated the practice of cricket into a discourse of cultural discipline was the idiosyncratic E. H. D. Sewell. One of only a few public-school-educated professional cricketers of the pre-war period, Sewell became a prolific writer of books on cricket and rugby characterized by their trenchant views and unreflecting, virile prosody. Sewell proposed a critical practice of cricket writing based on the concept of an elect who had experienced the cricket of both pre- and post-war periods. He positioned this elite remnant of cricketers and critics against a new, *de-classe* type of cricket writer who 'spring mainly from a section of our community which has arrived in our midst since the war,' there work seemingly redolent of 'the querulous spirit of the age which is the progenitor of such trash as Bolshevism' (Sewell 1931: 58–59). Sewell perceived that the same socio-economic forces that had produced the 'Bolshevist school' of cricket writing had infiltrated the cricket field and were busy insinuating themselves on the bodily practices of young English cricketers. His entire output therefore attached a political and moral imperative to the modalities of bodily performance in cricket:

The time has come to put in a word to try and save Cricket from Ugliness.

To make an effort to at least stay its downward progress on the slope atop of which Beauty sits enthroned.

More bluntly, but no less fervently put, I would ask all coaches and captains henceforth to ponder their rudiments; and, doing all in their power to stifle on-side [leg-side] dibs and dabs and pushes and general full-chested inelegance, to let the coming-on generation realize to the full that (1) *there is an off-side; and (2) that about ninety per cent of all the grace and beauty in stroke-play reigns there.*

It is a most regrettable but an undeniable fact that one seldom hears or reads the names mentioned of more that at most about half a dozen batsmen of the post-1920 cadres when the topic is elegant or attractive batting.

(Sewell 1946: 57; author's italics)

Sewell also transposed this political logic into the practice of bowling by berating the 'numerous awkward, *badly-brought up actions*' that he saw in inter-war cricket (Sewell 1942: 192). In a highly codified form cricket writers were anatomizing the contemporary reconfiguration of masculinity by transposing perceptions of the loss of organic political order into the logic of bodily practice.

In order to provide a utopian contrast to the fallen practice of inter-war cricket, writers constructed a pre-war 'Golden Age' by aestheticizing the amateur and professional divide which structured cricket's social relations until 1963. Amateurs or 'Gentlemen' were largely from the higher social classes and often excelled at the more genteel practice of batting; while professionals or 'Players' tended to be working- or lower-middle class, many of whom were involved in the more strenuous and less glamorous activity of bowling. Gentlemen and Players had separate dressing rooms and entered the field through different gates but were held to be equal under the laws. Cricket thus served to simultaneously obscure and highlight class distinctions. With the division between Gentlemen and Players becoming increasingly blurred, the inter-war construction of the Golden Age presented a more desirable typology of Anglo-British masculinities based upon social cohesiveness and clearly demarcated inequality under aristocratic benevolence. According to Cardus, pre-war amateur batsmen displayed their natural superiority through elegant and effortless bodily performance:

During the golden age of English cricket, the public school flavour could be felt as strongly as in any West End club. When Spooner or K. L. Hutching batted on a lovely summer day you could witness the fine flowerings of all the elegant cultural processes that had gone to the making of these cricketers; you could see their innings as though against a backdrop of distant playing fields, far away from the reach of industry, pleasant lawns stretching to the chaste countryside, lawns well trimmed and conscious of the things that are not done. (1945: 106)

Clearly Cardus was not only celebrating the skills of pre-war batsmen such as Spooner and Hutching but the economic conditions and social relations that supposedly enabled such performances of elite masculinity to arise.

Inter-war cricket discourse thus intersected with a broader contemporary critique of the shifting balance of class forces. In cricket writing this dislocation of the socio-economic order was represented by the new, more affluent, and upwardly mobile professional cricketers such as Walter Hammond. In Cardus's inter-war writings these professionals displayed modes of bodily performance that were interpreted as stylistic markers of dangerously democratizing social and economic forces. At the same time however, these relatively affluent professional cricketers disrupted cricket literature's feudal social vision by playing in a style very close to the aesthetic ideals of the pre-war amateurs. Cardus thus developed a spurious critical practice of qualified praise which he undercut by projecting into the field a series of aesthetic judgments based on assumptions concerning social class and masculinity. For Cardus such professionals lacked social breeding and were motivated by the accumulation of economic, rather than symbolic or cultural, capital: 'There have been 'stylish' professionals, of course...But the average "pro" usually hints at the struggle for existence in mean grasping places. Hammond is majestic, no doubt; but not in the *inherited* way that MacLaren was majestic' (1945: 70; Cardus's italics). Like the much-vilified middle-class suburban housing of the period, Hammond's bodily performance is presented as lacking authenticity. Cardus later explicitly implicated this critical practice in the contemporary reconfiguration of masculinity by complaining that such professionals, unlike W. G. Grace, 'wore feminine shoes of patent leather' (Cardus 1934: 117). When he wrote in his 1947 *Autobiography* that 'between 1926 and 1936 our cricket was as stereotyped as the council houses and flats and ribbon roads which more and more...symbolised post-war England' (123), he again connected perceptions of the bodily performance of cricket to a broader discourse of cultural decline and crisis.

Learie Constantine and black masculinity

Such critiques of contemporary metropolitan masculinity in cricket discourse also had an important imperial, and indeed racial, dimension. As sports historians have shown, sporting interactions between Britain and its colonies, and particularly cricket tours, had long been important moments of imperial interchange around which debates and negotiations as to the legitimate meaning of Anglo-British and imperial masculinities occurred (cf. Bradley; McDevitt). This was also the case when individual colonial players performed to British sporting audiences. The Trinidadian cricketer, Learie Constantine had visited England on a number of occasions in the 1920s with the West Indies team before playing for the Lancashire League club Nelson as a highly paid professional. An associate of both Cardus and James, both these authors wrote much about his unique playing style in such a way that revealed their radically different political perspectives. Cardus provided a preface to Constantine and James's *Cricket and I* (1933), although this was little more than an abridged version of his essay 'Constantine' which was reprinted in *Good Days* (1934). Another version of this piece exotically entitled 'Life, sunshine and lustre' appeared in the early 1960s, the years immediately preceding Trinidadian independence. Looking back at the Constantine of the 1920s, and employing many of the same images, metaphors, and tropes as in the two earlier pieces, the essay is nevertheless a more extensive appraisal of Constantine's cricket and of his cultural meaning, while the historical context of immanent decolonization gives the writing a new cultural and political resonance. As in the earlier essays Constantine's status as a 'representative cricketer' is conveyed through a list of confident generalizations about West Indianness, the emphasis being upon his intuitive and instinctive cricketing ability:

> He played like a sort of elemental instinctive force. Principle became impulse in him. He expressed in all of his motions on the field the West Indian temperament. His swift darts and twistings in the slips were directed by intuitions heated by West Indian blood; he bowled terrifically fast as every West Indian boy wishes and loves to bowl. He batted with a racial power, positiveness and agility – again, as every West Indian boy wishes and determines to bat.
>
> (Cardus 1963: 96)

Such generalizations place the piece within an ethnographic frame of reference in which Cardus's authoritative white voice defines his black object. Cardus frames Constantine at once as a noble savage, a primitive man, an infant, and an animal, hence the pleasure of spying on him from the elevated press box (a voyeuristic pleasure charged with latent homoeroticism) is permitted. Here cricket discourse absorbs the rhetorical strategies of High Imperial adventure fiction and travel writing with the press box acting as a 'noble coign of vantage' (Spurr 17):

> He drove with a velocity and power quite terrifying. From the high Press Box I looked down on the fury of primitive onslaught, beautiful if savage and violently destructive... Moreover, I was really scared at the power and velocity of Constantine's strokes – scared that someone in the field might not merely be hurt – this was to be expected – but perhaps killed. Yet there was no excess of muscular effort in Constantine's swift plunderings. It was the attack and savagings of a panther on the kill, sinuous, stealthy, strong but unburdened. The batsmanship of the jungle, beautiful, ravaging, marvellously springy, swift as a blow of a paw. He would pull the pace of Larwood square. His footwork leaped. He even played back defensively baring teeth.
>
> (Cardus 1963: 96–98)

The mixture of admiration and terror generated by the dynamics of Constantine's bodily performance typify the ambiguity of colonial discourse. While Constantine's performance shocks and unsettles the awe-struck English connoisseur or ethnographer, his stylistic authenticity places him in the valorized category of artist batsmen. For Cardus, Constantine's cricket embodies something akin to Ruskin's gothic style, with its primitivity, its unfinished 'savageness or rudeness.' Constantine's play represents a return to an aesthetically superior age; his play embodies an aesthetic that like Ruskin's art of the ancient world is 'healthier than those of modern time,' for then people were 'full of animal spirit and physical power... incapable of every morbid condition of mental emotion' (Low 35). Part of the discursive ambivalence of this text derives from its debt to this highly gendered discourse of Victorian cultural criticism in which the quality of manliness was frequently seen to exemplify true art. In attributing a positive axiology to Constantine at the level of the aesthetic, Cardus reminds us of Paul Gilroy and Simon Gikandi's assertions that the categories of race and ethnicity entered the often gendered debates about the crisis of metropolitan culture in the modern period. For Cardus the intense physicality and manliness of Constantine's cricket make it superior to the prevailing style of English cricket in the inter-war period (and, to a greater degree, the 1950s and 1960s). Cardus's writings on Constantine are essentially a discourse of national degeneration in which his object's virile cricketing style is aesthetically valorized over the moribund, unadventurous, and hence 'unmanly' modes of the increasingly professionalized cricket of both post-war periods. At the same time, in failing to civilize Constantine, the cricket field is a place of anxiety and bewilderment more than of imperial accomplishment. In this presentation of a distinctive black kinetics, the body and the body politic are symbolically conflated in such a way that simultaneously elicits fear and admiration on the part of the metropolitan observer.

From the 1920s the discourse and practice of cricket mediated, and contributed to, a broader discourse of national and imperial decline. As much cricket writing of the period shows, stylizations of masculinity enacted within the structured frame of cricket were interpreted as indicative of the health of the British nation and empire. Such discourse was comprised of issues of social class and race. Because of cricket's imperial scope discourses surrounding cricket were often ambiguous: although hopelessly racialized, Cardus's account of Constantine affords the colonial performance of masculinity a positive axiology. At the same time these stylizations are seen as indicative of imperial instability: in failing to discipline fully the male colonial body, cricket had not succeeded in its civilizing and disciplinary mission. Cricket was thus a field of masculine performance in which the tensions and contradictions of empire were re-enacted and played out. Furthermore, within the unlikely field of cricket, Anglo-British masculinity itself was open to performative revision.

Acknowledgment

Part of the writing of this chapter was undertaken as a Visiting Research Fellow at the Centre for Idraet, University of Aarhus, Denmark in November 2005.

Works cited

Arlott, John, ed. *From Hambledon to Lords: The Classics of Cricket*. London: Christopher Johnson, 1948.

Baucom, Ian. *Out of Place: Englishness, Empire and the Locations of Identity*. Princeton: Princeton UP, 1999.

Beldham, George W. and C. B. Fry. *Great Batsmen, Their Methods at a Glance*. London: Macmillan, 1905.

Bradley, James. 'Inventing Australians and Constructing Englishness: Cricket and the Creation of a National Consciousness 1860–1914.' *Sporting Traditions* 11 (1995): 35–60.

Cardus, Neville. *Autobiography*. London: Collins, 1947

——. *A Cricketer's Book*. London: Grant Richards, 1922.

——. *English Cricket*. 1945. London: Prion, 1997

——. *Good Days*. London: Jonathan Cape, 1934.

——. *The Playfair Cardus*. London: The Dickens Press, 1963.

Currie, F. Davison. *The Cricketer's Companion or the Secrets of Cricket*. London: George Routledge & Sons, 1918.

Frewin, Leslie, ed. *The Poetry of Cricket*. London: Macdonald, 1964.

Gikandi, Simon. *Maps of Englishness: Writing Identity in the Culture of Colonialism*. New York: Columbia UP, 1996.

Gilroy, Paul. *The Black Atlantic: Modernity and Double Consciousness*. London: Verso, 1993.

Henley, F. A. H. *The Boy's Book of Cricket*. London: G. Bell & Sons, 1924.

Hughes, Thomas. *Tom Brown's Schooldays*. 1857. Oxford: Oxford UP, 1989.

James, C. L. R. *Beyond a Boundary*. London: Hutchinson, 1963.

Judd, Denis. *Empire: The British Colonial Experience from 1765 to the Present*. 1996. London: Phoenix Press, 2001.

Lambert, William. *Instructions and Rules for Playing the Noble Game of Cricket, As Practised by the Most Eminent Players*. Lewes: Sussex Press, 1816.

Light, Alison. *Forever England: Femininity, Literature and Conservatism Between the Wars*. London: Routledge, 1991.

Low, Gail Ching-Liang. *White Skins Black Masks: Representation and Colonialism*. London: Routledge, 1996.

MacLaren, A. C. *Cricket Old and New*. London: Longmans, Green & Co., 1924.

McDevitt, Patrick F. *'May the Best Man Win': Sport, Masculinity and Nationalism in Great Britain and the Empire 1880–1935*. Basingstoke: Palgrave Macmillan, 2004.

Mosse, George. *The Image of Man: The Creation of Modern Masculinity*. Oxford: Oxford UP, 1996.

Nyren, John. *The Cricketers of My Time*. Ed. Ashley Mote. London: Robson Books, 1998.

Rutherford, Jonathan. *Forever England: Reflections on Race, Masculinity and Empire*. London: Lawrence & Wishart, 1997.

Sewell, E. H. D. *Cricket Up-to-Date*. London: John Murray, 1931.

——. *Cricket under Fire*. London: Stanley Paul, 1942.

——. *Well Hit Sir!* London: Stanley Paul, 1946.

Spurr, David. *The Rhetoric of Empire: Colonial Discourse in Journalism, Travel Writing, and Imperial Administration*. London: Duke UP, 1993.

Stevenson, John. *British Society 1914–45*. London: Penguin, 1990.

Williams, Raymond. *Marxism and Literature*. Oxford: Oxford UP, 1977.

6
'A Stoat Came to Tea': Camp Poetics and Masculinity

Antony Rowland

Abstract

While poetry has traditionally been regarded as the highest of literary genres and therefore frequently been associated with idealized male poets and their assumed gravitas, self-subverting forms of 'camp' poetics can be traced all the way to the Renaissance. The present essay takes camp poetics as a necessary corrective and self-criticism within a male poetic tradition and explores it in works by poets ranging from Donne to W. H. Auden and John Ashbery. In their works, excess, exaggeration, and strategic extravagance go side by side with often very serious concerns. A camp poetics provides masculinity with a kind of double vision inside which it performs itself while looking quizzically and critically at its own performance at the same time.

Camp poetics are an integral, and neglected, aspect of literary tradition. In relation to Sylvia Plath's monologues in particular, I have defined these poetics as instances of 'exaggeration, theatricality, insistent repetition and iteration, outrageous surrealism, overstatement, mock-amazement, melodramatic keening, vamping, bitchiness, sarcasm, inter-jections, incongruity, black comedy and queer poetics' (Rowland 2005: 28). Playful, self-conscious engagements with poetic form are rife from the Renaissance onward, yet such campy moments are often written off as light divergences from the real work of supposed lyrical trans-parency. F. R. Leavis famously attacked the extravagant indulgences of W. H. Auden's writing, but the latter's flippant verse should be regarded instead as a camp challenge to the dominant 'cool insistence' of the lyrical tradition.[1] Camp frivolousness can only be subservient to 'The greatest masculine art' if, as Robert Bly contends, the latter has to have 'what the Romans called *gravitas* – soberness, weight, and grief' (Bly, Hillman, Meade 95). 'We can feel gravity,' he adds, 'when we see great art' (by men).

Classical control over poetic diction and form has been – often unconsciously – construed as a masculine pursuit, as opposed to the effeminate dalliance with supposedly inferior forms such as the dramatic monologue. It is no coincidence that camp poetics are more often – but not exclusively – found in extravagant monologues. In contrast, the lyric – despite the recent interventions of linguistically innovative writers – often attempts to obscure its artifice by pretending that an uncomplicated, mimetic relationship exists between the text and the moon and duck ponds described therein. Auden's camp poetics were often associated with a (supposedly) concomitant moral and sexual deviancy. It is also no coincidence that the deviant textual strategies of camp poetics (in the form, for example, of queer monologues) have been derided as subservient to lyrical 'objectivity.'[2] Camp poetics call attention instead to the lyric, and poetry itself, as a *performance of form*, rather than an essential poetic distillation.[3]

By emphasizing that 'voices' in written poetry are partly an effect of form, camp poetics mirror the process in which campy performances of masculinity and femininity elsewhere call attention to the constructed nature of gender identities. In the work of male writers, camp poetics are often seen as a sign of queer effeminacy (as in Leavis's reaction to Auden's degenerate *Poems*), whereas for women writers they are signs of female masculinity. Critical illustrations of camp masculinity have encompassed the strutting insolence of Sylvia Plath's narrators (such as Lady Lazarus) and the rampant scolding of Carol Ann Duffy's anti-male characters (such as Frau Freud).[4] In fact, camp poetics highlight the binary gender associations of male writer/camp/queer/effeminate and female poet/camp/queer/masculine in such critical discourse that the poetics themselves at are pains to subvert.

These binaries partly ensue from the (inevitable) critical poverty of some of the terms that still predominate in Gender Studies. Judith Halberstam's groundbreaking *Female Masculinity* brilliantly illustrates how masculinity resides in, for example, lesbian (boilerplate) bulldaggers and stone butches; she argues that the concept of masculinities should be prised away from (straight) male bodies, which comprised the critical locus in Men's Studies until the late 1990s (1–5). The liberal proliferation of masculinity may be applauded, but Halberstam's critical illustrations are based on *a priori* gender constructions in which, for example, ebulliance and stoicism are rendered as masculine gender signs. Supposedly effeminate manifestations of the queer – such as femme lesbians and camp men – therefore have no part to play in her polemical study. In contrast, Lynne Segal argues that illustrations of queer masculinities are troubling in that they are paradoxically signs of a persistent patriarchy.[5] By focussing on instances of masculinity outside the realm of male power, she contends, gender critics take their eyes off the socio-economic ball; this critical blinkeredness means that patriarchy remains intact.

To return to a critical paradigm in which signs of masculinity are associated only with male bodies would, of course, be unthinkable after the advent of Judith Butler's theories of gender performance, and Queer Studies. What needs to be re-thought is the reification of masculinity. By this I mean the persistence of a masculine/feminine binary in Gender Studies, in which free-floating gender signs (such as aggression and timidity) are automatically categorized as instances of masculinity or femininity. This critical tenaciousness has contributed to the crisis in Men's Studies – as opposed to the oft-proposed crisis in masculinity – as it attempts to re-define itself after its 'first-wave' acceptance in academic circles during the 1990s.[6]

Camp poetics do not entirely escape such conceptual oppositions, but they do creatively wriggle across categorizations of straight men, queer femmes, and butchy disco bunnies. Instances of camp can be located in the performances of a straight hairdresser in *Brookside*, Russell Brand and 'the funny unchallengeable poofiness of a handsome straight boy in a country town,' as much as cross-dressing boys with their swishy boas pretending to be Greta Garbo, and David Hockney's pictures of 'the appealing insouciance of a sleeping young man's exposed bum.'[7] Yet when I mentioned the subject of this chapter to other academics, they mostly assumed that I was writing about a tradition of gay (male) poetry. Hence the versatility of camp (Fabio Cleto evaluates this phenomenon as its 'groundlessness') means that it is not, as some critics perceive, a term that became outdated after Stonewall and the Camp movement of the 1960s, or a simplistic symptom, now, of 'degayified taste.'[8] Camp poetics resulting from the affectations of poetic form can be located in the work of straight men, stone butches, or outrageously campy queers. Such rhetoric allows a focus on the performance of gender signs and poetic subgenres in the writing itself, rather than regarding the latter as an adjunct to the poets' own gender identities.

Having investigated the relationship between camp poetics and constructions of female masculinity elsewhere (cf. Rowland 2005), in this chapter I wish to uncover its often unnoted proliferation in the work of canonical male poets. More controversially, I argue that such queer poetics comprise a buried literary tradition. John Donne is our first camp poet.[9] Whereas deviant poetics are unthinkable in medieval devotional pieces, Donne's famous opening to 'The good-morrow' ('I wonder by my troth, what thou, and I/Did, till we lov'd? were we not wean'd till then?') comprises a camp aesthetics of agitation against what Leavis archly referred to as the dryness of the poet's contemporaries, such as 'Fulk Greville, Chapman, and Drayton' (qtd. in Attridge 44). Leavis refers to the lines' creation as 'The extraordinary force of originality'; Derek Attridge, as an exemplary instance of artistic inventiveness, and poetic singularity (44–46). They are also outrageously campy: the overblown interrogative calls attention to the self-referential form; these are poetics aware of the scandalous evaluation of human love in a devotional world of blood-lines, sin, and suffering.

As Rebecca Ann Bach has argued, it is anachronistic to consider Donne as an exemplary purveyor of male heterosexuality, since such gender identities were only formed in the eighteenth century. Of course, to queer Donne by labelling him a camp writer is equally anachronistic – since 'camp' was only coined in the nineteenth century to refer to 'actions and gestures of exaggerated emphasis' – but I do so in order to trace a neglected tradition of poetics which runs through Donne and Crashaw to Auden and Ashbery (Cleto 9). Such mannerist poetics (another anachronism) call attention – due to their exaggerated, theatrical, and insistent nature – to poetry as a *literary performance*, in contrast with the lyric's quiet insistence on its own transparency from the medieval period onward.

Mannerist poetics undercut (constructed) signs of normative masculinity, since the hyper-intensity of such writing eschews Bly's notion of classical *gravitas*. Mannerism is akin to the camp *spezzatura* or careless grace of Cavalier art. Developed in the twentieth century, the term describes (mainly Italian) sixteenth-century painting and architecture. Its affinity with camp poetics can be adduced from its resistance to classical rules: like Baroque art, *manneristi* writers such as John Lyly were attacked as artificial and affected. Linked movements such as Marinism and Gongorism were equally outrageous in their subversion of classical decorum with hyberbole and over-wrought intricacy. Such sumptuously indulgent writing offended classicist restraint; connections between mannerism, Marinism, and Gongorism have been made with the extravagant conceits of canonical writers such as Richard Crashaw, whose work contains shamelessly campy lamentations ('O these wakeful wounds of time! Are they mouths? or are they eyes?') (Crashaw 1993a:

1390). Such camp exaggerations, 'conscious of [their] status as performance,' highlight poetry's intrinsically 'rhetorical and incantatory' nature (Kendall 149).

As I have argued in relation to Plath's bees, the genre of poetry is so susceptible to camp because – like opera and musicals – it can turn a seemingly mundane incident into a glorious exaggeration or metaphysical dilemma (cf. Rowland 2005: 32). To pursue an entomological connection, when John Milton opines in 'Lycidas' that 'the Gray-fly winds her sultry horn' (444), he is only really writing about an insect buzzing. The philosopher Daniel Dennett argued that once language arrives on the evolutionary scene, we have to make room for 'all manner of biologically trivial or irrelevant or baroque (non-functional) endeavours: gossip, riddles, poetry, philosophy' (qtd. in Wainwright 5). To paraphrase Theodor Adorno (177), it is not necessary to sheer human survival to describe how a bee buzzes. Jeffrey Wainwright deduces that 'On [Dennett's] view, *all* poetry, including the most rhetorically purposeful, might be seen as "baroque"' (5).

Whereas mannerist writing in particular is consistent in its exaggerations, however, the focus in this chapter will be on poets who, on the whole, deploy camp poetics sparingly as a means of illustrating that democratic evaluations of writing can encompass theatrical zest as well as tub-thumping dirges. Hence camp poetics are a kind of controlled mannerism. They still rail against the high seriousness of art, since they can insert deviant sub-genres such as lowbrow burlesque into the supposedly highbrow genre of poetry itself. Traditional constructions of literary value have had a tendency to denigrate such tactical moves, but restrained, tragic lyricism can also dupe the reader into thinking that the lyric in front of them is *automatically* serious, transcendent, and transparent art of high aesthetic value. In contrast, the camp poetry of writers such as Auden aspires to the democratic inclusion of the 'jocoserious.'[10]

'[A]re they eyes?': Donne's camp opening

Donne's writing is usually construed as an early symptom of normative (heterosexual) masculinity, but the camp opening of 'The good-morrow' allows an alternative reading of the 'masculine perswasive force' that is often excerpted from 'Elegie 16 XVI. On his Mistris' and then applied to his *oeuvre* (*Donne Poetical Works* 99). This 'force' is already paradoxically bound up with a genre that, for post-Romantic readers, is inexorably constructed as effeminate, as opposed to the masculine classical control of prose. Wit may have been a sign of masculine virility in the seventeenth century, but for modern readers the exclamations, interrogatives, and self-dramatizations in Donne's love poems inevitably appear camp. (This rhetoric is also inextricable from Donne's misogyny, which – as Bach illustrates throughout her article – Donne's critics have been loathe to emphasize.)

Camp poetics are an aesthetics of agitation which rail against lyrical balance: in the case of 'The Sunne Rising,' they arise out of a preposterous hyperbole that can – for a moment – pretend that the lover's bed is the equivalent of the sun's center.[11] When Leavis and Attridge attribute genius and singularity (respectively) to the opening of 'The good-morrow,' they are reacting to the campy interrogative, which (equally preposterously) wonders whether the lovers in question were babies until they started indulging in each others' pleasures. Camp poetics thus comprise an energized language which contains its own winking critique. The interrogative highlights the hyperbole: this indicates that the reader may wish to read against the conceit (deciding that they were, after all, not babies but grown ups before they 'lov'd'). A more straightforward articulation (such as 'We were not wean'd, till we lov'd') would not encourage such readerly subversion to the same extent. Camp poetics thus encompass a self-questioning that emphasizes the artificial construction of subjectivity in poetry. Interrogatives suggest that the narrator is not sure about the offered conceits, just as the reader cannot be certain about the credentials of a persona after a two-line utterance.

My detection of camp poetics in Donne's rhetoric is not meant to set up a transhistorical metanarrative in which camp can be detected in all manner of writing from the medieval period onward, if only the reader were that way inclined. Leavis detects an 'extraordinary force of originality' in these lines which makes Donne a 'contemporary' in 1936 (qtd. in Attridge 44). However, an eighteenth-century reader would have been unlikely to encounter Donne 'as ... the living,' since the poet was then out of favor, when the rules of classical decorum once more held sway. Camp poetics are inextricably part of our own post-colloquial age: it was only in the twentieth century that pub characters were allowed to grumble in (mock-) epic poetry, and a poet could describe the machinations of the moon while not neglecting to point out that he was dying to urinate at the time.[12] Hence Donne's mock-chatty, conversational opening to 'The good-morrow' cannot help but appeal to twentieth- (and twenty-first-) century readers in a way that would have left Alexander Pope unmoved. Attridge (46) contextualizes Leavis's reaction to Donne's inventiveness by illustrating that he was responding unconsciously to a shift in modern criticism, which applauded 'directness of address, verbal ingenuity, and conspicuous intelligence married to intense feeling' (as in 'The good-morrow'). These are key components of camp poetics: Attridge's critical evaluation could be rendered in a different register as 'frank, flashy, showy and passionate.' All camp poets manipulate these cherished attributes in modern criticism.

In *The Singularity of Literature*, Attridge gently castigates instrumental-ist criticism that takes hold of an idea and then blunders into literary texts to prove its efficacy (6–10). My exposition of camp poetics in Renaissance literature might be accused of such instrumentalism, but it actually provides a critical vocabulary to explore, as Attridge puts it, the re-invention of invention:

> 'Discoveries' or 'rediscoveries' of artists of the past can, of course, be quite superficial, based on accidental similarities between the two cultural contexts, and in such cases the newly appreciated works are unlikely to be enjoyed as inventive or to spur fresh inventions. But if the new context relates to the earlier one in more profound ways, new possibilities of inventiveness in works and *oeuvres* (different but not entirely distinct from their original inventiveness) may come into being. This capacity for reinventing invention is at the heart of artistic survival. (47)

The 'new context' of camp poetics describes a form of invention not previously discussed in literary criticism. Rather than the detection of camp in Donne's poetry being an accidental similarity between twenty-first century poetics and Renaissance writing, the analysis of the interrogative opens out into undetected inventiveness in the work of other writers, such as Crashaw, Auden, Ashbery, Plath, and Duffy. (Camp poetics should also 'spur fresh inventions' in contemporary poetry.[13]) Leavis's reaction to innovations in 'tone, rhythm, dramatic presentation, language' (qtd. in Attridge 46) in the opening of 'The good-morrow' illustrates why Donne is our first camp poet (and why camp poetics are an inextricable part of modernity), as the lines play-fully call attention to these elements of poetry in a way not encountered before in the genre. Donne's self-conscious rhetoric makes us think of his scandalous speakers *as speakers*, rather than classical mouthpieces; uniquely, in terms of sixteenth- and seventeenth-century poetry, until the publication of the *Songs and Sonets*.

Such poetics stress the singularity of the poetry by commenting self-referentially on its structure, centuries before postmodern writing considered such textual strategies *de rigueur*. By stressing his innovations in rhythm, tone, and address, Donne allows the reader to dwell on the *performance* of the poem. As the narrator calls attention to his fanciful suppositions about human love, the poem enacts a 'verbal singularity' that includes the reader performing 'a *sense of its real-time unfolding*' (Attridge 71). (Jeffrey Wainwright (28) terms this the 'deliberate space of the poem.') Poems – with apologies to sub-genres such as the epic – usually need to be read as verbal devices unfolding in a single performance. Camp poetics highlight the controlling activity of the management of rhythm and tone across a poem; in other words, they are not mannerist just for the sake of wasteful extravagance.

Auden's orgy and Ashbery's stoat

Donne's campy extrapolation on a squashed flea as a site of atrocity ('Cruell and sodaine, hast thou since/Purpled thy naile, in blood of innocence?') calls attention to the apostrophe of a young narrator in a way unthinkable in the later, devotional pieces (*Donne: Poetical Works* 37). There is something constructedly youthful about camp: young poets' and narrators' extravagant meanderings can be contrasted with the wise, measured, and beautifully crafted lyrics of elder writers: Donne's career – like that of many other writers – encompassed both polarities, of course. John Keats's (mincing) performance of his own work in front of Wordsworth illustrates the contrast: the elder, Cumbrian poet famously wrote off the event as a 'very pretty piece of Paganism' (Haydon qtd. in Motion 215). Larkin associates campy apostrophe – such as Crashaw's 'O dart of love! Arrow of light!' – with youthful poetic excess in 'Sad Steps.'[14] Such projected interjections in his own writing ('O wolves of memory! Immensements!') are symptoms of an exclamatory and celebratory style that the older poet can only wince at, and pastiche (Larkin 169).

Donald Davie's depiction of Auden as a perfectly horrid little boy in short trousers when going about his serio-comic verse (qtd. in Smith 97) is instructive in this context. This critic perceives a self-indulgent solipsism in 'light' poems such as *Letter to Lord Byron* instead of a litany of deliberately camp techniques. The first two stanzas of the mock-epic set the campy tone of the entire poem: Auden is not afraid of the bad pun ('And then a lord – Good Lord'), deliberately crude, slangy rhyme (cash/pash [for passion]) and ribald humor, as he imagines Byron receiving fan-mail, including 'The correspondent's photo in the rude' (Auden 77). Davie mistakes camp poetics for formal immaturity: the serious frivolity elsewhere in the poem encompasses the bizarre expressed in a matter-of-fact tone (getting to sleep in Iceland is like 'returning after orgies'), outrageous rhyme (Geysir/plaisir; long/Continong), bitchy, off-the-cuff asides ('For all I know the Beatific Vision's/On view at all Surrealist Exhibitions'), interjected pastiche ('Byron, thou should'st be living at this hour!'), arch snobbery ('Someone may think that Empire wines are nice'), ironic affectation ('copper mines might, *faute de mieux*, be sound'), and tongue-in-cheek dismissals of literary critics ('Whose lives were uncreative but were good') (81, 83, 85, 86, 95, 89). Auden forges an apt, campy marriage between the Chaucerian stanza (rhyme royal with its jaunty ababbcc scheme) and light verse; playful pyrotechnics ensue rather than short-panted idlings.

Letter to Lord Byron contrasts frumpy lyrics with naughty light verse.[15] Whereas certain modernist texts require a 'spanner' for the reader's elucidation (the comment must be applied, partly, to T. S. Eliot, who is mentioned four – and seven – lines earlier), the narrator's ramblings are refreshingly 'gay and witty.' As Stan Smith points out (96), 'gay' had already accrued many of its modern associations by 1936: Auden is deliberately offsetting queer aesthetics against the masculinity of classicism; in his Oxford quads the dogmatism of 'Good poetry is … austere' rang 'clear' (78). (Hence Byron's suitability as a decadent muse: the Romantic poet's writing includes dedications to a choirboy, references to same-sex activities in his letters to C. Matthews and cross-dressing.[16]) For Davie, Auden's dilettante poetics prove inexcusably effeminate, but any such deviation from the lyric's 'cool insistence' should not be written off (using gender binaries) as inconsequential. Modern criticism adores the 'frank, flashy, showy and passionate' as long as such qualities do not result in overly light or comic forms of writing: hence Leavis's aforementioned comment that Auden could not marshal his material in a suitably (Eliotian) 'cool' manner.

The narrator of *Letter to Lord Byron* laments that because of such prejudice over aesthetics, light verse 'is under a sad weather' (80). In the stanza after this assertion, such critical frumpiness is undercut with campy self-deprecation ('Et cetera, et cetera. O curse,/That is the flattest line in English verse'). However, 'jocoserious' verse – or what the narrator calls 'conversational song' at the end of the poem (80) – does not, of course, eschew the austere entirely. Auden's interjections re the burgeoning technological age barely mask an impatient social critique, as the following lines reveal: 'Hail to the New World! Hail to those who'll love/Its antiseptic objects, feel at home' (82). After elucidating a vision of a classless society where 'the difference today is small/Of barmaid from the lady at the Hall,' the poet subverts such idealism with the bathetic litotes that 'It's sad to spoil this democratic vision/With millions suffering from malnutrition' (83). In a subsequent irony, the narrator notes that 'death is better, as the millions know,/Than dandruff, night-starvation, or B. O.'

Camp poetics here display ambivalence toward the objects of scrutiny: Auden's gormless lovers who gaze at electric stoves are comparable with the peanut-crunching crowd in Plath's 'Lady Lazarus.' The satire may be composed in an 'airy manner' (89), but it is also intensely scathing. Throughout the mock-epic, Auden damns with the faint praise of ironic litotes: scholars' lives were 'good,' idealist visions 'sad' and Iceland (apart from Reykjavik) 'a very nice land' (89, 83, 94).

Ashbery's camp poetics in poems such as 'Merrily We Live' from *Your Name Here* similarly deploy understatement for comic effect (Ashbery 10–11). The surreal opening, in which drums sometimes allow the unnamed narrator(s) to play just before closing time, is then undercut in the second line with the Audenesque litotes 'and that was nice' (10). By the end of the first stanza the reader has entered a typically bizarre Ashbery scenario in which a pub has put on a circus, and the clown is tired of having his bottom chewed off by a dinky donkey, who is similarly distressed by the fact that people keep trying to pin a tail on him, 'which was perhaps understandable.'

The seemingly throw away, coy, conversational diction that Ashbery often adopts in his poetry is a queer affront to the overly serious, masculine lyrics adored by poets at the front of the men's movement in the 1970s and 1980s, such as Robert Bly. The latter's (co-edited) collection *The Rag and Bone Shop of the Heart: Poems for Men* contains much pseudo-Lawrentian verse in which men dance in front of mirrors, alone, in order to reclaim their supposed masculinity diminished by the presence of women and babies.[17] In contrast, Ashbery's mock-diaristic poem records comically that 'Today a stoat came to tea/and that was so nice it almost made me cry' (11; note the understated 'nice' again). Tub-thumping, 'masculine' lyrics celebrating what Anne McNaughton calls the 'beautiful pebbles' between men's legs have little in common with the queer, incongruous juxtapositions in Ashbery's writing: deploying the classic surrealist technique of collating two separate images in order to create a comic third party, circuses take place in pubs, snowballs force their noxious way into halls and ermines come to tea (presumably, in their white winter coats) (Bly, Hillman, Meade 325). Clowns very rarely get their bottoms bitten in Robert Bly's poetry.

Ashbery's queer campiness may be an affront to the masculine lyric, but, as with Auden, this does not mean that his poetry can be dismissed as purely light. Indeed, critics often take the opposite view of Ashbery and mistakenly attempt to read his overtly playful work *as* lyrical. Like Auden's work, Ashbery's writing is often jocoserious. Comedy arises in 'Merrily We Live' from the arch ramblings of the possibly unhinged narrator(s) who shoves a variety of voices onto the poetic stage, but an alternative reading is possible in which we are listening to the imagined voice of an Alzheimer's patient. Faint, comic connections between lines (such as a noxious snowball suddenly smelling of violets) may be *de rigueur* in such (previously) avant-garde writing, but they could also be read as a sign of decaying brain transmitters. The poem contains the ghost of a dream-like story which is subverted by camp juxtapositions and switches in the narrative and interjections: after fearing that a nice (again) big tomorrow might come, the narrator sighs, 'Well, so long,' and implores the implied reader not to touch any breasts, 'at least until I get there' (11). These (dis)connections might be less a camp farrago for its own sake, and more a jocoserious piece which leads the readers into an uncomfortable position where they suddenly realize that they might be laughing at an Alzheimer's patient.

'Clusters of pollen blot out the magnolia blossoms this year': such a line would not be out of place in a masculine lyric, which would paradoxically be celebrating something as constructedly feminine as wax-like flowers (10). This opening to stanza two of Ashbery's poem is then immediately undercut with the rhetorical equivalent of a campy toss of the hand: 'and that's about all there is to it.' Such camp strategies proliferate in the work of Auden and Ashbery, yet they have not yet received the critical attention they deserve. Despite the poetics' subversive potential, they have not been able – by very dint of the fact that they are a queer, buried tradition – to detract from masculine lyrics' continuing predominance in mainstream contemporary poetry.

Lynne Segal writes throughout her 2001 article, in relation to queer (and other post-structuralist) readings of gender signs in literary texts, that it is all too easy to point out the subversive potential of queer phenomena such as camp poetics at the expense of reiterating that sites of male power still predominate in the social sphere. Whilst not forgetting Segal's edict, the aesthetic potential of such unrecognized queer poetics should not be underestimated. The efficacy of camp poetics appertains way beyond the genre of poetry: Vladimir Nabokov's rhetoric in *Lolita* should be recognized as an example of these poetics; when the tweenie sits on the narrator, Humbert senses the 'psychologically very friable texture of the material divide (pajamas and robe) between the weight of two sunburnt legs, resting athwart my lap, and the hidden tumor of an unspeakable passion' (Nabokov 59). The sometimes 'friable' connection between camp poetics and mental instability – as in the Ashbery poem – is indicated earlier in the novel when Humbert ensconces himself in an expensive sanatorium (35). Any analysis of camp poetics in the novel is beyond the scope of this chapter, but I hope that after essays such as this, their prevalence in literary tradition, and their challenge to subgenres of writing constructed as masculine, might be more easily recognized.

At the end of his discussion of the dominance of a plain, post-Movement style in post-war poetry, Jeffrey Wainwright asks 'whether an "ordinary" tone is what we want in poetry. Might we not want extraordinary speech, choice of words, a *diction*, that we do not encounter every day? At present, after half a century in which the…"unpoetic" manner has dominated poetry in English, we might think so' (33). Camp poetics comprise one possible example of such extraordinary diction. These are poetics which can comprise deviant signs of masculinity. They offer a challenge to the supposedly 'masculine' art of 'ordinary' post-Movement writing and classical *gravitas*.

Notes

1. Quoted in Stan Smith's exemplary discussion of Auden's light verse in his edited collection *The Cambridge Companion to W. H. Auden* (96). The object of the essay is not to denigrate the lyric entirely (as some linguistically innovative poets and critics have done), but merely to point out how, in the twentieth century, it began to be seen *as poetry itself*, to the exclusion of other forms, such as the monologue, the mock-epic, light verse, performance poetry, and so on. A glance at most of the mainstream poetry magazines and journals today would indicate that this conflation of a sub-genre (the lyric) with the genre of poetry as a whole persists in the twenty-first century. Many mainstream writers (such as Geoffrey Hill) subvert the lyrical form from within, of course, at the same time as the lyric is ultimately upheld as a site of poetic excellence. Others, such as Carol Ann Duffy, have made expansive use of the monologue form, but a critical tendency remains to praise Duffy's work before and after the monologue collections (*The World's Wife* and *Feminine Gospels*), and treat the monologues themselves as aberrations. The lyric's recent predominance is partly due to the supposition that a young poet should find their true voice (Malcolm Bradbury's early forays into creative writing at East Anglia comprise examples of this tendency). Coincidentally, 'true' voices tend to be 'discovered' in the sub-genre of the lyric rather than the monologue form; the latter, of course, highlights the artifice of poetic voice with its various narrators with a myriad of tones. Hence, critical suspicions have augmented about campy, versatile writers who are comfortable with an array of poetic forms (such as W. H. Auden), since they

do not adhere to a creative notion in which output has to be tied to an essential, poetic character (or 'soul'). In contrast, camp poems highlight, as I argue throughout this chapter, that *poetic voice is partly (and unavoidably) an effect of form* rather than an essential quality that creative writers have to dig deep to uncover, uncontaminated. Lyrics encourage a sober poetic voice instilled with gravitas, but such expression is only one possibility among many other poetic voices and sub-genres. Camp poetics tend instead toward the exuberant, witty (but not overly intellectual) poetic extravaganza.

2. When 'camp' was first coined, it was used chiefly 'by persons of exceptional want of character.' It proliferated in the 'slang of theatricals, high society, the fashion world, showbiz, and the underground city life' (Cleto 9).

3. Hence in what Cleto terms 'deliberate camp' (such as camp monologues), the focus is on 'the very act of [audacious] performance ... producing a failure of seriousness, acknowledging its "essence" in the unnatural, in the *inessential* and the contingent, and privileging form and style over message or content in self-(re)presentation' (24). Critics who (mostly unconsciously) regard the lyric as the only form of poetry can be exasperated by the monologue's focus on the artificial, inessential nature of the poetic voice. They may look for a 'true' voice elsewhere, which they mistakenly recognize in the equally artificial form of the lyric. Notions of authenticity are 'antithetical to camp which is so doggedly committed to artifice' (Cleto 407). As Susan Sontag notes, to 'perceive Camp in objects and persons is to understand Being-as-Playing-a-Role. It is the farthest extension, in sensibility, of the metaphor of life as theater' (qtd. in Cleto 25). A lyric can only be a lyric because it is simultaneously performing the role of a lyric. The poetic sub-genre that highlights the theatricality of being most openly is, of course, the monologue. And poetry's inherent, rhetorical theatricality is emphasized in camp poetics. However, such dramatic rhetoric does not necessarily result in an absolute 'failure of seriousness,' as Cleto claims. Christopher Isherwood contends that 'High Camp' contains 'underlying seriousness' (qtd. in Cleto 51). 'You're expressing what's basically serious to you in terms of fun and artifice and elegance.' Camp poetics may lampoon the lyric's po-faced seriousness, but they do not do so in order to discredit the genre of poetry in its entirety.

4. I include some my own work in this context, although in an article on Duffy I do point to the (inevitable) critical poverty of some of the terms still prevalent in gender studies, which I discuss later in this chapter (cf. Rowland 2003: 137–38).

5. Segal *passim*. '[W]hen a woman,' Segal argues, 'whether lesbian, bi- or heterosexual, can exemplify "masculinity"... its contingent, protean and inclusive character is such that, I fear, we may be in danger of bypassing rather than eroding its weighty cultural and symbolic intimidations and exclusions' (235). Literary texts find it all too easy to subvert normative/hegemonic/phallic/patriarchal masculinity, 'with this, *on its own*, not shifting its symbolic power' (245).

6. Roger Horrocks's *Men in Crisis: Myths, Fantasies and Realities* (London: Macmillan, 1994) is symptomatic of this supposedly calamitous masculinity. As Segal argues, 'The "masculinity in crisis" literature is problematic insofar as it ignores the central issue: the pay-offs men receive (or hope to receive) from their claims to manhood' (239). Whereas first-wave feminism

took approximately 70 years to reach its subsequent stage, men's studies had taken only about 30 years. This alacrity may be due to the fact that there is less at stake – in terms of winning, say, voting rights – than was the case with feminism. A scathing critic might comment that there was in fact very little at all at stake for men, who did, and still do, dominate cultural sites of power (parliament, the police, top executive posts, and so on).

7. The quotations are taken, respectively, from Alan Hollinghurst's novel *The Line of Beauty* (287) and Edmund White's 'Hockney, Art and Desire: Sunlight, beaches and boys' (16). The boa reference is taken from Cleto (51). (For the sake of assonance I have changed Marlene Dietrich to Greta Garbo in the quotation.) The hairdresser I am referring to in the (now defunct) Channel 4 soap *Brookside* was called Peter. In a delightfully campy moment he flounced off our screens after having an affair with the model Linda Lusardi, who was in fact the actor's real-life partner.

8. Cleto (9, 10). Cleto describes camp as a 'proper-groundless, mobile building without deep and anchoring foundations, a building devoid of the *stasis* potentially implicated by [a] diamond metaphor' (9). Rather than seeing camp as groundless in the sense of entirely escaping constructions of gender identity, I would argue that it cuts across, highlights, and subverts such identities. After Stonewall, camp became 'an embarrassment to the gay community, the sign of a pre-political gay identity' (Andrew Ross qtd. in Cleto 370). Perhaps this rejection accounts for the counter-proliferation of straight camp from the late 1960s onward (hence Cleto's conception of camp as potentially 'degayified taste').

9. I mean in the tradition of English poetry specifically, of course. Camp poetics to be found in alternative (and equally important) literature are beyond the scope of this chapter (which focuses on the Anglo-American tradition).

10. James Joyce coined the word: Stan Smith quotes it in his Auden essay (100).

11. 'Shine here to us, and thou art every where;/This bed thy center is, these walls, thy sphere' (*Donne: Poetical Works* 11).

12. I am referring here, of course, to T. S. Eliot's *The Waste Land* and Philip Larkin's 'Sad Steps.'

13. Some of my own work is enmeshed in this theory of camp poetics: the concept in this sense arose out of creative practice as much as gender theories.

14. Crashaw (1993b: 1396). Crashaw's unintentionally camp poetics are evidence of a baroque excess of religious passion, of course, in contrast with Larkin's pastiche of his youthful, Yeatsian, poetic self.

15. 'I like your muse because she's gay and witty/Because she's neither prostitute nor frump' (88).

16. I am referring here to the 'Thyrza' poems dedicated to the Cambridge choirboy Edleston (and not to a girl as originally suspected), letters to his friend Matthews using the word 'methodism' to refer to homosexual activities, and the cross-dressing in *Lara* (page Khaled is a woman) and *Don Juan* (in canto five Juan dresses up as a harem girl and the sultan falls for him). I am indebted to Professor Diego Saglia for this information.

17. I am referring here to William Carlos Williams's poem 'Danse Russe,' which, significantly, is the first poem in the collection (6).

Works cited

Adorno, Theodor. 'Commitment.' In *Aesthetics and Politics*. Trans. MacDonagh, F. Ed. Livingstone R., Anderson, P. and Mulhern, F. London: New Left Books, 1977. 177–95.

Ashbery, John. *Your Name Here*. Manchester: Carcanet, 2000.

Attridge, Derek. *The Singularity of Literature*. London and New York: Routledge, 2004.

Auden, W. H. *Collected Poems*. Ed. Edward Mendelson. London: Faber, 1976.

Bach, Rebecca Ann. '(Re)placing John Donne in the History of Sexuality.' *ELH* 72.1 (Spring 2005): 259–90.

Bly, Robert, James Hillman, and Michael Meade, eds *The Rag and Bone Shop of the Heart: Poems for Men*. New York: Harper Perennial, 1992.

Cleto, Fabio, ed. *Camp: Queer Aesthetics and the Performing Subject: A Reader*. Edinburgh: Edinburgh UP, 1999.

Crashaw, Richard. 'On the Wounds of Our Crucified Lord.' *The Norton Anthology of English Literature*. Vol. 1. 6th ed. London and New York: WW. Norton, 1993a. 1390–91.

——. 'To the Noblest and Best of Ladies, the Countess of Denbigh.' *The Norton Anthology of English Literature*. Vol. 1. 6th ed. London and New York: WW. Norton, 1993b, 1394–96.

Donne, John. *Donne: Poetical Works*. 1929. Oxford: Oxford UP, 1971.

Halberstam, Judith. *Female Masculinity*. Durham and London: Duke UP, 1998.

Hollinghurst, Alan. *The Line of Beauty*. London: Picador, 2004.

Kendall, Tim. *Sylvia Plath: A Critical Study*. London: Faber and Faber, 2001.

Larkin, Philip. *Collected Poems*. London: Faber, 1988.

Milton, John. 'Lycidas.' In *Poems of John Milton*. London: Nelson, n.d., 413–42.

Motion, Andrew. *Keats*. London: Faber, 1997.

Nabokov, Vladimir. *Lolita*. 1959. London: Penguin, 1995.

Rowland, Antony. 'Patriarchy, Male Power and the Psychopath in the Poetry of Carol Ann Duffy.' *Posting the Male: Masculinities in Post-war and Contemporary British Literature*. Ed. Daniel Lea and Berthold Schoene. Amsterdam: Rodopi, 2003. 125–40.

——. *Holocaust Poetry: Awkward Poetics in the Work of Sylvia Plath, Geoffrey Hill, Tony Harrison, and Ted Hughes*. Edinburgh: Edinburgh UP, 2005.

Segal, Lynne. 'Back to the Boys? Temptations of the Good Gender Theorist.' *Textual Practice* 15.2 (2001): 231–50.

Smith, Stan. 'Auden's Light and Serio-Comic Verse.' *The Cambridge Companion to W. H. Auden*. Ed. Stan Smith. Cambridge: Cambridge UP, 2004. 96–109.

Wainwright, Jeffrey. *Poetry: The Basics*. London and New York: Routledge, 2004.

White, Edmund. 'Hockney, Art and Desire: Sunlight, Beaches and Boys.' *The Guardian G2* 8 Aug. 2006: 16.

7
Lethal Enclosure: Masculinity under Fire in James Jones's *The Thin Red Line*

David Boulting

Abstract

War and masculinity have traditionally been intimately entangled – to the degree that the warrior ideal has become one of the crucial concepts of Masculinity Studies. The present essay looks at modern depictions of masculinity in war literature, especially at James Jones's novel The Thin Red Line *(1962). In it, both the typical 'hypermasculinity' of war scenarios and crucial cracks inside traditional norms of masculinity are traced. Among those are instances of effeminizing characters, homoeroticism and extravagant, excessive and irresponsible behavior, all the way to counterfeiting masculinity. Yet these 'paradoxes in thinking' of heroic masculinity are not averse to the creation of a mythic American self that bears a strong resemblance to that created in connection with the American West. Indeed they are part and parcel of such a performative creation in which they provide a necessary outlet within structures of containment and enforcement that would otherwise be unliveable. They are moreover responses to historical crises of such a mythical American selfhood. The presumed crisis of masculinity thereby joins a larger arrangement of supposed crises that nonetheless stabilize ideology.*

Battle lines

Established academic debates surrounding representations of gender and martial masculinities in American war literature have tended to focus on the literature of the cataclysmic Civil War, on more canonical representations of World War II like Mailer's *The Naked and the Dead* (1948) and, most intensely of all, on the deluge of literary responses to America's long war in Vietnam. The centrality of Vietnam to these debates owes a good deal, of course, to that war's suggestive defeat of a muscular Western superpower by a more slightly built 'third world' opponent. Susan Jeffords's seminal, and still very persuasive, account of the gender battlefield, *The Remasculinization of America: Gender and the Vietnam War*, also undoubtedly served to focus debates about war, gender, and representation on the Vietnam era. As a result of the pervasiveness and intensity of those debates, the conventional identification of the feminine as enemy or threat is therefore well known and readily perceptible in many modern (and indeed postmodern) American war narratives. Less well explored, until recently, is the notion that normative masculinity and culturally constructed masculine ideals also figure as potent enemies in a long-standing tradition of American war narratives, both during and well before the cultural-historical context of the Vietnam War.[1] The following chapter explores representations of masculinity in James Jones's 1962 novel *The Thin Red Line*, and argues that the soldier subject's preconceived ideals of military manhood constitute one of a series of deterministic enclosures in a novel dominated by images and instances of containment and entrapment. The performance of tough, heroic, or hypermasculine male identities repeatedly debilitates free will and channels men toward often futile encounters with death and danger in the novel. The sources of those performances in prewar American culture, in particular in representations of the American West, are a further point of focus for the chapter.

Set during the fighting for the Pacific island of Guadalcanal of 1942–1943, *The Thin Red Line* draws extensively on James Jones's own experience of that campaign as a US Army infantryman. As Norman Mailer observed in 1966 in *Cannibals and Christians*, Jones is primarily concerned in *The Thin Red Line* with communicating and illuminating 'the feel of combat, the psychology of men' (112). In particular, it is the psychology of the *enlisted* man that most interests Jones. He presents the infantryman's war as a shifting complex of conflicts and threats in which enemies both interior and exterior to the soldier subject proliferate. The Japanese enemy in Jones's novel often constitute a lower order of threat to the men of C Company than their own ambitious commanders and the Byzantine military, political, and social structures that loom behind them.

Idealized notions of manliness and a powerfully conditioned requirement to show courage, or at least stoicism, in the combat zone occupy a central position in this complex of threats. Typically, they are culturally marked as specifically American in character and origin. The conventions, norms, fantasies, and taboos associated with appropriate soldierly conduct function in the novel as a restrictive or destructive agency rather than one that is empowering or socially cohesive. Susan Gubar identifies the sanctuary of a 'bonding born of brotherhood' as a central feature of much of the broadly anti-war war literature generated after World War II (251). Jones's infantrymen, in contrast, seem at war with each other and internally with themselves as much as with the Japanese. And the male lore (and consequently *law*) performed within the imaginary enclosure of the combat unit seems to steer them toward annihilation rather than into a sheltering enclave or *laager* of mutually supporting and empowering comradeship.[2]

Immediately after volunteering for a particularly dangerous assignment, Private Doll (feminizing names abound in the novel) finds himself,

> biting the inside of his lip so hard that it brought tears to his eyes. He was wishing he could do worse: bang his head up and down on a rock; bite a whole chunk out of his arm. Why did he do things like this to himself? Why did he?
>
> (*The Thin Red Line* 235)

Shortly afterward, Sergeant Bell reconnoitres a Japanese strongpoint without orders to do so and at enormous personal risk, though '[w]hy he did it even Bell himself never knew' (273). Even the saturnine and cynical First Sergeant Welsh, who despises the army and the government above all other adversaries, runs across open ground through massed enemy machine-gun fire to help a fatally wounded man only to ask himself: 'Why in the Name of Foolish Bastardly God had he ever done it in the first place? Sobbing audibly for breath, he made himself promise never again to let his screwy wacked up emotions get the better of his common sense' (260). Actual or apparent acts of courage are often driven by less than honorable motives in the novel. Frequently they are performances for the benefit of superiors (the ambitious Doll) or peers (the outfit's staple tough-guy, Queen), and sometimes they are so hysterical in character (as in Welsh's case, above) that the apparent absence of agency or free will undercuts them and renders them uncomfortably similar to 'uncontrollable' flight.

It is important to note from the outset that Jones intertwines his critique of the traditions of idealized masculinity with repeated efforts to link (especially through the use of animal imagery) men's violent and warring tendencies with genetic inheritance as well as cultural heritage.

For James R. Giles, '[a]ll of Jones's characters are, in fact, doomed by the same inter-related causes: the animal nature of man and the anonymous nature of modern technological society' (198). I would argue that, while Giles is broadly right, *The Thin Red Line* suggests that nature and nurture work in concert as drivers of male battlefield behavior. And if his characters are sometimes exhilarated by war, then Jones seeks to communicate that uncomfortable fact without passing judgment on them. Jones's own attitudes toward war and its cultural and evolutionary origins were complex and fraught with ambivalences. While he is deeply critical of culturally constructed masculine ideals in *The Thin Red Line*, he also expresses in the text and elsewhere the concern that individual courage and morality are being squeezed out by massive mechanizing and homogenizing social and economic forces.[3]

Jones's novel choreographs the author's own struggle with new and old models of masculinity at a time when wider debates and conflicts on the same issue were gathering at the fault-lines of an American society and culture progressing toward the upheavals of the sixties and away from the more stable and conformist fifties. Jones wrote that he wanted his son 'to be brave and strong, not to run away, to fight back when he has to,' while also recognizing the existence of 'a paradox in [his] thinking.' 'I also want my boy to be gentle,' he wrote, '[t]hat's the goal I'm really striving for' (qtd. in MacShane 224). Elsewhere, he claimed that he regarded bravery as the 'most pernicious of virtues' and 'a horrible thing.' 'The human race,' he felt, 'has it left over from the animal world and we can't get rid of it' (qtd. in Giles 196). Steven R. Carter observes that, although Jones's conflicting attitudes to courage and masculinity were difficult to resolve, they functioned as a valuable source of 'creative tension' in his writing (82). Carter claims at the outset of his 1998 reappraisal of Jones's writing, that Jones 'spoke out against the insensitivity and foolhardiness of the Hemingway code of manhood and sought to replace it with restraint, compassion and adult love' (1). Carter also quotes Jones's 'Letter Home' for *Esquire* in December 1963 in which 'he asked what had Hemingway "done to us with all his big macho bullshit" ' (ix). Certainly, there are those who would argue that Jones (and perhaps Carter, too) do an injustice to Hemingway, but the point is clearly made nevertheless: Jones was deeply concerned at the damage wrought on men, and especially soldiers, by idealized images of the heroic male self.

Jones's exploration of masculinity and the soldier subject is mapped and analyzed here by focusing on its two major axes in the text: first, performed masculinity and mythic constructions of the American male self and, second, the diminishing place of the individual soldier in mass industrialized modern warfare (what Jones (1975: 86) later dubbed 'corporation war'). The chapter also briefly explores something of Jones's ambivalence to masculinity, courage, and modern war, contrasting the ways in which it stymies and encloses the soldier subject with some of the ways in which it appears to liberate him.

Male fictions

In keeping with its psychological realist mode, a large proportion of the novel's narrative is devoted to exploring the prelude to combat; studying the vocabulary of men's inward and outward responses to this stage in their martial evolution.[4] Three interconnected episodes in the novel's first two chapters form the principal contexts through which Jones examines the interplay of men's outward performances and interior subjective processes. Explosive internal voices and impulses must repeatedly be sealed in, albeit sometimes incompletely or imperfectly, and the outward spaces in which these containments occur also speak of claustrophobia and unhealthy – even lethal – encroachments, of leaks, contaminations, and invisible dangers. The hull of a troopship with its overcrowded compartments, a thick area of jungle near their first night's bivouac, and a hastily improvised burial site, are the chambered spaces in which these performances are played out. The first involves a stolen pistol; the second, a bloodstained shirt; and the third, the remains of Japanese war-dead.

While most of the men are fretting about the possibility of an air raid and the disembarkation, Private Doll sets out to steal a pistol from one of the other units waiting aboard the troopship. One of the most ambitious and ruthless of Jones's characters, Doll has been radically shaped by the realization of a fundamental truth about men: 'Nobody was really what he pretended to be. It was as if everybody made up a fiction story about himself, and then he just pretended to everybody that that was what he was. And everybody believed him, or at least accepted his fiction story' (14). Doll's consuming need to acquire a pistol takes on new meaning in the light of his attitudes to counterfeit manhood. It becomes part of an identity-building process. The 45 automatic is one of the manufactured pieces that compose this artificial entity, a piece of regalia without which the costume – or uniform – of identity is incomplete.

The narrative weight of Doll's pistol is also better understood when considered in relation to another symbolically charged pistol in Jones's fiction. Jones had already explored many of these themes in detail in his 1959 symbolic novel *The Pistol*, in which Pfc Richard Mast, a soldier on guard duty at the time of the Pearl Harbor attack (as Jones himself had been) tries to avoid returning the pistol he had been issued when he went on duty. Mast becomes convinced that the pistol is the only viable defence against 'his personal enemy, his devil' (118): a Japanese major he imagines is trying to hack him in two with a samurai sword in some future battle of the war that has just begun. Other soldiers, equally convinced that they need its protection, repeatedly try to steal the pistol from Mast. Finally, impassively unaware of its talismanic properties, the weapon is casually repossessed by a supply clerk ('[t]he personification,' in Mast's mind, 'of absolute, inexorable, impersonal Authority') (154).

When, later in *The Thin Red Line*, Doll imagines with abject horror the prospect of being captured by the Japanese and 'dragged back over the crest [of Hill 209] into the midst of those jabbering, Emperor-worshipping savages,' he relives an archetypal Western colonialist nightmare: engulfed, cut-off from the sustaining order of civilization, doomed to a death not clean and soldierly and machine-forged, but 'manual' and distinctly dirty (145). Doll's pistol is an industrial-age defence against an enemy that lives, for him and for his peers, in a benighted feudal past. Intertwined with long-standing anti-Asian racist discourses, American propaganda and popular culture in the aftermath of Pearl Harbor had quickly come to figure the Japanese enemy as culturally backward, and even 'more barbarous and diabolical than his German counterpart' (Dower 37).

Doll's pistol signifies a particularly American brand of mythic masculinity. It is more than a badge of authority or special status (though, since side-arms were typically issued to officers, it is surely that too). Its potency draws on both American industrial superiority and on America's unique cultural heritage: the iconic gunslinger, steady-handed, and cool-headed. Acquired by the application of guile and bravado, Doll regards his weapon as an index of his own, well-developed brand of American ingenuity and individualism. It is therefore the perfect defence against an enemy he has been taught to perceive in terms of a homogenous, slave-like mass (resembling 'photographic prints off the same negative' according to Frank Capra's 1945 film *Know Your Enemy – Japan*). Popular wartime discourses linking the Japanese enemy with the Native American further shape the context of Doll's actions (and those of Richard Mast in *The Pistol*). John Dower, for example, notes the common use of the term 'Indian fighting' by correspondents and US troops to describe jungle warfare against the Japanese forces (152). While Richard Slotkin records that, in April 1942, *Life* explicitly linked the US defeat on

Bataan to Custer's last stand, 'rationalizing' the former as 'a heroic sacrifice intended to buy time' (319).

Mythic constructions of the American West are referenced – and ironically undercut – soon afterward in the narrative, as the men of C Company first enter the Guadalcanal jungle. Having disembarked just in time to avoid an enemy air attack, the men march inland to their designated bivouac. A group of C Company men decide to leave the safety of the bivouac to investigate what lies inside the towering jungle's edge that looms nearby. During this childlike game of exploration the men happen upon the debris of a recent action. The first evidence they find of the battle is a US Army-issue shirt, bloodstained and torn at the entry and exit points of a Japanese bullet. In a further allusion to the frontier West, the shirtsleeves have been cut short and shredded with a sharp blade 'to look like the old-fashioned fringe of the plainsmen' (68). Above all, the shirt's 'cowboy fringe' references cultural *representations* of the West; its maker sought to forge a link to the touchstone of American myths of the frontier. Such representations had experienced something of a renaissance in the build-up to America's entry into the war. Paul Schrijvers notes that,

> [a]fter World War I, movies in particular ensured that the legacy of the frontier lived on in powerful images. In the three years preceding the Japanese attack on Pearl Harbor in 1941, the Western movie genre suddenly underwent a remarkable revival as it became part of a larger effort to renew the patriotic optimism of Americans that had been dealt hard blows by the Great Depression. Its percentage of Hollywood's total production tripled in this short period. (4)

Leo Braudy also argues that a 'crisis of male individuality' driven by World War I and the Great Depression was answered by an atmosphere of 'masculine redefinition' in the 1920s and 1930s. That redefinition saw an explosion of new, harder-edged heroic American individualists: the 'adventurers, detectives and cowboys, whose exploits filled the mass-market pulp magazines' (Braudy 436–38).

When one of the two men holding the shirt up for perusal releases his corner and steps back, 'the first man straightened his arm out so the shirt would not touch him, and continued to hold it. And there it dangled, like some forever windless flag symbolic of the darker, nether side of patriotism' (*The Thin Red Line* 70). Jones was well versed in the iconography of the Pacific war: in the 'Special Note' that prefaces the novel, for example, he claims that he set the novel on Guadalcanal rather than on some 'entirely fictional island' because of 'what Guadalcanal stood for' to Americans of his generation (it was the first Allied counter-offensive in the Pacific and the American victory there carries some of the same symbolic weight as the Allied victory at El Alamein or that of the Soviets at Stalingrad). The bloody shirt or 'flag' described here inevitably invites comparison with that other iconic flag image associated with the US campaign in the Pacific: Joe Rosenthal's photograph of US Marines raising the Stars and Stripes on Iwo Jima (and the subject of Clint Eastwood's 2006 film, *Flags of Our Fathers*). Susan D. Moeller, in her book on war photography, *Shooting War*, describes this as the most famous photograph not only of the Pacific theater or even of World War II, but of *any* war (225). In the image, the Marine furthest from the point at which the base of the pole is being driven into the ground is reaching up, stretching his fingertips toward the shaft of the pole. Jones's image here, of a 'flag' untouchable and taboo, is the absolute antithesis of Rosenthal's perfect image of soldiering as heroic masculine labor and triumph of collective effort.

For Jones's untried infantrymen, the flag is untouchable because what it signifies is unmentionable. The limp and tattered 'flag' of the bloody shirt stimulates personal speculations among the men about the possibility and potential causes of their own violent deaths. A kind of psychic archaeological find, it necessitates not only a reconstruction of the recent past but also private contemplations of a certainly violent future. The shirt seems less something merely retrieved from the jungle than something figured forth from the unconscious, from a dream-world of secret and terrifying imaginings, a kind of collective and collaborative hallucination. We are told that:

> A curious sense of unreality had come over all of them with the discovery of the shirt. The dripping, gloomy, airless jungle with its vaulted cathedral-like ceiling far above did not serve to lessen it. Fighting and killing and being struck by death-delivering bullets which keyholed through you, were facts. They existed, certainly. But it was too much for them to assimilate, and left them with a dreamlike nightmare feeling which they couldn't shake off. (71)

This peep through the keyhole into the as yet unglimpsed world of combat returns us to that rhythmically occurring theme in the narrative of lethal and often provisional enclosures, chambers, and spaces that are subject – like the soldier's body – to sudden and unexpected rupture. Here it is not only a narcissistic sense of self and self-worth that has been punctured and laid open to (partial) view, but also that inner chambering of fears and anxieties that can only be shared wordlessly, as in the group's unified but silent contemplation of the shirt.

That the wearer of this fringed shirt sought irrationally (and unsuccessfully) to armor himself with this peculiarly American talisman points the reader back toward Doll and his myth-invested pistol. Though he ultimately survives the campaign, Doll's substitute six-gun is no kind of protection at all in a war that features long-range artillery and air-raids, land mines and invisible snipers, malaria, and permanent mental derangement. 'Mother! Mother!' Doll will later scream repeatedly and in a 'high falsetto' as he charges hysterically toward the enemy, not in a moment of cool-headed courage, but rather because, 'in an ecstasy of panic, terror, fear and cowardice,' he 'simply could not stand it any longer.' Not insignificantly, he loses his rifle during the same action (289–90).

Immediately following the discovery of the shirt the members of this impromptu and unofficial scouting party make a second and infinitely more macabre discovery – that of a mass grave packed with Japanese battle dead. Socially and culturally transmitted models of idealized male behavior are again at the center of both the soldier's performed behavior and the interior anxieties these performances seem designed to camouflage. At the center of the episode is the company's biggest and strongest member, Corporal Queen. Queen is acknowledged by his peers as the largest and toughest man in the company. He has a reputation to maintain as 'a myth had grown up around him' and 'once Queen discovered it ... he had – with a strange welcoming sense of having at last found his identity – done everything he could to live up to it' (64). Queen's masculine identity has been constructed for him by 'an amorphous collection of small men in the outfit, men who adored and longed for a size and strength they themselves would never have' (64). All that remains for Queen to do is to step into this ready-made shell and operate as best he can within its narrow confines. The disjunction between Queen's interior and performed male selves recalls Doll's earlier reflections on the nature of masculine identity, his realization that '[n]obody was really what he pretended to be' (14). If Doll is, at least temporarily, liberated and empowered by this new-found knowledge, Queen seems only to be imprisoned. 'Remembering how to act,' we are told, 'required a great deal of Queen's time and energy ... It tired him' (65).

It is in order to retain his reputation for fearlessness that Queen leads the way into the jungle in the first place. He soon discovers that the obligations attendant on his elevated in-group status are ratcheted up to an entirely new level in the combat zone. Maintaining the value of his stock here entails far greater risks than were required in the old life of barrack and bar-room where violence, though it played a central part, was of an entirely different order. He forces himself forward despite the 'horrible results' (65) that his imagination constantly places in his path (the soldier's silent, interior battle with that most dreadful of enemies, his own imagination, is one to which Jones repeatedly returns). Snakes figure largely in Queen's anxieties; appropriately enough, since it is a kind of disembodied masculinity that most threatens him here. Appropriate, too, since the jungle seems increasingly to signify a blasphemous inversion of the American Eden. (Queen cannot help but view the riotous jungle foliage through the distorting lens of an idealized memory of American landscapes: 'No American would ever let his woodlot get into any such condition as this' (64), he tells himself.)

It is in the 'un-American,' encroaching enclosure of the jungle (the outer edges of which form a 'high wall' of 'jostling' leaves) that the party find the mass grave (62). Here, Queen finds a more sustained performance of fearlessness is called for. The hysterical defiling of the grave that follows is a response to the discomfiting power of the shirt/flag, a ritual tussle with death intended to deny the overwhelming anxieties that the shirt has dredged up from where it, too, had been hastily interred.

> Eagerly in the dim light, more than glad to forget the shirt, the men hurried over and began to clamber up onto the mounds to inspect – with a sort of painful, lascivious masochism – what they one day soon would be up against themselves. It was beyond these mounds, where it had remained hidden from their view because of them, that the mass grave lay. (72)

Embedded in Jones's careful paradigmatic selections – 'eagerly,' 'clambering,' 'lascivious masochism' – we find a lexis associated with childhood or adolescence: the men, having completed their 'chores,' have slipped away from the quasi-parental or patriarchal authority of their superiors and gone exploring. The awe-inspiring and alien jungle stands in for the dark and threatening, folklore-haunted forest of childhood and fairytale alike. It is clear that this is a place appropriate to the performance of a male rite of passage.

When a few of the men step out onto the surface of the grave, they instantly begin to sink into 'the dirt and dead' before 'cursing savagely' and leaping back onto 'solid ground' (73). It seems that the

Japanese dead have not entirely surrendered the capacity to discomfit their enemy, and Queen, the tacitly recognized leader of the party, now initiates ritualized revenge, freighted with symbolic potential:

> Queen looked back at the rest challengingly. His face seemed to say that he had suffered enough personal indignities for one day and by God now he was going to get even.

> 'Looks like this one was a healthy spec'men. Ought to be somethin worth takin [*sic*] home on some of them,' he said by way of preamble, and leaning forward seized [a] shod foot.... (74)

Others begin to follow Queen's lead, to outdo each other as they 'boisterously desecrate' the enemy dead. Yet the corpses remain stubbornly interred. A grotesquely comic struggle between living and dead now ensues, one from which Queen clearly cannot back down without loss of face.

Queen finally succeeds in dragging a Japanese corpse from the earth. His 'victory,' however, is short lived.

> From the grave a new smell, as distinct from the former greenish-coloured one as if they derived from different sources, rolled up like an oily fog from around the muddy body and began to spread. With dismayed curses and astonished, pained exclamations of consternation the men began to back off, then finally just simply turned and fled.... (79)

The detachment's symbolic confrontation with the enemy and with death itself is, for all their bravado, a pyrrhic victory at best. This precombat jungle interlude continually returns to one of the novel's central themes: the exponentially increasing demands associated with maintaining the essentially fictional male selves behind which the central characters have retreated. Rather than armoring the vulnerable male subject these male fictions ironically often force the soldier to expose himself to further risk. Queen 'really had had no intention of disinterring the leg or the body at the other end of it. He was only showing off,' but when Hoff joins in and then his rival Doll discovers a highly prized Japanese bayonet, Queen must up the ante in the face of a perceived leadership challenge (75).

Once the foul gas is released from the grave, Doll is terrified that his own mask will slip: 'Doll was trying very hard not to throw up...there was a strong urge in his throat to swallow repeatedly... It was not enough to refrain from vomiting; if he kept swallowing someone would be sure to notice... And that was unthinkable. He couldn't allow it. Especially with Queen standing not far from him' (79). In the current situation the stakes are relatively low, but once the unit is in combat a man attempting to prove his courage risks an even less profitable encounter with death than Queen's. Gender identity in this climate threatens to become a deterministic prison, a claustrophobic enclosure like the iron womb of the troopship that brought them here.

'They thought they were men'

Crucially, the grave desecration episode shows Queen and the others de-individualized, acting irrationally but in concert. Still untested in battle, their atrocity is not driven by brutalizing encounters with the (living) enemy or by extended combat stress. Capering at the grave's edge and striving to outdo each other, it is these men who seem bestial or simian and not, as in so many American popular and propaganda discourses, the Japanese enemy (John Dower (84), charting anti-Japanese wartime propaganda, notes that '[w]ithout question... the most common caricature of the Japanese by Westerners... was the monkey or ape'). Jones's ironic treatment of mythic American masculinities is particularly evident here, as he erodes the imaginary distance between the supposedly self-determining American individual and a Japanese counterpart typically constructed in Western eyes as drone-like and utterly de-individualized.

Even in these early phases of the narrative, before the men have seen the living enemy, Jones's imagery is explicitly working to confound conventional romantic views of the American soldier as patriotic volunteer, the citizen-soldier who lends the weight of his individual skill and personal bravery to the pursuit of collective goals. American propaganda imagery frequently sought to represent the GI as the direct descendant of earlier idealized American males who had swapped plowshares for swords, did what needed to be done, then swapped them back again: the minutemen who drove out the English, and the Indian fighters who cleared the West's hostile terrain for settlement. It is Bell, the most cerebral of the central characters, who most succinctly (inwardly) expresses the absurdity of this conceit:

They thought they were men. They all thought they were real people. They really did. How funny. They thought they made decisions and ran their own lives, and proudly called themselves free individual human beings. The truth was they were here, and they were gonna stay here, until the state through some other automaton told them to go someplace else, and then they'd go. But they'd go freely, of their own free choice and will, because they were free individual human beings. Well, well. (284)

Jones's infantrymen repeatedly resemble animals or machines (recalling the dominant tropes of Stephen Crane's imagery in the Civil War novel *The Red Badge of Courage* (1895)).[5] The individual infantryman is revealed in *The Thin Red Line* as both an uncomprehending mechanical component in the arcane machinery of division, battle group, army, and state; and uncomprehending animal, driven by the equally unknowable complexes of sense, emotion, and instinct. These two interpretative schema are, however, complementary rather than contradictory. The infantryman behaves under stress in accordance with a combination of conditioned and instinctual or innate factors, in either case his responses to stimuli are thus in a sense 'mechanical,' performed without the conscious mind or the exercise of free will being fully engaged.

Fife, Welsh, Bell, and a handful of other C Company men are able to perceive in their own government a deadly threat: a terrifying and implacable machinery that determines their fate not as individual men but as huge blocs of military resource. Similarly, Fife's experience of combat and its aftermath seems to demonstrate the equally deterministic and inescapable operation of an interior government. During the battle for the village of Bunabala, Fife discovers 'that he was really much braver than he'd thought, and this gave him real joy' (490). His pride in his ability to function as a 'real soldier' during the action – to advance, to give commands, to kill the enemy – is short-lived, however (514). As the effects of an increasingly customary 'combat numbness' wear off, all of his old fears return unabated. The 'swashbuckling' role he performs in front of the new, untested recruits is exposed to him as a pitiful sham and, finally, he is 'forced to face up once again to the same old fact he had always known. He was a coward' (514). Just as the Depression had robbed so many men of the traditional indicators of their manhood, so the war again repeatedly 'unmans' them. Receiving and giving wounds, killing and dying heroically, proving one's worth under duress: many of the conventional indicators of masculinity in combat are rendered meaningless or, at least highly dubious, in Jones's world of war.

However skilfully Fife fabricates and performs an elaborate synthetic self, this is only sustainable either while there is no imminent physical threat or he is sufficiently anaesthetized by 'combat numbness.' Shifting interior forces constantly threaten to overthrow this convenient fiction since at any other time, he realizes, his body may rebel in an instant and betray what he considers to be his 'natural' and ineluctable cowardice. Most acute and most fully explored in the novel through the character of Fife (though present to some degree in almost every major character), the terror of exposure as a coward constitutes one of the most potent sites of threat to Jones's soldier subjects. The warring forces of instinct, innate character, and social and cultural conditioning likewise consti-tute one of the most vivid scenes of conflict in *The Thin Red Line*. The same men fight and flee, they kill with 'savage joy' at one moment and cower at another (342). Throughout it all, in Jones's conception of war, they are 'automatons' driven variously by fear, the fear of displaying fear, fear of authority and censure, arbitrary motives rooted in character and disposition, peer pressure, powerful forms of social and cultural train-ing, and military training and socialization (285). Repeatedly enclosed and trapped, however, they absurdly persist in seeing themselves as 'free individual human beings' (284). With the possible exception of the handful who (like Welsh) have been liberated into an intense and mis-anthropic cynicism, they presumably insist on this only because they have been trained to believe it is what they are currently fighting and dying for.

'A savage joy'

Guadalcanal itself figures in Jones's novel as one of a series of enclosures: concentric and overlapping, physical and metaphysical, and actual and imaginary. The island, a tropical paradise from the perspective of the troop transport's deck, soon mutates into a prison without (obvious) walls or guards ('[a]fter all, where was anybody going to run away to on this fucking island, that they needed guards?' (390), they muse). Para-doxically, the island (and the war in general) is also, at other moments, a space of liberation and licensed (or at least tolerated) transgression. The novel's delineation of lethal deterministic enclosures is periodically destabilized and rendered ambiguous in this effort to illustrate war's capacity to provide specifically male forms of 'relief' or 'reward.'

When Doll kills his first enemy soldier, he experiences both guilt and pleasure:

> Doll felt guilty. He couldn't help it. He had killed a human being, a man. He had done the most horrible thing a human could do,

worse than rape even. And nobody in the whole world could say anything to him about it. That was where the pleasure came from. Nobody could do anything to him for it. He had gotten by with murder. (210–11)

When C Company, having flanked Hill 210, are able to attack a Japanese bivouac from the rear, catching the enemy off-guard, the ensuing massacre generates an 'ebullient mood,' and there is a 'shooting jamboree' that resembles 'some sort of declared school holiday from all moral ethics' (339–40).

Guadalcanal may be a hellish labyrinth of mud and jungles and fortified hill groups, but its resemblance to the conventional tropical island paradise periodically resurfaces in the narrative. Journeying back from the line at the end of Chapter 7, the men watch 'the peaceful looking sun-dappled shade of the wheeling groves, with the bright sea and the sound of the surf only a few yards away' (482). That night men bathe 'bareass nude' by moonlight (484). The island thus also becomes a homosocial utopia of sorts where forbidden lusts are freely exercised. Homosexual activities, for example, are made permissible by the absence of women, though they must still be conducted discreetly. Christina S. Jarvis argues that,

> Although still caught up with cultural definitions of masculinity, the men [of C Company described in *The Thin Red Line*] are free to explore alternative homosocial bonds and actions discouraged within cultural gender norms... [and] can engage in homosexual activities without being labelled 'queer'. (96)

Perhaps, however, Jarvis underestimates the residual power of cultural gender norms even in this more liberated milieu, or the limited and clearly defined (if unspoken) ways in which the boundaries of proscription can be moved. When Doll propositions Carrie Arbre, he is horrified to discover that Arbre has misunderstood the precise nature of his advances and taken Doll for '[a] real fairy' (494): Doll had assumed Arbre was going to be the 'girl' in this particular relationship, which 'wouldn't make [Doll] queer, it would only make Arbre queer' (496). In an environment where masculinity is beset by countless enemies, where men stand to lose their manhood either figuratively by exposure as cowards or literally by the physical injury many (including Bell) fear above all others, it is perhaps unsurprising that few will voluntarily allow themselves to be positioned in passive or feminizing roles in relation to their peers. Nevertheless, many others, such as Bead and Fife, are able to negotiate the 'new' rules and exchange sexual favors, albeit with some awkwardness (126–30).

Other, more visible forms of explosive release are also evident. A kind of male hysteria grips individuals or groups of C Company men at a number of points in the narrative, either during periods of high stress or as they seek to release that stress by drinking and fist-fighting.[6] Having been 'blooded' in combat and then relieved for a rest period, C Company are left to pursue 'a wild mass bacchanalian orgy' without interference from the military authorities (483). Nine fist-fights take place in a single night (490), 'almost everybody vomit[s] one or more times' (490) and several get down on hands and knees and bay at the moon 'like wolves or hounds' (484). While elsewhere in the narrative Jones suggests the lurking dangers and base mistruth of hypermasculinity, the naturalist in Jones, seeing a feral streak in all men, presents this homosocial orgy as a riotous carnival of the masculine. It is a salacious and spectacular celebration and a source of brutish comedy in the novel. From the perspective of his own experience, too, Jones perhaps has reason to see something joyous in the unrestrained re-affirmation of the living male self among men returned from a private and collective confrontation with death. The novel's enclosing or pressurizing forces are periodically balanced by such instances of wild release or sly escape (as in the novel's many acts of overt and covert military insubordination).

'They cannot understand how we could hate it, and still like it'

The 'orgy' of the masculine described above is only superficially unifying. It is a ritual in which men expiate the fear and passivity they have been forced to endure under fire (they are often, in the novel's early actions, forced to remain prone under enemy fire for extended periods). Jones clearly, explicitly, and repeatedly critiques normative masculinity and the influence of the idealized 'hard-boiled' models of masculinity prevalent in American culture in the novel. Nevertheless, as the animalistic 'orgy' described above suggests, Jones finds the sources of men's violence and self-destructiveness to be more wide-ranging than cultural conditioning alone. For Jones, something in men answers the call of war. His is a carefully weighted appraisal of both war's horror and its seductions. In the often autobiographical *WW II: A Chronicle of Soldiering*, Jones wrote: 'Some [servicemen] are actually sorry to come home and see [the war] end. Even those of us who hated it found it exciting, sometimes. That is what civilian people never understand about their returned soldiers, in any war, Vietnam as well. They cannot understand how we could hate it, and still like it' (45).

The Thin Red Line therefore anticipates many of the controversial texts and debates engaging men's relationship with war that would follow in the wake of the Vietnam War. Michael Herr, who famously mused: 'I think that Vietnam is what we had instead of happy childhoods' (195), observed that many correspondents in Vietnam – and he is careful to include himself in the category – spent years 'trying to piece together their very real hatred of the war with their great love for it, that rough reconciliation that many of us had to look at' (178). Herr, writing against the grain of nineteenth- and twentieth-century literature's conventional depiction of war as a grim, if necessary and sometimes even noble endeavor, shows the distasteful spectacle of men enchanted by – and sometimes revelling in – war. Likewise, Vietnam veteran William Broyles Jr stirred criticism in 1984 by addressing the unspeakable question of 'Why Men Love War.' Before Herr or Broyles had broached this uncomfortable subject, however, Jones had already done so in *The Thin Red Line*, dispassionately reporting not only the power of war to entrap and dehumanize men but also its power to awe men, sometimes even to liberate them, and to leave them, like Jones (and later Herr, Broyles and countless others), forever ambivalent about their experiences and uncertain as to the source of their nostalgic feelings toward them in later years.

A feminist approach to these texts would be quick to point out that the forms of liberation from conventional values enjoyed by soldiers under such conditions have all too often been exercised at the expense of women or, indeed, of other oppressed groups. There are also appalling risks in showing the exhilarating in war (as Francis Ford Coppola's take on the Air Cavalry in *Apocalypse Now* was clearly intended to do): so self-evidently that there can be little purpose in rehearsing them here. But Jones's great combat novel, like Stephen Crane's before it, is committed to leaving nothing out. Little is served by telling men new lies about war to wrap around the old. And ultimately Jones's novel moves beyond the story of men's multiple entrapments in the wartime Army. As Joan Didion observed, 'James Jones had known a great simple truth: the Army was nothing more or less than life itself' (64). *The Thin Red Line* also illuminates an emergent American society in which the subject is increasingly militarized, pressed into pursuing the goals of the state rather than the self, atomized, and 'numbed.' First Sergeant

Welsh makes explicit the connection between the dehumanization and collectivization of soldiers and that of civilians. He delights in predicting (for the patriotic Staff Sergeant Storm) an American future shaped by these very forces of massive, silent enclosure:

> 'You know what it is, don't you? You realize what's happened, what's happening.' Welsh's eyes brooded across Storm's face. 'There aint [*sic*] any choice. There's no choice left for anybody. And it aint only here, with us. It's everywhere. And it aint going to get any better. This war's just the start. You understand that.' (83–84)

Simultaneously men, animals, and machines – during one engagement Queen howls and roars like 'some flesh and blood tank' (342) – Jones's infantrymen act under the powerful combined influence of social and genetic determinants. And under attack from forces within and without, to the front and to the rear, the models of male toughness and independence to which they seem doomed to aspire offer neither protection nor consolation. In Jones's cosmos of remorselessly warring forces, much of the violence is internecine: as harmful to its agent as its intended target (and neatly miniaturized in the running battle between privates Tills and Mazzi). The codes and characteristics of contemporary masculinity serve to prise C Company's men apart and stifle discourse on the subject of their deepest fears and anxieties. They are channelled not only toward often ill-judged encounters with the enemy, but also toward interactions with each other in which they perform idealized and hypermasculine identities and so alienate their only reliable sources of succor and support.

Notes

1. The relatively recent expansion of academic interest in representing masculinities includes two works of particular relevance to the issues discussed here: Christina S. Jarvis's *The Male Body at War: American Masculinity During World War II* (2004) and Leo Braudy's *From Chivalry to Terrorism: War and the Changing Nature of Masculinity* (2003).
2. Exploring the psychological impact of the Vietnam War on its American veterans, Jonathan Shay elects to call this particular form of love *philia*, defining it as the 'passion of care that arises between soldiers in combat' (40).
3. See, for example, Jones's comments on *Go to the Widow-maker* quoted in the final chapter of Giles (199).
4. Jones talks extensively about what he terms 'the evolution of a soldier' in *WW II: A Chronicle of Soldiering*. His clearest account of what he understands by the term is given in a chapter titled 'Soldier's Evolution': 'I think that when all the

nationalistic or ideological propaganda and patriotic slogans are put aside, all the straining to convince a soldier that he is dying *for* something, it is the soldier's final full acceptance of the fact that his name is already written in the rolls of the already dead. Every combat soldier, if he follows far enough along the path that began with his induction, must, I think, be led inexorably to that awareness. He must make a compact with himself or with Fate that he is lost. Only then can he function as he ought to function, under fire' (43; author's italics).

5. This date refers to the first publication of the text as a complete novel. It had appeared as a newspaper serial in the previous year (cf. Katz xiv).

6. I have used the term 'hysteria' here not to denote a diagnostic category but in the broader sense of a 'morbidly excited condition' ('hysteria,' def. 2, *Oxford English Dictionary Online*). Though the behavior of Jones's infantrymen described here is clearly linked to combat stress, it should not be confused with the psychoneurotic 'hysterical' symptoms associated, during World War I, with what was then termed 'shell-shock.' French professor of neurology, Jean-Martin Charcot (1825–1893), pioneered the study of hysterical symptoms (such as the paralysis of limbs) as a response to trauma and succeeded in convincing his peers that hysteria could afflict men as well as women (Shephard 8–10). The later work in this field of Freud, Janet, and others who had studied under or been influenced by Charcot is generally better remembered.

Works cited

Apocalypse Now. Dir. Francis Ford Coppola. Perf. Martin Sheen, Marlon Brando and Robert Duvall. Zoetrope Studios, 1979.

Braudy, Leo. *From Chivalry to Terrorism: War and the Changing Nature of Masculinity*. New York: Vintage, 2003.

Broyles, William, Jr. 'Why Men Love War.' *The Vietnam Reader*. Ed. Walter Capps. London: Routledge, 1991. 68–81.

Carter, Steven R. *James Jones: An American Literary Orientalist Master*. Chicago: U of Illinois P, 1998.

Didion, Joan. 'Goodbye Gentleman-Ranker.' *Esquire* 88 Oct. 1977: 50–64.

Dower, John. *War Without Mercy: Race and Power in the Pacific War*. New York: Pantheon, 1993.

Flags of Our Fathers. Dir. Clint Eastwood. Perf. Ryan Phillippe, Jesse Bradford and Adam Beach. DreamWorks SKG, 2006.

Giles, James R. *James Jones*. Boston: Twayne, 1981.

Gubar, Susan. 'This is My Rifle, This is my Gun: World War II and the Blitz on Women.' *Behind the Lines: Gender and the Two World Wars*. Ed. Margaret Randolph Higgonet and Jane Jenson. London and New Haven: Yale U P, 1987. 227–59.

Herr, Michael. *Dispatches*. London: Picador, 1979. [1977].

Jarvis, Christina S. *The Male Body at War: American Masculinity During World War II*. DeKalb: Northern Illinois U P, 2004.

Jeffords, Susan. *The Remasculinization of America: Gender and the Vietnam War*. Bloomington: Indiana U P, 1989.

Jones, James. *The Pistol*. New York: Dell, 1973. [1959].

———. *WW II: A Chronicle of Soldiering*. New York: Ballantine Books, 1975.

———. *The Thin Red Line*. 1962. London: Hodder & Stoughton, 1998.

Katz, Joseph. ed. *The Portable Stephen Crane*. Harmondsworth: Viking Penguin, 1986.

Know Your Enemy – Japan. Dir. Frank Capra, Joris Ivens. Writ. Frank Capra et al. US War Department, 1945.

MacShane, Frank. *Into Eternity: The Life of James Jones, American Writer*. Boston: Houghton Mifflin, 1985.

Mailer, Norman. *Cannibals and Christians*. London: Granada, 1979. [1966].

Moeller, Susan D. *Shooting War: Photography and the American Experience of Combat*. New York: Basic, 1989.

Schrijvers, Paul. *The GI War against Japan: American Soldiers in Asia and the Pacific*. Basingstoke: Palgrave Macmillan, 2002.

Shay, Jonathan. *Achilles in Vietnam: Combat Trauma and the Undoing of Character*. New York: Scribner, 2003.

Shephard, Ben. *A War of Nerves: Soldiers and Psychiatrists 1914–1994*. London: Pimlico, 2002.

Slotkin, Richard. *Gunfighter Nation: The Myth of the Frontier in Twentieth-Century America*. Norman: U of Oklahoma P, 1998.

8

In their Fathers' Footsteps: Performing Masculinity and Fatherhood in the Work of Les Murray and Michael Ondaatje

Katharine Burkitt

Abstract

The performance of masculinity is always rife with contradictions and conflicts. However, as theorists such as Hazel V. Carby, Gayatri Chakravorty Spivak, Frantz Fanon, and, more recently, Stephen M. Whitehead and Frank J. Barrett have suggested, in a postcolonial context this performance is even more precarious and political. This chapter considers the implications of performing masculinity in the work of Australian poet, Les Murray and that of Sri Lankan-Canadian writer, Michael Ondaatje. It will engage, for the most part, with Les Murray's Fredy Neptune *(1998) and Michael Ondaatje's* In the Skin of a Lion *(1987). These texts explore performances of masculinity against the backdrop of twentieth-century histories that are characterized by complicated cultural and social exchanges. In both novels, all identity is transnational and the writers' representations of race and nationality also have implications for the performance of gender. These works deal with postcolonial histories, although they are not radical discussions of race, or focussed on black masculinities. Yet, both writers seek to dismantle a secure sense of white Western masculinity and question the patriarchal paradigm of the nation-state. As they reveal the unstable performance of masculinity, other forms of self-identification are also demonstrated to be similarly insubstantial. This is most overtly shown through the novels' focus on the physical performance of masculinity and its lack of sustainability, as the protagonists' male bodies become signifiers of gender that are aged, numbed, emasculated, damaged, or exploited. Not only is this focus on the physical a direct reference to the corporeality of any performance of masculinity, but these symbols of man-liness are also tied into a construction of identity that is predicated on the physical attributes of race. This problematic masculinity is refracted into the discussion of nationality through both texts' centralization of the father and son relationship. The homosocial families that Murray and Ondaatje envisage reconceptualize the family unit and abandon the restrictive binaries of gen-der. If, as has been suggested by Anne McClintock (1997) and David H. J. Morgan (2001), the nuclear family is an iconic representation of national identity that upholds the patriarchal ideal, these texts abandon the female part of this model and thereby demonstrate its restrictions. The potentially patriarchal remains of the family unit is destabilized through the unreliable performance of masculinity, as the masculine identity that is inherited and re-learned from generation to generation is revealed to be an empty performance. In this context, this chapter will argue that in Murray and Ondaatje's work, to follow in ones father's footsteps is to perform a paradoxical masculinity that unmasks the stereotypes of maleness, and disrupts a patriarchal sense of nationhood.*

The performance of masculinity in a postcolonial context is always problematic and provisional. As has been skilfully documented by a number of theorists including Hazel V. Carby, Gayatri Chakravorty Spivak and Frantz Fanon, this demonstration of masculinity is a negoti-ation of power and in situations fuelled by postcolonial, racial tension, the stakes become even higher. In line with this, Stephen M. White-head and Frank J. Barrett suggest that '[t]he (power) relations among men produce subordinate and marginal masculinities, such as those which surround homosexuals and non-white men' (8). These 'marginal masculinities' form much of the discussion of this chapter, although they are not necessarily figured as the 'homosexuals and non-white men' that Whitehead and Barrett suggest. Rather, in the work of Les Murray and Michael Ondaatje the shifts of power that heighten those performances of masculinity are explored through the familiar images of the male body and the father figure. The authors' engagements with male protagonists often exclude any other conceptual standpoint, and both writers use clichéd signifiers of masculinity, most notably the overt masculine violence of Ondaatje's early work.[1] However, despite these potentially rigid conceptualizations of masculinity, both writers demonstrate the unsettling role of 'subordinate and marginal masculinities' and destabilize binary constructions of gender by fore-grounding the performance that is involved in any demonstration of manhood.

Les Murray and Michael Ondaatje are divergent figures, an Australian poet and Sri Lankan-Canadian novelist and poet, respectively. Their status as postcolonial writers is not straightforward: Murray is inherently rooted in his own Australian context, an aspect of his poetry that is repeatedly reiterated through his deployment of Australian colloquialisms, so that even non-Australian events are imbued with an Australianess. In contrast, Ondaatje's sense of the postcolonial is closely tied to his own immigrant experience in the UK and Canada, and is often figured through the exploration of Western figures, or the clashes between cultures. Therefore, for the most part of their careers, both writers have focussed on their own versions of settler communities, using, in different ways, their histories and myths to explore contemporary issues and envisage transnational relationships. Les Murray's *Fredy Neptune* and Michael Ondaatje's *In the Skin of a Lion* will inform much of the discussion in this chapter. These texts are respectively Murray and Ondaatje's most detailed explorations of masculinity; bearing this in mind, they will retain the focus of this chapter, although I will also refer to other works. There are great differences between the texts: Murray's is a verse-novel, while Ondaatje's is written in prose and is the prequel to his 1992 bestseller, *The English Patient*. However, both writers seek to unmask the performance of masculinity through their self-consciously stylized male protagonists and the filial relationships that dominate both texts. In the first section of this chapter, I will consider the way in which the performance of masculinity is figured corporeally, as both texts explore the way in which men's bodies are sites which determine social inclusions and exclusions. In the second section, I will suggest that these demonstrations of problematic and marginalized masculinities are further complicated in the context of father and son relationships. In the work of these writers, the family becomes a wider symbol of a nationhood that is based upon similarly complex, male-orientated, intergenerational relationships that are not always as secure as their performances imply. This paradigm foregrounds the unstable performance of manhood and fatherhood, and provides a space to consider the complex notions of race and masculinity that inform the work of these writers as they disrupt the old certainties of gender, race, and nationhood.

Stereotypes and the performance of masculinity

In both Les Murray's *Fredy Neptune* and Michael Ondaatje's *In the Skin of a Lion*, the performance of masculinity is constructed in retrospect, and is explored through the recollection of a homosocial history. This is figured, in both texts, as a corporeal masculinity, which relies on the literal physical performance of the male body. Although this is a potentially clichéd and outdated version of male identity, both writers engage with this truism of male identity in order to explore masculinity from their complex and diversely postcolonial standpoints. Both texts also engage with recorded histories to structure their narratives; as such, they propound the way in which the construction and performances of masculinity has become increasingly problematic in the late twentieth century. This distance induces a further complex binary between the body of the ageing male writer and that of his actively male protagonist. In the work of both writers, therefore, the exploration of male identity is explored through the deployment of recognizable stereotypes of manliness which point toward the performative nature of all masculinities, and gender more generally.

The most notable of these in Ondaatje's work is his representation of the American outlaw Billy the Kid in *The Collected Works of Billy the Kid*. This mythical masculinity has been made familiar through oral narratives and more recently, and widely, through the Hollywood Westerns. Billy the Kid is a familiar figure entrenched in discourses of masculine violence, illicit sexuality, drunkenness, and subversion of social control. Ondaatje's engagement with the myth of Billy the Kid and contemporary media highlights Kenneth MacKinnon's belief that, 'mass media play a particularly important role in creating the fantasies of "hegemonic masculinities"' (10). This link between the mass media and the construction and circulation of gender identity is crucial in highlighting the insubstantial nature of all gender construction and its performative nature, and further drawing attention to a hierarchy of masculinities. Ondaatje's Billy the Kid complicates this hierarchy; he is a symbol of an anti-heroic masculinity that is reliant on cinematic, racial, and cultural stereotypes. But rather than reinforcing MacKinnon's 'hegemonic masculinities,' Billy is an outsider that provides Ondaatje with a framework to question, and reveal, the performance of this mythical masculinity and its insubstantial nature. Furthermore, Ondaatje does not overlook the paradox that renders Billy both masculine ideal and outlaw, but uses this problematic position to explore the role of the excluded masculine subject.

This preoccupation with male figures located on the borders is replicated in Murray's work, perhaps even more explicitly. Although Murray's exploration of the role of the male outsider culminates in *Fredy Neptune*, one of the most notable examples of Murray's engagement with a specifically male outsider is in his early poem, 'An Absolutely Ordinary Rainbow':

> But the weeping man, like the earth, requires nothing,
> The man who weeps ignores us, and cries out
> Of his writhen face and ordinary body
>   . . .
> Evading believers, he hurries off down Pitt Street.

> (*Collected Poems* 30)

This poem is both a polemic of religious enlightenment and an exploration of the role of the male outsider who marks himself as such, something that Murray retains an interest in throughout his career. In this passage, the 'weeping man' undermines his own manhood as 'weeping' is a practice more normally associated with women than men, however clichéd an image that may be. In Murray's poem this ambivalence draws attention to the corporeal act of performing masculinity, while also pointing toward the inherent differences between the masculinity and femininity. In 'An Absolutely Ordinary Rainbow,' this is set within a specifically urban Australian context as the man 'hurries off down Pitt Street,' an image which contrasts with the weeping man who 'like the earth, requires nothing.' This suggests a division between urban Australia and Murray's sense of the 'earth' which contributes to the sense of inherent Australian masculinity that I will discuss in relation to *Fredy Neptune* later in this chapter. However, it also roots Murray's quasi-mythical narrative in a material Australia, thus tying the overt performance of religion and masculinity into a context which is specifically national.

Michael Ondaatje's *In the Skin of a Lion* (57) utilizes a similar juxtaposition of myth and specificity in his exploration of the disappearance of the real-life figure of Ambrose Small, the reclusive tycoon. Small acts as both a signifier for a specific historical moment in Canadian history and a particular characterization of successful Western manhood that is based on wealth and status. As such he acts as spoil to Patrick Lewis's masculine identity which is constructed through his working man's body (Fraser). As millionaire, media tycoon and owner of theaters in Toronto, Ambrose Small comprises one of MacKinnon's 'hegemonic masculinities.' Significantly, it is in Small's actual disappearance that his status is fully reiterated through the mass media as '[t]he press leapt upon every possibility' (58). For Ondaatje masculinities are constructed through myths and stereotypes; but he seeks to undermine rather than endorse those truisms of male identity, and interrogate cultural stereotypes in a way that recalls Homi K. Bhabha's notion of mimicry:

> It is from this area between mimicry and mockery, where the reforming, civilizing mission is threatened by the displacing gaze of its disciplinary double, that my instances of colonial imitation come. What they all share is a discursive process by which the excess or slippage produced by the *ambivalence* of mimicry (almost the same, *but not quite*) does not merely 'rupture' the discourse, but becomes transformed into an uncertainty which fixes the colonial subject as a 'partial' presence. (123)

For Bhabha, the act of mimicry is ambivalent, and destabilizes the original through the 'colonial imitation.' It is this 'colonial imitation' of received versions of Western and 'hegemonic' masculinity in the work of Ondaatje and Murray that demonstrates their commitment to postcolonial critique, and locates them most convincingly as postcolonial writers. In the context of their work, performances of recognizable masculine identities operate, 'so that mimicry is at once resemblance and menace' (Bhabha 123). For both writers, national identity is a postcolonial concern as their problematically masculine figures are revealed to represent similarly problematic notions of nationality. These complex notions of national identity provide a lens to critique entrenched notions of Western masculinity, as the male bodies of their protagonists call attention to the way in which all identities are performed.

Like Patrick's body in *In the Skin of a Lion*, in *Fredy Neptune* it is Fred's physicality which draws attention to his performance of masculinity. This masculinity becomes a vital contingent in his 'cracking normal' (1998: 9) as he consciously takes on and acts out the physical role of the Australian male in the face of his social displacement and physical numbness. While Murray is at pains to demonstrate that Fred's loss of his bodily self engenders a reconstruction of his identity on every level, it is undertaken from an inherently masculine perspective as the sexual and social conventions that he is forced to perform are foregrounded. The clearest way in which Fred's masculinity is performed is through his physical strength which is the by-product of his numbness. If this strength marks him out as hypermasculine, the numbness to which it is directly related ensures that all human contact, and most notably Fred's sexual feeling, is eradicated. As such, his masculinity becomes an untouchable performance based on Fred's social conditioning rather than any inherent maleness. Throughout the text, his strength remains a potent symbol for this performance of identity as he is forced to consciously consider his actions and their social implications:

> Oh, please Mister come help him! A woman was crying
>   at my side. This engine's tipped back on him!
> I ran with her, down the freight yards. Men were collecting
> round a ship's diesel engine, half off a flatcar, with snapped chains
> and awful agonised yells under it. I could hear the man would die
> No time for holding in. I got two good holts on big Otto
> And heaved at him, against all his iron inclinations.
> I'll bet you could have cut pump-washers off my ring
> That morning as the Digger said. No more give than Gibraltar-
> The others had been hopeless, poking at him with planks.
> And then he moved! I didn't feel it but could see it.
> A gap! Getting. Higher. Between his. Bolt flange and the dirt.
> The crushed. V-trench. The flange had made. Up. They slid the
>   man out. (138)

This passage draws attention to the performed nature of Fred's masculinity as he considers whether to reveal his super-strength and decides: this is 'no time for holding in.' Thus he self-consciously utilizes his physical capabilities and acts out the role of the hero. This whole passage is constructed within the clichéd terms of a superhero narrative, and Fred enacts a parodic version of Bhabha's mimicry and undermines the status of the hyperbolic discourse through his quotidian language and ordinariness. Fred's language roots him in a wider colonial context: when he suggests that 'Big Otto' has 'No more give than Gibraltar' he imbues the very specific, masculine, working-class context of the American ship builders with imagery of the British Empire. Fred's battle with the ship's engine becomes a symbol for the struggle between man and machine, as he 'got two good holts on big Otto,' and reveals the underbelly of technology as men's lives are put at risk by their own creations.

Murray's passage draws attention to the role of the machine through very specific naming of its parts, 'Bolt flange and the dirt. / The crushed. V-trench' and repeated use of caesuras which emphasize each clause. The binary of man and machine is complicated as Fred 'heaved at him, against all his iron inclinations,' and the explicit gendering of 'big Otto' draws attention to the fact that this struggle is fought within an entirely masculine space. This metaphor acts with a double purpose: it reiterates what John MacInnes has called the 'fetishistic image of masculinity' (324) that is propagated by modernity, as the physical image of man pitched against machine looms large. It also foregrounds the mechanical nature of Fred's performance of his own identity, as his male body becomes aligned with the body of the 'ship's diesel engine' and focuses on its mechanized and feelingless nature. Therefore, the body and its functions becomes a space to explore the physical dangers that are involved in manual labor, while drawing attention to the fact that it is a largely male undertaking.

The role of physical labor in the performance of masculinity is also at the heart of Ondaatje's *In the Skin of a Lion*. Like Murray's *Fredy Neptune*, at times this text celebrates the male body to the point of fetish; like Fred's, Patrick's body is the symbol of his male identity and there is a potency in its physical nature that becomes the focus of Ondaatje's text. This is a potentially narrow frame of reference, although it does allow for a full exploration of the way in which masculinity is a spectacle. Just as Fred Boettcher's physical numbness reveals the performed nature of his masculinity, so Patrick Lewis's male body is at once celebrated and objectified as he performs that manual labor which makes him a man:

> Hazen Lewis and his son rode up to the split rock. The large man walked around the logjam. He drilled in a plug of dynamite and lit the fuse. He got the boy to shout the warning and the logs went up into the air, on to the bank, and the river was free.
>
> In difficult cases Patrick would remove his clothes and grease himself down with oil for the crankcase of the steam donkey. He dove into the ribbed water and swam along the logs. Every half-minute wherever he was he had to raise his hand to assure his father. Eventually the boy located the log his father had pointed to. He caught the charge thrown out to him, crimped the blasting cap on to the fuse with his teeth, and lit the powder.
>
> He re-emerged from the water, walked back to the horses and dried himself with the towels from the packsack, like his father not even turning round to watch. A river exploded behind him, the crows leafing up. (17)

Like in *Fredy Neptune*, this passage foregrounds the physical nature of masculinity in the context of manual labor. Patrick becomes part of the machine, 'He caught the charge thrown out to him, crimped the blasting cap on to the fuse with his teeth, and lit the powder,' in a way which foregrounds the links between man, labor, and machine and also emphasizes the mechanical nature of his human body as it aligns Patrick with the explosive he is setting and the jam of logs. This focus upon the mechanized nature of Patrick's body emphasizes its physical performance and highlights the insubstantial nature of his masculinity and all socially constructed identity.

Their work as loggers sets Hazen and Patrick in a homosocial context which is reiterated and made hierarchical by the focus on their familial relationship and the repetition of the word 'father.' It is significant that this passage comes early in the novel and sets the context for the text, which deals explicitly with notions of masculinity throughout. Ondaatje's interest in the male-line re-inscribes the lack of the feminine, particularly as here the focus is on Patrick's young male body. It is the adolescent male who 'would remove his clothes and grease himself down' and, while this is posited as a purely practical act, it also ironically invites the male gaze, unlike the explosion which he sets but does not watch. Thus, even in the context of this entirely male community, Patrick's masculinity is demonstrated to be more of a performance than the spectacle of the logs exploding. This upsets notions of 'hegemonic' masculinity by forcing Patrick into a feminized role, and the questionable masculinity of his male body remains in view throughout the text. It is further reiterated in the figures of Caravaggio and Nicholas Temelcoff, where the feminization of their male bodies is more explicitly linked to their immigration and the concomitant problematic national status, thus explicitly tying notions of gender and race together in the context of the feminized masculine body.[2]

In the Skin of a Lion presents an early twentieth-century Toronto which is characterized by the, largely male, immigrants who literally construct the city by building its infrastructure. This physical construction of Toronto remains at the heart of the novel and is imbued with the nationalities of its workers; thus tying the exploration of masculine identity that the novel undertakes into a specifically Canadian postcolonial context. However, as Carol L. Beran suggests: 'By choosing to write about groups "hopelessly predestined to insignificance," Ondaatje challenges the traditional patterns of Canadian thinking'. *In the Skin of a Lion* presents a Canada that is always filtered through the community of loggers that opens the text. Ondaatje's Canada mirrors Murray's almost completely homosocial sense of Australia, while also using the loggers to demonstrate that it is possible to be on the social margins, even in your own county: 'Patrick has clung like moss to strangers, to the nooks and fissures of their situations. He has always been alien, the third person in the picture. He is the one born in this country who knows nothing of the place' (Ondaatje 1987: 163). As Patrick clings 'like moss to strangers' he consciously performs a marginal masculinity that is awkward and peripheral: he's a logger, an outsider in a community of immigrants, a prisoner and a terrorist. As such, his performance of masculinity, which is rooted in the Canadian, working-class, masculine tradition becomes a paradoxical symbol of his outsider status in terms of both his nationality and his gender.

This tension between a masculine national tradition and otherness is mirrored in *Fredy Neptune* as Fred is cast as an authentic rural Australian male, an aspect of his identity which is reiterated throughout the text by Murray's use of colloquial language and diction:

> The language Fredy uses when he speaks is English. It's essentially the sociolect I'm describing, rural men's talk of my father's youth. Earlier in the century, when Australia was more comfortable with a proletarian identity, this language was widely enjoyed and valued.
> (Murray 2002: 67)

Murray highlights the anachronistic nature of the language that Fred uses, while also drawing attention to the fact that it is has always been marginal, a 'sociolect.' In this context, *Fredy Neptune* is a celebration of the 'rural men' of 'his father's youth': explicitly a class and gender-based identity which has now become obsolete in the face of what Murray calls Australian 'gentrification' (2002: 68). This already complex identity is complicated further as Fred's dual nationality means that he is a foreigner, both at home and away. Therefore, Murray too disrupts 'the traditional patterns' of his national thinking and, through a stereotypical figure that represents Australian 'rural men,' critiques both notions of male identity and notions of Australian nationhood. His is a performance of masculine identity that is rooted in the past and is in many ways problematic as it is both nostalgic and idealized, something I will discuss in more depth later. However, like Ondaatje's marginal protagonists and his engagements with modern myths it also points toward the potential for constructing masculine and national identities from outside the social norms, and, as I will consider in more detail in the following section, explicitly destabilizes the old signifiers of patriarchy.

Performing masculinity, fatherhood, and nationality

In the second section of this chapter I will consider the way in which the problematically marginalized masculine identities that Murray and Ondaatje explore come to signify their versions of postcolonial nationhood. This is most notable in the various versions of fatherhood that they explore. In both writers' work the father and son relationship, a symbol of masculinity that is inherently tied to notions of collectiveness and genealogy as well as those of patriarchy and male dominance, becomes a metonym for their very specific understandings of nationhood. As Stella Bruzzi suggests, fatherhood is a role to be consciously adopted and performed:

> 'Father' is a word that signals the actual individual who takes on the patriarchal role within a family, although even here the meanings are various. 'Father', for instance is a very different tenor to 'dad': more formal, less comforting. But what is it to be a father? The phrase 'to father a child' refers merely to the act of successful insemination, although 'to be a father' suggests some measure of nurturing and familial involvement. However, 'father' is also a more abstract, nebulous term than 'dad', the father, but not the dad, can be a symbolic ideal. (vii)

For Bruzzi, fatherhood is a performance, both actual and linguistic, that an 'individual' 'takes on,' as she discusses the 'patriarchal role' of the father, and suggests the nuanced way in which the term and its derivatives might be deployed. Her notion of fatherhood is rooted within the family context, but she also foregrounds the way in which this is a 'nebulous' notion that can be a 'symbolic ideal,' based on traditions of masculine identity and patriarchy. Likewise, the role of the father and son relationship in Ondaatje's *In the Skin of a Lion* is largely emblematic, particularly as the marginalized homosocial community of loggers becomes a paradigm for all family relationships while also contributing to Patrick Lewis's sense of 'being alien, the third person in the picture.' By the end of the text, postcolonial Toronto is symbolized by more complex and cross-gendered family relationships as Patrick is left with only his stepdaughter Hana. In a similar way, Murray's poetry points toward the importance of his father, and the role of fathers, in his conception of Australian identity. As Murray points out in the previous passage, this is particularly notable in *Fredy Neptune* as his father forms the socio-linguistic basis for his protagonist's poetic voice. However, Cecil Murray also plays an allegorical role in Murray's early work, much of which explores the way in which his Australian identity is rooted in the outback.

The role of the father in the work of these writers serves a number of purposes. Both writers are preoccupied with their own personal relationships with their fathers, and in their work, the symbol of the father is also a complex representation of masculine and national identities, while fatherhood is also revealed to be a performed role rather than an inherent state. Anne McClintock's discussion of the role of the family in the representation of the nation is a fruitful way of conceptualizing the role of the father in the work of Ondaatje and Murray. She draws attention to the gendered nature of the nuclear family, which also acts as a wider symbol of the nation, and points toward its clichéd but anachronistic nature: 'A crucial question thus remains for progressive nationalism: Can the iconography of the family be retained as a figure for national unity, or must an alternative, radical iconography be developed?' (110).

Although it is, in some ways, problematic to apply McClintock's feminist reading of the nation to the work of either Murray or Ondaatje, her call for an 'alternative, radical iconography' is mirrored in their work. Their nuanced versions of masculine identity explore nation as an inherently gendered state, while also revealing the limitations of McClintock's paradigm. Rather than upholding patriarchal tradition, both writers interrogate the male–female gender binary by revealing the performed nature of masculinity and all identity. Although their focus is on the male-line in the context of family frameworks, the almost complete absence of the feminine ensures that they avoid thinking about gender in binary terms, and their alternative family units not only complicate notions of the family, but also complicate the ideal of 'national unity.'

The masculine nature of Murray's representations of the family form the basis of his own vision of his homeland and more widely the sense of his own personal and national identity. It is a particularly male-orientated version of Australia, which is often conceived through the figure of his father. This is at some level a practicality, as Cecil Murray was a widower; yet, his focus on the male-line demonstrates a shift away from the iconography of the nuclear family that McClintock finds so restrictive. In 'Evening Alone at Bunyah' he engages with the figure of his father, who is out of place and out of date, and draws attention to the performative nature of his masculine identity and the increasingly tenuous link between the poet and his family:

> My father will be there now, at a hall
> in the dark of the country, shining at the waltz,
> spry and stately, twirling at formal speeds
> on a roaring waxed plank floor.
> The petrol lamps
> sizzle and glare now the clapping has died down.
> They announce some modern dance. He steps outside
> to where cigarettes glow sparsely in the dark,
> joins some old friends and yarns about his son.

(Collected Poems 15)

In this poem, Murray recalls his father in a self-consciously nostalgic and regional setting that draws attention to the conceptual and actual distance between the two men. He romantically envisages Cecil 'in the dark of the country, shining at the waltz,' in a way that sets him spatially and temporally apart from his son. However, Murray's focus remains on his father's contradictory performance of his masculinity that vacillates between the formal dance in which he appears 'spry and stately' and his 'yarns about his son.' This is also a linguistic clash as the colloquial 'yarns' sets the context of Murray's vision clearly within outback Australia. Murray's use of the word 'country' here suggests that his imaginative scope encompasses Australia, rather than just his father who acts a metonym for his homeland. The male-line is foregrounded here and consequently it is a homosocial notion of Australianess which Murray engages with most fully. This is reiterated throughout the poem as the figure of Cecil Murray explicitly provides a poetic vision of Australia: 'This country is my mind. I lift my face/and count my hills, and linger over one' (*Collected Poems* 15). His sense of nation is a vision of masculine collectiveness, of the poet and his father, a very specific sense of his place of home as he counts 'my hills,' all of which contribute to wider national notion of Australia, which retains Murray's sense of masculinity and marginality.

For both writers, the family connection provides the strongest link between the performance of male identity and nationality. In line with David H. Morgan's suggestion, there is potential for the framework of the family to undermine the traditions of gender relations. Therefore, as their allegorical engagements with their own family units unsettle notions of masculinity and gender, more generally, they also problematize notions of nation:

> Masculinities located, if not anchored, in family relationships, may provide one mode of 'doing masculinity'. Or, alternatively, the increasingly fluid contexts of family life might provide a basis for increasing questioning of the oppositions between men and women, masculine and feminine.
>
> (Morgan 230)

Morgan suggests 'doing masculinity' which is always a performance, and points out that there is more than 'one mode' of operating. As changing notions of the family actually undercut gender stereotypes, in contrast to McClintock, Morgan retains the notion of masculinity as central to the notion of the family. The 'increasingly fluid contexts of family life' suggest a disruption of the old certainties of gender, and perhaps also other social categories including, race, nationality, and sexuality. Therefore, the allegorical use of this 'fluid' sense of family represents the complexities of postcolonial nations in a nuanced way. Whether either Ondaatje or Murray ever fully undertakes this critique is questionable; however, they both represent unconventional family units that, while retaining a focus on the masculine explore alternative identities within that structure, and demonstrate masculinity to be something provisional and performed rather than inherent. At times, these masculine identities also operate in line with Bhabha's mimicry, as I discussed more fully earlier on, to demonstrate the stereotypical nature of performances of masculinities by revealing the way in which they operate. This is particularly notable in Murray's work as a sentimental representation of his ageing father becomes a eulogy to Murray's nostalgic, regional, and homosocial Australia.

Murray's stereotype of fatherhood operates in a similar way to the clichéd versions of masculinity that are explored in *Fredy Neptune* and *In the Skin of a Lion*, and goes further to emphasize the distance and limited nature of stereotypes. Ondaatje's *Running in the Family*, a fictional memoir based on his Sri Lankan family, also valorizes this notion of the past as it recalls the figure of Ondaatje's father, Mervyn:

> It was two and a half years later, after several letters about his successful academic career, that his parents discovered he had not even passed the entrance exam and was living off their money in England. He had rented extravagant rooms in Cambridge and simply

eliminated the academic element of the university, making close friends among the students, reading contemporary novels, boating, and making a name for himself as someone who knew exactly what was valuable and interesting in the Cambridge circles of the 1920s. He had a good time, becoming briefly engaged to a Russian countess, even taking a short trip to Ireland when the university closed down for its vacation. No one knew about this Irish adventure apart from an aunt who was sent a photograph of him posing slyly in uniform.

(*Running in the Family* 31)

Ondaatje's father is represented as a performer throughout *Running in the Family*. He is a carnivalesque figure whose mimicry is invariably revealed in a way which destabilizes any notion of authentic identity. In the above passage, what might be read as a clichéd and stereotypical version of Ondaatje's heritage is also a comment on the postcolonial nature of his family and Sri Lanka. Ondaatje draws attention to the financially interspersed nature of Sri Lanka and the UK as his father 'was living off their money in England.' There is a reversal of the expectations of the colonial relationship as his Sri Lankan parents fund Mervyn's English experience, although the conventional nature of the archetypal Cambridge undergraduate is notable. Mervyn, however, acts in line with Bhabha's mimicry: there is no substance to his performance of undergraduate identity, even though it is based upon recognizable conventions. His 'Irish adventure' further complicates the role of the postcolonial immigrant who becomes involved with the British forces. This is a specifically masculine display of his Anglophilia; however, this performance of his British and male identity remains covert and hidden. Rather than reifying colonial relationships, Mervyn subverts not only the expectations of his parents, but also those of the Cambridge community, and the British armed forces, that he mimics. His performance is an inauthentic version of masculinity and nationality, and draws attention to itself as such.

As both writers present limited and nostalgic versions of national identity and masculinity, they concomitantly draw attention to the way in which these identities are performed with varying degrees of success. 'Evening at Bunyah' represents a nostalgic vision of Murray's father who is valorized for his position in Murray's past, but also lacks potency and centrality. In a similar way, Melvyn Ondaatje is a carnivalesque figure who is both historicized and made childlike, thus similarly reneging the ideals of the Western masculinity that he appears to embrace. Both these figures operate on the postcolonial margins as they demonstrate, in line with McClintock, social inclusions and exclusions: 'despite many nationalists' investment in the idea of popular *unity*, nations have historically amounted to the sanctioned institutionalization of gender *difference'* (McClintock 89). Again, the focus for McClintock is on the way in which binary notions of gender are inherent within the construct of the family and the nation. However, in the work of Murray and Ondaatje, this 'institutionalization of gender *difference'* is undermined by an interrogation of masculinity and a focus on masculine figures who operate outside, and sometimes in direct opposition to, the nation. Ondaatje's work, in particular, locates the exploration of postcolonial social contexts outside the normative constructs of nation, family and gender. This is notable in *In the Skin of a Lion* where the entirely male community of loggers is used to demonstrate Patrick's otherness, but is also found in his other texts. For instance, in *The English Patient* where the residents of the Villa San Girolamo form a family unit that crosses boundaries of nationality, gender, and race the performance of masculine identity is explored from various cultural positions.

If, in line with McClintock's argument, the family structure is a model which accommodates both the exploration of gender relationships and those of nationhood, in *Fredy Neptune* the father and son relationship is a pessimistic metaphor for the future of Australia. Murray's notion of masculine identity is the opposite of McClintock's 'forward-thrusting, potent' (90) masculinity, most explicitly demonstrated in the figure of Fred's son, Joe, who is a physically maimed war veteran:

> Next doors came in, and skittered back from Hans a bit:
> *He's all right*, I said. *My brother. He's been away. He's harmless.*
> They had the phone and I was wanted on it. *Your brother?*
> Laura was ringing from Brisbane. Joe was fine, don't worry,
> A young strong fellow with a tin left foot, he'd get preference,
> He could even dance again, as if he ever had in our bush camp-
> Then she told me what she thought of this comfort she'd
>   been given.
> *Prepare yourself, love. Joe's not the boy he was. He's savage.*
> *Lay in a lot of smokes.* I pulled some very long strings
> To get cartons of Camel and Lucky Strike and Ardath.
> Our yellowy ghost of a son
> Horrified me to look at him. And he seemed glad it did.
> *The atebrin tan, Dad. I'm not as fucking yellow as some.*
> And he limped to his room with tin squeak in his left boot
> And lay there smoking, a hundred, a hundred and fifty a day.

(Murray 1998: 242)

In this passage the performance of masculine identity becomes a national concern as Laura repeats the official description of Joe's injuries: 'Joe was fine, don't worry, A young strong fellow with a tin left foot.' This is in contrast with the realities of the war veteran who is 'not the boy he was' and is repeatedly referred to as inhuman, 'our yellowy ghost of a son,' and inhumane, 'savage.' These contrasting images draw attention to the way in which masculinity is performed in a post-war context, and the versions of masculine identity which underpin nationalist propaganda. The focus is on Joe's physicality which he embraces as a signifier of his identity, as it renders him gleefully abject: '[it] Horrified me to look at him. And he seemed glad it did.' The performance of Joe's masculinity becomes a depraved and ghoulish demonstration of his post-traumatic shock and the shame of a nation. Murray explores the very real pain that is involved in witnessing the curtailment of youth and masculinity: 'I'm not as fucking yellow as some.' Joe's yellowness becomes a physical signifier of the impact of the war on Australian men, which also hints at the politics of race through Murray's focus on color; furthermore, this is coupled with the demotic 'fucking' which also suggests a moral degradation. Alongside this, the family figures as an allegory for a grieving post-war nation while Fred and Joe's intergenerational, masculine relationship is a symbol of Australia's problematic future. It is notable that Fred's family is transnational: it includes Hans, the autistic German man, a metaphor which is an extension of Fred's own Australian/German identity, and points toward an acceptance of the divisions and conflicts which are inherent within both the self and the nation. In this context, Joe and his consciously performed masculine identity are pessimistic symbols for the future of the Australian nation as he 'lay there smoking, a hundred, a hundred and fifty a day.' The nostalgic and fixed representations of intergenerational masculine identities that have characterized *Fredy Neptune*, and Murray's work more generally, are abandoned here. Fred and Joe's father and son relationship is an angry prediction for the Australian nation as it points toward the insubstantial and divisive nature of the performance of masculinity and all identity.

Ondaatje's *In the Skin of a Lion* ends on a more positive note, although the homosocial social unit with which the novel began has been entirely replaced by the cross-gendered stepfamily made up of Patrick and Hana:

They stopped at the Ford and unlocked the passenger door. He was about to climb over into the driver's seat.

– Do you want to drive? He asked
– Me? I don't know the gears.

– Go ahead. I'll talk the gears to you till we are out of town.
– I'll try it for a bit. (256)

Patrick and Hana destabilize notions of the family as they are not blood-relatives and are both orphans, thus fulfilling that 'alternative, radical iconography' that McClintock insists upon, while still maintaining a broad paradigm of the family. Ondaatje eschews the tradition of the passing of knowledge through the male-line in favor of a cross-gendered relationship, and the above passage contrasts with the earlier piece where Patrick is a logger. As Patrick who was 'about to climb over into the driver's seat' surrenders control to the feminine Hana the focus on homosocial relationships that the text has maintained up to this point is complicated. In allowing Hana to take the driving seat, Patrick revokes the privilege of his paternal and gender status and allows her to perform masculinity. This is a paradoxical ending with potentially conservative implications as the gendered family unit is reinstated, albeit a new and reconsidered form of family, and it does provide a space for the exploration of femininity, that has been barely visible in the text up to this point. It also has implications that are carried through *The English Patient*, as the boundaries of gender are complicated and confused, more overtly than in its predecessor.

In these texts, therefore, intergenerational relationships provide a space to explore the changing performances of masculinity, and also have implications for the national identities, as Fred and Patrick's offspring become problematic vectors of their fathers' identities. Each writer's concept of marginalized masculine identities that exist interstitially in transnational contexts informs their constructions of complex and multi-faceted identities that frustrate monolithic representations of gender and nationhood. Both texts end with complex gender relations, as Fred's son is unmanned and Patrick has only a daughter. In abandoning or undercutting stereotypes, masculinity and nationality are revealed to be performances and the binaries of gender and traditions of patriarchy are destabilized. In this way, in the work of Murray and Ondaatje, following in one's father's footsteps is not a patriarchal tradition, but a mode of revealing the way in which all identities are conscious and unstable performances.

Notes

1. Much of Ondaatje's early work features overt masculine violence, it is, however, most notable in *The Collected Works of Billy the Kid: Left Handed Poems* and *Coming Through Slaughter*.

2. The most detailed characterization of Nicholas Telemcoff and David Caravaggio focuses on their masculinity and their status as immigrants. The most notable passage of characterization of Telemcoff is from pp. 36–48 of *In the Skin of a Lion*, which focuses on his part in the construction of the Bloor Street Viaduct in Toronto. Caravaggio is characterized as 'an exotic creature' (188) as part of the section that he's fully introduced in (183–215).

Works cited

Beran, Carol L. 'Ex-Centricity: Michael Ondaatje's *In the Skin of a Lion* and Hugh MacLennan's *Barometer Rising.' Studies in Canadian Literature* 18.1 (1993): 71–84. 12 Dec 2009. <http://www.lib.unb.ca/Texts/SCL/bin/get.cgi?directory= vol18_1/&filename=Beran.htm>.

Bhabha, Homi K. *The Location of Culture.* 1994. London: Routledge, 2004.

Bruzzi, Stella. *Bringing up Daddy: Fatherhood and Masculinity in Post-War Hollywood.* London: British Film Institute, 2005.

Carby, Hazel V. *Race Men: W.E.B. Du Bois Lectures.* Cambridge: Harvard UP, 1998.

Fanon, Frantz. *Black Skin, White Masks.* 1952. New York: Grove Press Inc, 1967.

Fraser, Kathleen D. J. 'Small, Ambrose Joseph.' *The Dictionary of Canadian Biography Online.* U of Toronto 2000. 12 Dec 2009. <http://www.biographi.ca/009004-119.01-e.php?&id_nbr=7709&interval=25 &&PHPSESSID=5foa3nl0hpdldak2odgf9p16n2>.

MacInnes, John. 'The Crisis of Masculinity and the Politics of Identity.' *The Masculinities Reader.* Ed. Stephen M. Whitehead and Frank J. Barrett. Cambridge: Polity, 2001. 311–29.

MacKinnon, Kenneth. *Representing Men: Maleness and Masculinity in the Media.* London: Arnold, 2003.

McClintock, Anne. ' "No Longer in a Future Heaven": Gender, Race and Nationalism.' *Dangerous Liaisons: Gender, Nation & Postcolonial Perspectives.* Ed. Anne McClintock et al. Minneapolis: U of Minnesota P, 1997. 89–112.

Morgan, David H. J. 'Family, Gender and Masculinities.' *The Masculinities Reader.* Ed. Stephen M. Whitehead and Frank J. Barrett. Cambridge: Polity P, 2001. 223–32.

Murray, Les. *Collected Poems.* Manchester: Carcanet, 1991.

——. *Fredy Neptune.* Manchester: Carcanet, 1998.

——. 'How Fred and I wrote *Fredy Neptune.' Les Murray and Australian Poetry.* Ed. Angela Smith. London: Menzies Centre for Australian Studies, 2002. 65–78.

Ondaatje, Michael. *The Collected Works of Billy the Kid: Left Handed Poems.* 1970. Basingstoke: Picador, 1989.——. *Coming Through Slaughter.* 1976. London: Bloomsbury, 2004.

——. *The English Patient.* 1992. London: Bloomsbury, 2007.

——. *Running in the Family.* 1982. London: Vintage, 1993.

——. *In the Skin of a Lion.* London: Picador, 1987.

Spivak, Gayatri Chakravorty. 'Can the Subaltern Speak?' *Marxism and the Interpretation of Culture.* Ed. Cary Nelson and Lawrence Grossberg. Champaign: U of Illinois P, 1988. 271–315.

Whitehead, Stephen M. and Frank J. Barrett. 'Introduction: The Sociology of Masculinity.' *The Masculinities Reader.* Ed. Stephen M. Whitehead and Frank J. Barrett. Cambridge: Polity P, 2001. 1–26.

9

Seeding Asian Masculinities in the US Landscape: Representations of Men's Lives in Asian American Literature

Wendy Ho

Abstract

Asian American masculinities emerge out of the everyday realities of men's embodied lives and thus should be understood as organically growing out of the intersections of local and global contexts. The literary texts of David Mas Masumoto, a Japanese American writer and peach farmer, who lives in the San Joaquin Valley in California, portray work, family, community, and the environment in a nuanced ecological and ethnic framework, yet also the multiple tensions faced by Asian American men as they negotiate notions of masculinity across diverse geopolitical borders, social and cultural formations, and networks in diasporic communities. They display transformative formations of masculinity that move away from the aggressive, martial cultural nationalist models of the 1960s and 1970s that were being constructed in the ferment of Asian American cultural and literary politics and calls for social justice and recognition. Land and the care of the environment as well as the cultivation and sustainability of families and communities are the embodied heart of his narrative and practice. His is a self-reflexive attentiveness, respect, and sensoriality that savor the minutiae of daily life and work, the fluctuating rhythms of actively inhabiting and engaging with a bio-diverse world.

Within the past two decades, the field of Asian American studies has begun to more actively address research on the important and complex aspects of Asian American masculinities.[1] In this essay, I provide a theoretical perspective on the subject of Asian American masculinities, grounded in contemporary Asian American literary cultural politics and US history. Then I conduct an analysis of one writer's works in order to draw out subtle aspects of the study of Asian American masculinities. Specifically, I discuss the texts of David Mas Masumoto, a Japanese American writer and peach farmer, who lives in the San Joaquin Valley in California. I examine the development of his understandings of work, family, community, and the environment in a nuanced ecological and ethnic framework. This framework is worth exploring in its linkages to more transformative formations of masculinity that move away from the aggressive, martial, and cultural nationalist models of the 1960s and 1970s that were being constructed in the ferment of the Asian American literary and cultural nationalist movement that demanded recognition and social justice. Key to my analysis is the recognition that Asian American masculinities emerge out of the everyday realities of men's embodied lives and thus should be understood as organically growing out of the intersections of local and global contexts.

A number of Asian American scholars, writers, artists, and community activists continue to explore new ways to better articulate and represent male identities and knowledge formations in relation to social experiences, cultures, histories, and political understandings of the world. For example, they work to denaturalize cultural conceptions and representations of masculine formation by examining how racialized ethnic masculinities are constituted in relation to mainstream US culture, society, and history, how new practices or styles of classed masculinity develop in relation to national or imperial constructs of masculinity, or how often marginalized ethnic masculinities seed themselves within and beyond the field of gendered and sexualized norms in both US and transnational geographies. It is very possible that these often invisible, marginalized and sometimes appropriated masculinities can suggest alternative, more open-ended formations of masculinity than have not been previously theorized or understood in their own right.

Early discussions among Asian Americans during the turmoil and ferment of the 1960s and 1970s on masculinity often concentrated on issues of Asian American emasculation. Sadly, a number of early cultural nationalists like the influential Asian American writer Frank Chin identified with the socially and emotionally deforming and exclusionary practices of a white racialized masculinity that disempowered men as well as women, families, and other diverse communities. They tried to empower and regulate Asian American men by valorizing certain traditional forms of masculinity as heroic or by focusing on the tragedy of not being able to be traditional – for example, that they regret not having been 'men' enough to protect their women or to be authoritarian patriarchs in control of their women and children. From Chin's warrior standpoint, Asian American men forced to confront terrible humiliation for the sake of the family are not perceived as heroic. In Chin's definition of an Asian American moral universe the individual 'Chinaman I' trains to fight like the war god Kwan Kung. Daily living is male camaraderie, fighting, and revenge. Life is daily war (1991: 35). Chin talks a great deal about the heroic as it is – more often than not – referenced to men and written by men: the peach blossom oath of individualized fighters, the ethics of war, military strategy and statecraft, private and popular revenge, memorized sets 'on the ethic of life that is war,' fraternal organizations of triads and tongs, and criminal gangs of warriors and outlaws. In the absence of 'manly' and 'strong' father-models, integrity, honor, and loyalty are transferred to a predominantly fraternal culture of gangs, brotherhoods, triads, or outlaws, who inhabit the marshes, woods, or urban Chinatowns, wreaking havoc and revenge on a corrupt and racist ruling white patriarchal, capitalist, and imperialist nation-state. Chin has long favored a more openly aggressive, belligerent stance and style of writing which do not kowtow to Western racism and imperialism by denying traditional Chinese myths, and history, which do not require one to spill one's guts. Moreover, the fighter-writer, according to Chin, must carry over these skills into his writing: 'As a rule of style and literary activity, . . . the fighter writer uses literary forms as weapons of war, not the expression of ego alone, and does not fuck around wasting time with dandyish expressions of feeling and psychological attitudinizing. The individual is found in the act of war, of not selling out, not in feelings' (1985: 112).

Studies on Asian American masculinity have emerged from contemporary feminist discussions as well.[2] Early on, Asian American feminists noted the significance and importance of Asian American masculinity as a site of contestation. For example, in her poem/essay, 'Letter to Ma,' Merle Woo challenges writers like Frank Chin on many different fronts. She recognizes the multiple oppressions of racism, sexism, and classism confronted not only by her mother but also by her father. She describes the psychological, emotional, and bodily damage to her mother and how it has affected her own life and struggles with self-abuse. Likewise, she observes the complex social and economic violence that humiliates and dehumanizes her father in front of his family and community, grinding him down to the bone in US contexts. Woo, moreover, is concerned about Chin's ridicule and dismissal of lesbian and gay identities and experiences in erecting a particular homophobic performance of masculinity. Like a number of Asian American women and other feminist women of color writers, Woo does not choose to leave men, women, and their distressed ethnic families or communities behind. Even when fiercely critical, they often return to – not escape – these geographies of love, pain, anger, and memory to construct their critical narratives and politics. Despite their temporary, and sometimes necessary, separations and border-crossings (emotional, imaginative, and physical), their narratives often remain deeply linked with the primary sites of family and community, not only as a personal choice but also as a social, cultural, historical, and political site for interrogation and intervention.[3] There is much promise in the marginalized in-between spaces for what David Theo Goldberg calls 'affirmative resistance':

> It is ... only on and *from* these sites, the social margins, that the battles of resistance will be waged, the fights for full recognition of freedoms, interests, claims and powers, for the autonomy of registered voices, and the insistence upon full incorporated social institutions, resources, *spaces*.... After all ... to change one's geography – not only to move from but equally to transform one's spaces and its representation – may well be to change one's world. (205)

More recent gender, sexuality, and queer studies approaches have continued to challenge attempts to construct a less 'feminine' warrior masculinity by contrasting the masculinity in Chin's work with that of scholars who allow for alternative masculinities. In her essay, 'Of Men and Men: Reconstructing Chinese American Masculinity,' King-Kok Cheung argues that 'Chinese American men, and Asian American men in general, who are seldom allowed by the dominant culture to perform "masculine" roles, are self-driven to rehearse gender norms' (173). Cheung argues, 'Asian American writers should no doubt continue to expose and combat Asian sexism, but they must also guard against internalizing and reproducing racial stereotypes, thereby reinforcing the deep-seated biases of the American reading and viewing public' (176). She critiques Frank Chin's essay, 'Come All Ye Asian American Writers of the Real and the Fake' for its 'patriarchal prescriptions,' especially for reproducing violence as key to masculinity, despite her sympathy for his attempt to re-conceive Asian American masculinity (177). Instead, she advocates considering the Asian American 'poet-scholar' as a model for Asian American masculinity, in contrast to images of Asian American violence that mimic dominant forms of masculinity and those based on traditional stereotypes of Asian American male passivity and asexuality (Cheung 2002).

In just this decade, important work has focused on masculinity within and in relation to queer literary and cultural studies.[4] There are now a number of book-length studies on Asian American masculinity that explore literary and cultural productions. In *Chinese American Masculinities: From Fu Manchu to Bruce Lee*, Jachinson Chan argues that queer literature and scholarship provide alternative models of resistance to dominant white masculinity. He suggests that 'gay masculine constructs offer alternative strategies to resist the effects of a hegemonic model of masculinity: particularly, gay models of masculinity allow straight men to confront an inherited homophobia and the conventional masculine fear of effeminization' (138). David Eng's book *Racial Castration: Managing Masculinity in Asian America* explores the intimate relationship between gender and sexuality on the racial formations of Asian American men. Eng applies a predominantly psychoanalytic paradigm to an analysis of Chinese and Japanese American texts. He explores the intimate linkages between racial and sexual differences, stereotypes and fantasies; that is, the relationships between gender and sexuality on the racial formations of Asian American men. As he states, 'racial fantasies facilitate our investments in sexual fantasies and vice versa. As such, they must be understood as mutually constitutive, as drawing their discursive legibility and social power in relation to one another' (2). Finally, Daniel Kim's *Writing Manhood in Black and Yellow: Ralph Ellison, Frank Chin, and the Literary Politics of Identity* examines how African American and Asian American conceptions of masculinity function in relation to each other. He shows how the language of gender and sexuality is used to frame metaphors of emasculation and the psychological trauma of racism on men of color. In focusing on how homosexuality functions as a form of 'feminizing racism' in their work, Kim shows how these writers come to define literary work as a 'cultural and political activity capable of producing the most virile and racially authentic forms of manhood' (back cover).

Despite the depth and diversity of texts listed here, even these critical works do not begin to draw attention to the very broad range of Asian American male and female creative writers working to expand the critical literary fictions of masculinity that often go under the general and broad category of 'Asian American.'[5]

II

Asian American men have not historically had the opportunity to fit seamlessly into white heteronormative notions of masculinity in the US; it may be more fruitful to seriously engage in the making of practices that have the potential to reconfigure ways of theorizing and articulating new social and cultural spaces and relations in the US landscape. We must search for potentially democratizing and improvizational social and political formations of Asian American masculinities that do not simply duplicate or reify traditional white hegemonic patriarchal and nationalist ideals or practices. The historian Gail Bederman has examined the cultural reconfigurations of masculinity between 1880 and 1917 as they shifted from more self-restrained, moral notions of ideal manhood in the Victorian period toward new and more individualized, aggressive, and sexualized constructions that were intimately embroiled in the discourses and institutions that were attempting to define a superior and civilized white US nation-state and empire. White masculinity and civilization were often defined against constructed narratives and representations of a racialized primitive, inferior, weak, and/or effeminate masculinity and nation in various Asian contexts.[6]

The model US citizen has been frequently represented by strong, stoic, heroic male figures – the rugged individualist on the physical or metaphysical frontier of the American West. This figure of history, legend, and myth is typified in the white hunter, gunman, cowboy, frontiersman and other pioneer heroes, fictional and real. They are self-reliant, emotionally independent, hard-working and endlessly resourceful, larger-than-life characters, explorers, warriors, and tamers of the wilderness and constructors of a white nation-state (Bederman). These representatives of a certain type of American heroic manhood also manifest a dark side in their practice of manhood in society; namely, the brutal massacre of the Indians, slavery, internment, the exploitation of the poor and weak, the accumulation of massive fortunes, and the arrogant, immoral contempt for the cultures of a whole range of subordinated groups. Native Americans, Mexican Americans, African Americans, and Asian Americans were exploited as slaves or as cheap labor, made to toil without families, citizenship or basic human rights, or terrorized by racist governmental policies, lynchings, and massacres.

These types of white heroic manhood were appealing to racist white males in the State of California, whose historical origins in the nineteenth century (as well as the twentieth century) were very much embedded in racialized white-supremacist ideologies, discourses, and institutions, which 'were used to inscribe racial difference and divide humankind into distinct categories of people. These notions provided the basis upon which white European immigrants differentiated themselves from the diverse ethnic populations they encountered during their expansion into the Far West' (Almaguer 7). In a similar vein, President Teddy Roosevelt, according to Gail Bederman, advanced the notion of a 'virile imperialism' by building a 'claim to political power on his claim to manhood':

> Roosevelt drew on 'civilization' to help formulate his larger politics as an advocate of both nationalism and imperialism. As he saw it, the United States was engaged in a millennial drama of manly racial advancement, in which American men [meaning white men] enacted their superior manhood by asserting imperialistic control over races of inferior manhood. To prove this virility, as a race and a nation, American men needed to take up the 'strenuous life' and strive to advance civilization – through imperialistic warfare and racial violence if necessary. (171)

We need new models of masculinity that move toward an 'erotics of life' rather than toward one hell-bent on conquest, violence and death to other individuals, groups and communities, and living environments (cf. Lorde).

III

In contrast to these ideologies, practices, and representations, I argue that there are many less visible spaces of masculine identity formation and knowledge beyond the panoptic gaze. They exist despite the regulation and discipline of hegemonic masculinity and the normative institutions and practices of the nation-state, for example, at marginalized and often exploited ethnic and immigrant sites, in poor and working-class inner city and rural communities and geographies beyond the city proper. In these imaginative and material in-between spaces some men practice alternative, more fluid forms of masculinity that are intimately linked to families, communities, hybrid networks and environments. They critically challenge delimited stereotypes or representations of 'private' or 'domestic' sites of struggle and survival by adjusting to dual or multi-income family needs, to taking care of children and doing familial work, to maintaining a nurturing, stable home environment or community, to living with independent women all as part of an understanding of virile and heroic masculinity. Making acts of transition between ways of life and gender systems, becoming a different sort of man may *seem* like being less of a man from some perspectives, but it can also be seen and defined as meaningful and ful-filling work and relations rather than as 'dysfunctional,' 'pathological,' 'effeminizing,' 'sell-out' or 'model minority.'

It is very important to tell the stories of men as individuals, fathers, sons, husbands, friends, workers, lovers, and artists at the tangled inter-sections and distances of love, pain, and anger if we are to contemplate new formations of masculinity. Asian American men, after all, are cru-cial to familial and/or community and social networks and survival processes, especially considering the long social, legal, and political his-tories of denying them access to their own critical understandings and narratives of self, their families and ethnic communities, and geogra-phies in the US.[7] These critical understandings and narratives are often haunted by the residual and persistent traces of emotional, communal, cultural, historical, and/or geopolitical legacies linked to other countries of origin and to other diasporic sites of belonging.

IV

In this exploratory vein, I think the Japanese American writer-farmer David Mas Masumoto articulates one refreshing alternative understand-ing of masculinity that counters narratives or mythologies that project a more violent and war-like spectacle of masculinity, that tie into projects of racism, imperialism, and colonialism, the conquest and regulation of peoples and land or environment as a masculine activity or enter-prise. Masumoto's representation of masculinity links self to others and human to environment. While he does not discuss masculinity as dis-tinct from these other issues, through my reading of his work I seek to engage with and articulate how his experiences and visions of farming, community, family, and self offer a useful alternative Asian American masculinity within the context of the contemporary US.

Masumoto lives in the vast agricultural region known as Central Valley, California. He grew up in the 1950s in the Valley as a third-generation Japanese American *sansei* and lives in a 90-year old farm-house with his wife Marcy, two children Nikiko and Korio, and his parents in Del Rey, California. In his books *Country Voices: the Oral His-tory of a Japanese American Family Farm Community* (1987), *Epitaph for a Peach: Four Seasons on My Family Farm* (1995), *Harvest Son: Planting Roots in American Soil* (1998), *Letters to the Valley: A Harvest of Memo-ries* (2004), *Four Seasons in Five Senses: Things Worth Savoring* (2003), and *Heirlooms: Letters from a Peach Farmer* (2007), he provides a personal and collective understanding of his daily experiences as a Japanese American small family farmer in a rural and agricultural community. Through a lifetime of collecting and sifting through the bits and pieces of his family and community history, he discovers a rich legacy of toil and suffering as well as survival and strength in his family and community as they make their way from the rural agricultural regions of Japan to California in the early to mid 1900s. His stories reclaim a subjectivity and agency in an alternative voice and embodied (not abstract) practice that challenge the dehumanizing racialized representations of Japanese Americans in US popular culture as well as the formal governmental and legal discourses and bureaucratic structures that have attempted to define, regulate, and punish Japanese Americans. These stories are narrated within a social-economic history in the US that is situated within a chaotic and transient world of labor, poverty, erasure, and violence – where one is constantly configured in mainstream culture as a displaced person, a permanent stranger, an alien, a homeless outsider, a disloyal, second-class citizen.

More specifically, Masumoto's texts shift the reader's gaze away from the dominance of urban cityscapes and paradigms to see or interpret the traumatized lay of the land and the people who live on it – how men, women, and families survive in fluid transnational spaces that are not in the city, and yet, are very much linked to urban issues, needs, and practices. Though there are Asian American historians writing about diverse ethnic rural and agricultural spaces, much work still remains to forefront the rich multiplicity and nuances of neglected ethnic rural and agricultural life experiences, communities, and histories, especially at the complex intersections of race, gender, sexuality, class, and transnationality.

In his daily walks on the land, Masumoto is visited by ghosts of relatives, migrant laborers, farmers, and families that have occupied, worked, and reclaimed the desert lands for agriculture. 'A sense of history lives in these farms, each with private histories, buried memories, and families married to their lands. A farm carries an inherited legacy, the ghosts of the past daily walk through each vineyard and orchard' (1987: 3). They drift in and disperse punctually with the winter tule fogs, reminding him of the stories of his family and Japanese American community as they confront both natural and human forces that have forcibly uprooted, transplanted and bulldozed them through the landscape made fertile and rich by their hopes of new beginnings, new roots. They migrate back to these sites with their untold or unfinished stories, refusing to depart, refusing erasure from and dispossession of the land they have cultivated and claimed with their bodies and spirits. Told from their standpoints, the land can tell stories that make visible the chaotic and violent shifts in social-economic and political power that have shaped and still shape the fertile Valley landscape and culture in California and the West.

Where are these critical memories and narratives of struggle and endurance of an individual, his family, and Japanese American community in the transformation of the land and the making of culture and community in California and the West? In the formation of the US nation-state? Diverse ethnic people and communities have transformed the social, economic, and political landscapes of the Central Valley and state of California with their histories, knowledge formations, traditions, and practices; and yet their rural and agricultural histories have been substantially excluded or neglected within foundational US metanarratives. The journalist Helen Zia refers to the 'MIH' (Missing in History) – those haunting presences both living and dead that testify to a missing or marginalized past and present not centrally resurrected in a number of family histories or in mainstream tellings of social, economic, cultural, legal, and public histories in the US.

Within this context, Masumoto's stories narrate a fierce desire for a place to root and sustain (not escape or avoid) a family, a community, a cultural, historical, and political identity and practice. That is, the search for a semblance of stability and permanence – even if temporary, vulnerable and against great odds – becomes profoundly understandable for individuals and groups with long social and cultural legacies and practices sutured to land and family, but who are forced to wander continuously like tumbleweeds from one place to another through California and the US. To be permanently displaced or mobile is not an ideal way of life or condition for everyone. Unmoored from kin, long farming roots and lands in rural, agricultural Japan, entering port cities and moving through the plantations of Hawai'i or the reclaimed tule swamps and desert internment camps in the US, many Japanese nevertheless sought new homesteads, communities, and lands to settle, cultivate, and nurture even as they kept and transformed the traditions, memories, and affiliations of former distant homeplaces in their ever-changing present and future circumstances in the US. Masumoto's stories provide us with a window into fuller and more complex perspectives on such ethnic masculinities as they are practiced within rural agricultural labor and small family farming and community sites. He charts an intimate narrative that portrays his daily negotiations, emotions, compromises, and dilemmas in enacting a more radically oppositional politics of identity (masculinity), community social formation, and ecological survival of the environment.

More broadly, Masumoto's politics are intimately allied to his developing understanding of ecological models and practices for sustaining the land. Masumoto has linkages to Carlo Petrini's Slow Food movement that seeks 'to catalyze a broad cultural shift away from the destructive effects of an industrial food system and fast life: toward the regenerative cultural, ecological, social, and economic benefits of a sustainable food system, regional food traditions, the pleasures of the table, and a slower and more harmonious rhythm of life.'[8] His texts construct an understanding of masculinity that interweaves his multiple identities (son, father, husband, farmer, Japanese American, writer, and so on) to family and community, culture and history. His resisting narratives and practices help to de-center the centrality of profit, commodification, competition, individual, and monocultural approaches that have dominated the Central Valley and the mainstream narratives of the Western frontier. It is a movement away from what Vandana Shiva describes as a Eurocentric notion of property that privileges capital investments as investment and perceives these capital returns as the only right that is to be protected. She asserts that 'non-Western indigenous communities and cultures recognize that investment can also be a labor of care and nurturance. Rights in such cultural systems protect investments beyond capital. They protect the culture of conservation and the culture of caring and sharing' (130). Though not himself free from the compromises and dilemmas exacted in living within a capitalist social-economic structure, Masumoto works actively toward this goal of a 'culture of conservation' and 'culture of caring and sharing' within Japanese American legacies and cultural practices that do not simply duplicate the same hegemonic and capitalist power arrangements/relations and laboring geographies that have so seriously impacted the Central Valley landscape and its workers and communities. The models of impersonal and abstracted corporate, agribusiness farming represent a techno-rational logic, history, and way of utilizing the land, producing crops, and relating to individuals and communities that is often related to normative or privileged notions of white hegemonic masculinity and power. Masumoto does not choose to duplicate these models within his own life and daily practices farming his family's land and caring patiently for his beloved old peach trees and grape vines, and extended family and communities. His is not a choice for violent masculinity that seeks to dominate or ravage the land or people; it is not a masculinity that marks its separation from women, children, or its escape from an ethnic community.

Masumoto's stories demonstrate how important it is to engage and contest both the social-economic and political landscape that commodifies land, individuals, and communities to its needs for power and profit, that have stripped racialized ethnic individuals, families, and small family farming communities of their voices, homesteads, and livelihoods, their experience and understandings of shared places in the defining and making of public history and social relations and policy. The Central Valley's history has included atrocities and brutalities against communities of color who have lived and worked on the land but have not benefited greatly from the fruits of their own sweat labor and suffering. They have often been literally and figuratively erased from the landscape in order to construct and privilege an untroubled pastoral representation of an enlightened Western civilization and capitalist democracy, or a myth about rugged/self-reliant individualism, or the conquest history of the Western frontier and wilderness by a heroic white yeoman-citizenry class. As Don Mitchell has argued,

> images have been repeatedly called up to valorize and celebrate the 'way of life' that California agriculture had become by the turn of the century. *Only* by erasing – or completely aestheticizing – the workers who made that way of life is its celebration possible. *Only* by seeing California purely as a landscape view can we see beauty without understanding the lives of the damned who are an integral part of the beauty. And that move, erasing the traces of work and struggle is precisely what landscape imagery is all about.[9]

In *Epitaph for a Peach*, *Harvest Son*, and *Four Seasons in Five Senses*, Masumoto outlines his very embodied discoveries for a way to live and farm that works with rather than against nature, to structure a cooperative, sustainable relationship with the natural world that is not rooted in conquest, dominance, exploitation, or erasure. He isrespectful of old cultural traditions in his family history in Japan and the US yet realizes that life and farming require a flexibility and openness to innovation, experimentation and risk-taking. It requires new habits of being and more transformative ways of observing and relating to the people and minutiae of the environment. He abandons his old farm-work schedules, set to a calendar, and learns the need for patience and for flowing with the ever-changing rhythms and unpredictability of nature. He curbs his impulse to find quick fixes, to constantly regulate chaos or wilderness, or to remove the variability that comes with each farm year or season. He learns he cannot always be in control of situations, and must learn to fail without winners or losers (1995: 65). In more ways than one, 'the farm becomes a test of the unconventional, a continuous experiment, a journey of adaptation and living with change.... I am learning to live with chaos' (1995: 37). As a small family farmer, Masumoto must engage a range of practical ethical dilemmas such as grappling with the wages, health and treatment of his migrant seasonal workers. He also chooses to re-examine his use of types of fertilizers and pesticides, altered and cover crops, seeking less abusive ways of farming and exhausting an environment that sustains him and his family farm community. He is well aware of the weight of the actualities that bear down on his decisions. He functions, after all, within a world that has his family farm competing for their social and economic survival against real Central Valley corporate agribusiness.

Rather than a reductive monoculture or monocropping practice, Masumoto recognizes the importance of cultivating complexity and biodiversity in the environment and in society. He confesses that his desire to experiment with planting cover crops had little to do with increasing the profit of his land or with some grand or abstract philosophy for changing the world. At root, Masumoto tells us it had to do with love – the graceful renewal and reciprocation of love: his wife Marcy was pregnant with their first child and she was tired of the gray earth of winter outside her kitchen window. He 'did it for her dreams of spring walks through the soft clover with the baby in her arms, breathing in the fresh scent of spring growth. I did it for reasons that seemed disconnected with farming at the time' (1995: 8). And yet, his farm becomes a rich ecological habitat for insect life, blooming flowers, and cover crops that not only rejuvenate the earth but also renew the body and spirit in its transformative desire for beauty, passion, pleasure, spontaneity, creativity, and hope. By Thanksgiving, they have 'a smiling, cooing child and a germinating cover crop, its green leaves poking through the soil crust. Both child and crop grew through the winter and by spring we took walks through the fields, picking fresh peas and beans and letting ladybugs tickle her soft baby skin' (1995: 8). Planting and growing a family and farm 'demand that you believe in the magic and the mystery of life' (1995: 9). In the face of difficult survival and possible extinction, Masumoto chooses to affirm life and another day of struggle, another kind of wealth far beyond money and commodities consumption within a capitalist system. Land and the care of the environment as well as the cultivation and nurture of culturally hybrid families and communities are the embodied heart of his narrative and practice.

This sensitivity is further applied to the cultivation and nurture of families and communities. His individual politics of identity is related to a belonging within a family and community working together. The singular 'I' aligns with the collective – a self-in-community listening, sensing and attending to the feelings, memories, and silences of family members who endured the Japanese American internment and its aftermath or to an elderly father's conversation as an affective and political practice of sociality and resistance against legacies of injustice and dehumanization of subordinated farm families and communities living in the cold heartland of the Central Valley and in the US.

Farming for David Mas Masumoto is an integrated, embodied habit of being and daily practice that weaves together a meaningful work life with his personal and communal life in society. His is a self-reflexive attentiveness, respect, and sensoriality that savor the minutiae of daily life and work, the chaotic rhythms of actively inhabiting and engaging with a biodiverse world. The bottom line for him is not money: 'When I first started, I realized I would never make a fortune in farming, but I hoped I could be rich in other ways – and maybe, just maybe, my work would create some other kind of wealth in the process' (1995: xi). As Gerald Haslam notes, 'Family farms and personal farming bespeak a different philosophy, a far more intimate relationship with nature, than does agribusiness; it is a vision less economically productive but by no means less wise. "The ultimate goal of farming is not the growing of crops but the cultivation and perfection of human beings," suggests philosopher Masanobu Fukunoka' (qtd. in Johnson, Dawson, Haslam 208). And David Masumoto's stories contribute to this 'other kind of wealth,' to other understandings of masculine identity, subjectivity, and agency in relation to his significant coordinates to family, land, and community, to transnational and local rural farming histories tied to multiple, ever-changing social and cultural heritages affiliated to Japan and continued in the US.

Notes

1. I thank the *Journal of International Law and Policy* at the University of California, Davis's Martin Luther King School of Law for creating interdisciplinary space for me to discuss and write about the experiences of Japanese Americans, David Masumoto and small family farms in an earlier essay. I also thank my friend and colleague Kent Ono for spurring me on to continue work on this exploratory essay on Japanese American masculinities.
2. See, for example, Elaine Kim; Wong; Lowe; Espiritu; Cheung 1998; Cheung 2002; Rachel Lee; Ho; Chu.

3. In foregrounding women writers like Maxine Hong Kingston, Amy Tan, and Fae Myenne Ng, Wendy Ho sought out models beyond hegemonic masculinity and Asian American cultural nationalism in order to suggest more fulfilling options for men and their families, communities, and/or societies. See, for example, Ho 195–243.
4. The emergent field of Asian American queer studies contributes greatly to masculinity studies by examining its relations to race, gender, and sexuality not only in US frameworks but also transnational ones. See, for example, a range of early anthologies that discuss these concerns in local and global contexts in the US and abroad: Quang Bao and Hanya Yanagihara; Eng and Hom; and Leong; Nakayama. Besides the books by Jachinson Chan, David Eng and Daniel Kim mentioned in the text, see the articles and books that rethink Asian American masculinity and sexuality studies by: Fung; Gopinath; Manalansan.
5. A sampling of other interesting studies that include some discussions of Asian American masculinity formations in specific ethnic communities are those by Espiritu and España-Maram. In other literary and cultural studies, see Chu; Chuh; Rachel Lee; Li; Ma; Nguyen; Palumbo-Liu; and San Juan, Jr. In Asian American Studies theater and performance text studies, there are discussions most often of Frank Chin's plays and David Henry Hwang's M. Butterfly: See for example, Moy; Shimakawa; and Kondo.
6. For example, see Robert Lee; Moy; and Creef.
7. A majority of early immigrant Asian American men – single or married with kin, wives, and families in their original homelands – were denied the traditional markers of masculinity in the US well into the twentieth century: fatherhood, providing for women and families, companionship-sexuality, citizenship and naturalization (Naturalization Act of 1790) and ownership of land (1913 California Alien Land Act bars aliens from owning land). It is important to tease out the stories of Asian American men and their understandings of masculinity, and to be attentive to the historicized emotional, social, and physical genealogies and negotiations within their families and communities that are variously affected by factors such as race, ethnicity, class, gender and sexuality, and immigration histories.
8. Petrini cover flap. See also Appendix with an excerpt on the Manifesto on the Future of Food (251–53).
9. Mitchell (20). See also Schenker.

Works cited

Almaguer, Tomás. *Racial Fault Lines: The Historical Origins of White Supremacy in California*. Berkeley: U of California P, 1994.

Bao, Quang and Hanya Yanagihara, eds. *Take Out: Queer Writing From Asian Pacific America*. New York: Asian American Writers' Workshop, 2000.

Bederman, Gail. *Manliness and Civilization: A Cultural History of Gender and Race in the United States, 1880–1917*. Chicago: U of Chicago P, 1995.

Chan, Jachinson. *Chinese American Masculinities: From Fu Manchu to Bruce Lee*. New York: Routledge, 2001.

Cheung, King-Kok. 'Of Men and Men: Reconstructing Chinese American Masculinity.' *Other Sisterhoods: Literary Theory and U.S. Women of Color*. Ed. Sandra Kumamoto Stanley. Urbana and Chicago: U of Illinois P, 1998.173–99.

——. 'Art, Spirituality, and the Ethic of Care: Alternative Masculinities in Chinese American Literature.' *Masculinity Studies and Feminist Theory: New Directions*. Ed. Judith Kegan Gardiner. New York: Columbia U P, 2002. 261–89.

Chin, Frank. 'This is not an Autobiography.' *Genre* 18 (Summer 1985): 109–30.

——. 'Come All Ye Asian American Writers of the Real and the Fake.' *The Big Aiiieeeee!: An Anthology of Chinese American and Japanese American Literature*. Ed. Jeffrey Paul Chan et al. New York: Meridian, 1991. 133–56.

Chu, Patricia. *Assimilating Asians: Gendered Strategies of Authorship in Asian America*. Durham: Duke U P, 2000.

Chuh, Kandice. *Imagine Otherwise on Asian Americanist Critique*. Durham: Duke U P, 2003.

Creef, Elena Tajima. *Imaging Japanese America: The Visual Construction of Citizenship, Nation, and the Body*. New York: New York U P, 2004.

Eng, David and Alice Hom, ed. *Q&A: Queer in Asian America*. Philadelphia: Temple U P, 1998.

Eng, David L. *Racial Castration: Managing Masculinity in Asian America*. Durham: Duke U P, 2001.

España-Maram, Linda. *Creating Masculinity in Los Angeles's Little Manila: Working-Class Filipinos and Popular Culture, 1920s–1950s*. New York: Columbia U P, 2006.

Espiritu, Yen Le. *Asian American Women and Men*. Thousand Oaks: Sage, 1997.

Fung, Richard. 'Looking for My Penis: The Eroticized Asia in Gay Porn Video.' *How Do I Look?* Ed. Bad Object Choices. Seattle: Bay Press, 1991. 145–68.

Goldberg, David Theo. *Racist Culture: Philosophy and the Politics of Meaning*. Cambridge: Basil Blackwell, 1993.

Gopinath, Gayatri. *Impossible Desires: Queer Diasporas and South Asian Public Cultures*. Durham: Duke U P, 2005.

Ho, Wendy. *In Her Mother's House: The Politics of Asian American Mother-Daughter Writing*. Walnut Creek: AltaMira Press/Rowman & Littlefield, 1999.

Johnson, Stephen, Robert Dawson and Gerald Haslam. *The Great Central Valley: California's Heartland*. Berkeley: U of California P with the California Academy of Sciences, 1993.

Kim, Daniel Y. *Writing Manhood in Black and Yellow: Ralph Ellison, Frank Chin, and the Literary Politics of Identity*. Stanford: Stanford U P, 2005.

Kim, Elaine. ' "Such Opposite Creatures": Men and Women in Asian American Literature.' *Michigan Quarterly Review* 29.1 (1990): 68–93.

Kondo, Dorinne K. *About Face: Performing Race in Fashion and Theater*. New York: Routledge, 1997.

Lee, Rachel. *The Americas of Asian American Literature: Gendered Fictions of Nation and Transnation*. Princeton: Princeton U P, 1999.

Lee, Robert. *Orientals: Asian Americans in Popular Culture*. Philadelphia: Temple U P, 1999.

Leong, Russell, ed. *Asian American Sexualities: Dimensions of the Gay and Lesbian Experience*. New York: Routledge, 1996.

Li, David Leiwei. 'The Production of Chinese American Tradition: Displacing American Orientalist Discourse.' *Reading the Literature of Asian America*. Ed. Shirley Geok-lin Lim and Amy Ling. Phildadelphia: Temple U P, 1992. 319–32.

Ling, Jinqi. 'Identity Crisis and Gender Politics; Reappropriating Asian American Masculinity.' *An Interethnic Companion to Asian American Literature.* Ed. King-Kok Cheung. New York: Cambridge, 1997. 312–37.

Lorde, Audre. *Sister Outsider: Essays and Speeches.* New York: Crossing Press, 1982.

Lowe, Lisa. *Immigrant Acts: On Asian American Cultural Politics.* Durham: Duke U P, 1996.

Ma, Sheng-Mei. *The Deathly Embrace: Orientalism and Asian American Identity.* Minneapolis: U of Minnesota P, 2000.

Manalansan IV, Martin F. *Global Divas: Filipino Gay Men in the Diaspora.* Durham: Duke U P, 2003.

Masumoto, David Mas. *Country Voices: The Oral History of a Japanese American Family Farm Community.* Del Rey: Inaka Countryside Publications, 1987.

———. *Epitaph for a Peach: Four Seasons on My Family Farm.* New York: HarperSanFrancisco, 1995.

———. *Four Seasons in Five Senses: Things Worth Savoring.* New York: WW. Norton & Company, 2003.

———. *Harvest Son: Planting Roots in American Soil.* New York: W.W. Norton and Company, 1998.

———. *Heirlooms: Letters from a Peach Farmer.* Berkeley: Heyday Books, 2007.

———. *Letters to the Valley: A Harvest of Memories.* Berkeley, California: Great Valley Books/Heyday Books, 2004.

Mitchell, Don. *The Lie of the Land: Migrant Workers and the California Landscape.* Minneapolis: U of Minnesota P, 1996.

Moy, James. *Marginal Sights: Staging the Chinese in America.* Iowa City: U of Iowa P, 1993.

Nakayama, Thomas, ed. *Asian Pacific American Genders and Sexualities.* Tempe: Arizona State University, 1999.

Nguyen, Viet Thanh. *Race and Resistance: Literature and Politics in Asian America.* New York: Oxford University Press, 2002.

Palumbo-Liu, David. *Asian/American: Historical Crossings of a Racial Frontier.* Stanford: Stanford U P, 1999.

Petrini, Carlo. *Slow Food Nation: Why Our Food Should Be Good, Clean, and Fair.* Trans. Carla Furlan and Jonathan Hunt. New York: Rizzoli Ex Libris, 2005.

San Juan, E., Jr. *Racial Formations/Critical Transformations: Articulations of Power in Ethnic and Racial Studies in the United States.* Atlantic Highlands: Humanities International Press, 1992.

Schenker, Heath, ed. *Picturing California's Other Landscape: The Great Central Valley.* Berkeley: Heyday Books, 1999.

Shimakawa, Karen. *Asian American Body on Stage.* Durham: Duke U P, 2002.

Shiva, Vandana. *Tomorrow's Biodiversity.* New York: Thames and Hudson, 2001.

Woo, Merle. 'Letter to Ma.' *This Bridge Called My Back: Writings by Radical Women of Color.* Ed. Cherríe Moraga and Gloria Anzaldúa. San Francisco: Kitchen Table/Women of Color Press, 1981. 140–47.

Wong, Sau-ling Cynthia. *Reading Asian American Literature: From Necessity to Extravagance.* Princeton: Princeton U P, 1993.

Zia, Helen. 'Staying Positive Through the Backlash.' *Public talk.* University Club at the University of California, Davis. 15 Nov. 2005.

10
From Glam Rock to Cock Rock: Revis(it)ing Rock Masculinities in Recent Feature Films

Lucia Krämer

Abstract

After a brief general outline of the depiction of rock in film, this essay investigates the constructions of rock masculinities in the feature films Rock Star, Almost Famous, Still Crazy, *and* Velvet Goldmine. *The essay reads the first three films as representative of the dominant strategies of representing male rock stardom in streamlined independent cinema. Despite the pretence of (comically) debunking the discourses of authenticity, rebelliousness, and gender prevalent in various forms of 'cock rock' through a representation of masculinities in crisis and a moralistic guidance of sympathy, these films actually rely on and support a construction of rock as a male cosmos streaked by homophobia, misogyny and a gendered conception of fandom.* Velvet Goldmine, *in contrast, is marked by a narrative structure and a discussion of ideas that deliberately uphold ambivalences and uncertainties on the topics of art, stardom, theatricality, love, and sexuality. Despite these differences all four films share a celebratory attitude toward rock music and, through a technique of historical distancing, convey nostalgia for an idealized state of rock. This nostalgia, however, refers to the spirit of rebelliousness and authenticity rather than the gender conceptions in the glam and cock rock spheres of the 1970s and 1980s.*

A book on the performative aspects of masculinity should address the sphere of rock, since rock is a predominantly male cosmos, and the widespread equation of rock with a lifestyle of sexual excess is based on a version of masculinity whose emphasis on virility and sexual prowess projects an almost archaic image of man. This is, however, only one of a number of various kinds of masculinity to be encountered in the multi-faceted world of rock, which covers a variety of styles and comes with almost as many variations on the notions of masculinity associated with it. Rock musicians perform gender on various levels, the most obvious one being the stage show itself. The off-stage performance of an individual lifestyle, which for rock musicians is often expected to be one of self-destructive debauchery, is another way of projecting gender notions. Moreover, rockers of course construct gender and sex in the more general sense of Butler's concept of performativity[1] through acts that are not restricted to the public or semi-public performance areas of stage and backstage life. In this essay, I would like to go beyond this triad of performative spheres by analyzing the presentation of rock masculinities in another performative medium: the fiction film. The main questions of this essay therefore relate to the strategies by which filmmakers have engaged and reworked dominant discourses of rock for a medium that has a different core audience and relies on different, in particular narrative, ways of creating emotional appeal. I will concentrate especially on the discourses concerning gender in general and masculinity in particular, as well as the discourses of rebelliousness and authenticity to which they are inextricably linked in the world of rock.

Just as rock is not a homogeneous sphere, film is of course an extremely variable medium with production contexts, distribution strategies, and target audiences varying from one cinema segment to the next. After a short introduction to rock films in general, I will therefore restrict my analysis to four films whose production contexts, generic nature and thematic emphasis are similar enough to guarantee comparability. At the same time they were among the most visible and widely seen films on rock in their period of origin and can therefore be considered to belong to the more influential recent fictional works on rock. The films chosen for analysis[2] are *Still Crazy* (dir. Brian Gibson, 1998), *Almost Famous* (dir. Cameron Crowe, 2000), *Rock Star* (dir. Stephen Herek, 2001) and *Velvet Goldmine* (dir. Todd Haynes, 1998).[3] These works do not only share a thematic emphasis on male rock stardom and the theme of performing (gender);[4] by depicting rock careers that happened 35 or 25 years ago, all four films moreover implicitly or explicitly juxtapose the past and the present and the gender models that come with them. Since it must be expected that a considerable portion of the films' audiences has no first-hand knowledge or memory of these times, one must also discuss the purposes and effects of this juxtaposition.

Rock has been a popular subject with filmmakers since its beginnings. In a book published in 1987, Linda J. Sandahl listed more than 400 rock films for the period 1955–1986 alone. Nowadays, music channels broadcast music videos into millions of households and, since the second half of the 1990s, a large number of concert films and documentaries have been released each year. Most of these films are commissioned by the musicians themselves for purposes of promotion and are aimed at those who are already fans or at least interested in the artists or their music. They are usually released straight onto DVD (or formerly video), in order to avoid the considerable costs related to distributing a feature film (promotion, prints), the need to appeal to a much more heterogeneous audience and the exposition to a critical discourse that is more interested in the cinematic than the musical.

When rock films today make it onto the big screen, we should therefore ask why they do so. A look at some recent films implies that at least with documentaries one reason – apart from the general appeal of rock music and spectacular stage performances – could be a 'different-angle approach.' Not only have filmmakers recently rediscovered several musicians who had been marginalized in rock historiography,[5] they have also tried to present prominent rockers in a new light. *Metallica – Some Kind of Monster* (dir. Joe Berlinger, Bruce Sinofsky, 2004), for example, concentrated on the psychological conflicts within one of today's most revered rock bands and their effects on the creative process. The voyeuristic appeal which such an approach can provide is also exploited in the biopic genre, where stage performers and entertainers have long been among the most popular subjects (Custen 6, 84/5). *The Doors* (dir. Oliver Stone, 1991), *Tina – What's Love Got To Do With It* (dir. Brian Gibson, 1993), and the more recent *Walk the Line* (dir. James Mangold, 2005) are among the most famous examples of musical biopics from the past two decades and exemplify the tendency of filmmakers to choose well-known subjects, when they want to reach a larger audience.

With rock stars, fame very often comes as a form of notoriety, which can hold a sensationalist appeal for non-rock audiences (and film audiences are to a great degree non-rock audiences). Rebelliousness and an anti-establishment stance – 'sticking it to the Man,' as the main character in Richard Linklater's film *The School of Rock* (2003) puts it – are still key discourses of rock, and they are associated with a life-style of excess that includes promiscuous sex, drug abuse and the squandering of money. However, in most rock films this 'dark side' of the business is juxtaposed with the music as a point of admiration. The live performance especially is very often represented as a spiritual (communal) act and/or authentic self-exposure by the artists.[6] Both of these aspects carry over into films, such as those discussed in this essay, whose stories may be set in the rock business, but which do not pretend to depict real people. Such films will not fulfil voyeuristic desires of seeing a real life revealed or cater to the admiring fans of a particular artist. Yet due to the choice of a rock setting they automatically foreground the dominant discourses of rock.

The following analysis will first concentrate on *Rock Star, Almost Famous*, and *Still Crazy* before moving on to *Velvet Goldmine*, which, despite its thematic similarities, presents a different kind of rock with different gender conceptions from the three other films. It is also formally more experimental and seems to be aimed at a different audience and will therefore be treated separately, as an exception to the norm. *Rock Star, Almost Famous*, and *Still Crazy*, in contrast, can be grouped together as representative of the dominant strategies of presenting male rock stardom in streamlined independent cinema,[7] where today most fiction films on rock originate. All three films are set in a rock cosmos with clear-cut gender roles mirroring those prevalent in the dominant forms of rock in real life. These are dominated by the image of male (white) performers who are supposed to be authentic and original creative artists and interact with their fans in a strictly heterosexual and male-dominated framework. The male hegemony of this rock cosmos is evident, for example, from its historiography, which has consistently written female musicians out of rock history (Jensen 175). Fan activity, too, is differentiated and ranked according to the sex of the fans, with male fandom being regarded as a connoisseur engagement with music and as identificatory involvement with a star image, while female fandom 'appears solely as heterosexual interest in the male star image.' This implies, of course, that female fans are clueless about music and hence inferior to male fans (Jensen 3), which in turn suggests that musicians playing for a predominantly female audience cannot be truly authentic artists. In Simpson's analysis, girls are 'very much a part of the rock and roll legend, [yet] they often come behind drinking, drugs and the music itself in priority and then seem to be valued only in terms of what exchange they bring between "the guys" ' (192).

In a similar vein, Jensen argues that the figure of the female groupie has ultimately not come to attest to a celebration of heterosexuality in rock. Instead, it has facilitated an institutionalization of heterosexuality within a misogynist power structure that bolsters the male rock stars' status and images of virility and that potentially contributes to a male homosocial musical sphere connoted with a threat of sexual violence (264).

The most extreme forms of 'cock rock'[8] in which masculinity is most obviously equated with virility and an often aggressive sexuality are the various forms of heavy metal, where potentially feminizing attributes like long hair or make-up and theatrical clothing are counteracted by an extreme flaunting of heterosexuality:

> So many heavy metal artists look like your worst nightmare of an amateur drag queen, or plumber's mate tranny, but they are careful to atone for this by cussing and swearing, pulling 'babes', drinking cold tea out of Jack Daniel's bottles at breakfast and being unable to form a sentence without the customary phrase 'fuckin' faggot!'
>
> (Simpson 203)

This is the social setting of Stephen Herek's *Rock Star*. Set in 1985, the film tells the story of Chris Cole, a young singer who idolizes the heavy metal band Steel Dragon and is himself the front man of a Steel Dragon tribute band. He is thrown into the crazy world of heavy metal stardom after being chosen to replace the original Steel Dragon band singer. Cameron Crowe's film *Almost Famous*, set in 1973, also has a rather naive outsider as the protagonist forced to come to grips with the world of rock, even if this time it is not the world of hard rock: 15-year-old William Miller, an aspiring journalist, gets the chance to go on tour with rising rock band Stillwater and, like Chris Cole in *Rock Star*, encounters the excesses and madness of the rock circus, by which he is both attracted and repelled. In contrast to *Rock Star* and *Almost Famous*, *Still Crazy* is not a period piece, but shares their narrative core of presenting a learning process. The film is about the struggles of veteran band Strange Fruit, who attempt a comeback reunion 20 years after their split-up in the 1970s. The forty-somethings, who try to cash in on the retro wave, are obliged to confront the inevitable changes they have undergone since their heyday of glory, be it in social status, fame, or age.

In the tradition of Rob Reiner's cult classic *This is Spinal Tap* (1984) all three films approach the rock business from a more or less comic angle, with a stronger (*Rock Star*, *Almost Famous*) or weaker (*Still Crazy*) emphasis on the underbelly of the rock circus as a world of sex, drugs, and conflicting egos. However, all three films clearly show the personal conflicts within the bands or their entourages and the toll that the life of rock stardom takes on the musicians, many of whom are troubled by problems of health, money, or identity loss. The rock masculinities depicted in the films are therefore usually masculinities in crisis. All three films adopt an unequivocal moral stance toward rock stardom, since the happy endings for the protagonists only occur under the condition that they leave behind the rock lifestyle and instead follow their 'real' vocation.

In accordance with what has been said about heavy metal, the excesses that are implied in the films are greatest in *Rock Star*, and the necessity of the band members to project determined aggression and virility and to assume a persona both on stage and in the media is shown most exhaustively in this film. This applies to details like musicians padding the front of their trousers in order to give the impression of a large penis as well as to more pervasive role playing. For example, Chris Cole, who is American, adopts an English accent on stage and in interviews in order to fit in with the British band Steel Dragon, and he even takes on a new name. After a while Chris starts to run the danger of complete identity loss, because in order to fulfil his new role as Steel Dragon front man he has to adapt to a life style of promiscuous sex and drugs. This is his job, as the amoral drummer A. C. explains to him, since the economic well-being of the band depends on the projection of a rock star image:

> You see, you got all these birds out there dreaming about having it off with you. And that makes the guys want to be you. And the guys are the ones who buy the records. So if the chicks don't want you, the guys are gone. Put it this way, your job is to live the fantasy that other people only dream about. (70.48–71.07)

This view of women as a means to an end points to the rampant misogyny in the world of *Rock Star*. During concerts, for example, the stars' wives must remain backstage in 'the henhouse,' and the groupies who come to pleasure the stars must bring their 'pussy passes.' The film implicitly supports this misogynist discourse by presenting the groupies as brainless and the stars' wives as utterly cynical and mercenary creatures. In contrast, the groupies in *Almost Famous*, who define themselves as 'band aids,' garner at least some respect from the spectator because their interest lies as much with the music as with the stars' images. This view of the girls is not necessarily shared by the band members in the film however, since at times they seem to harbor more affection for their tour bus Doris than for the teenagers they sleep with. Eventually, the band manager even sells the 'band aids' to another group for $50 and a case of Heineken. In keeping with the gender conventions of the rock world in *Almost Famous*, a female DJ and a female fact checker at *Rolling Stone* magazine, that is, two women who have garnered jobs in the predominantly male world surrounding rock music, are presented in a completely different way from the hyper-feminine groupies. The fact checker, for example, seems to feel compelled to put on extremely bossy behavior in order to evade the equation of femininity and sexual objectification. Since this character opposes the protagonist however, the guidance of sympathy toward her is negative so that once again the film implicitly aligns itself with the discourse of rock as a brotherhood of men.

Yet the filmmakers have also included at least one very strong female character in each film to counteract such a misogynistic discourse, possibly in order to escape accusations of political incorrectness. In *Almost Famous* this character is William Miller's mother; in *Rock Star* it is Chris Cole's girlfriend and manager Emily; and in *Still Crazy* it is Karen, the band manager of Strange Fruit and former girlfriend of band guitarist Brian. Both Emily and Karen are attractive, independent, and adept businesswomen who overcome the gender clichés of rock because of their love for music. Moreover, the filmmakers use the strategy of guiding the spectators' sympathies against the musicians' misogynistic attitude toward women by making it the main obstacle in the fulfilment of romantic love stories: the rock cliché of quick and promiscuous sex is pitted negatively against the bourgeois notions of romantic love predominant in mainstream film. Thus, in *Rock Star*, Emily's relationship with Chris breaks apart when he adopts a typical hard rock lifestyle. Similarly, in *Still Crazy*, Karen leaves Brian, a heavy drug user, because she does not want to see him die. In *Almost Famous*, finally, the leading 'band aid' Penny Lane, who falls in love with Stillwater guitarist Russell, is driven to attempt suicide because she realizes that while she may have been loved by him in the make-believe world of tour life, she will not be able to carry this relationship over into the real world, where Russell has a girlfriend.

While the representation of women in the three films therefore partly confirms and partly contradicts the dominantly misogynist rock discourse, the representation of male homosexuality is far less balanced. The patriarchal world of rock is built on intense homosocial bonding between men which, as many critics have pointed out, often carries more or less obvious homoerotic traits. The focal point of hard rock concerts, which Simon Frith has called 'a masturbatory celebration of penis power,' is, as Horrocks emphasizes, not women but the male artist himself,[9] and considering the striking predominance of male fans, the display of the male body by heavy metal artists is intended for other males rather than women (Horrocks 144).

Despite these homoerotic overtones, however, overt mutual sexuality between men is unacceptable in 'cock rock,' and homophobia rampant. This exclusion of homosexuality from the discourses on masculinity in rock may be one reason why the filmmakers take up the topic at all. However, despite their apparently debunking attitude toward the dominant gender roles in the rock business, their treatment of the topic actually relies on and cements prevalent discriminatory attitudes.

Almost Famous, Still Crazy, and *Rock Star* all contain instances of intense male bonding, most obviously among the rock fans. In *Almost Famous,* for example, William's mentor Lester Bangs glorifies the relationship between uncool men like William and himself; they find a home in rock, not by identifying with the stars but in their common appreciation of music. There is also intense bonding among the band members, for whom the bands often function as surrogate families despite recurring tensions. Yet male homosexuality in the films is only good for comedy, which depends on the incongruence of gayness with a cock rock image. In the climactic scene of *Almost Famous,* for example, the Stillwater band plane is caught in an electrical storm. In fear of death the band members start confessing intimate secrets to each other. After everyone has had their say, the drummer, who is at the bottom of the band hierarchy anyway, cries out that he is gay and thus provokes an embarrassed silence with overtones of shock. The intended comic effect of the scene is reinforced by the fact that this coming-out is instantly rendered superfluous when the flight captain announces that the danger of the electrical storm is over. The gay character thus becomes a figure of ridicule as well as of pity.

Rock Star shows a very similar treatment of the story's male homosexual character, Steel Dragon lead singer Bobby Beers. One of the reasons why he leaves the band is the fact that he is no longer able to put up with the homophobic remarks and attitudes of the other band members. It is also obvious that his attempts to project a hard rock life style amount to a denial of his own personality. Even though his anger and narcissism make him appear a slightly pathetic figure, he therefore commands the sympathy of the spectator when he quits the band. At the very end of the film, however, the film implicitly aligns itself with the discriminatory attitude of the rock cosmos it seemed to debunk. Beers turns out to have become the lead dancer in an Irish tap dance show *à la* Riverdance. This change underlines the insincerity of Beer's former image as a hard rocker, and his description of his new art form as a substantial, healthy, and honest form of expression also seems unjustified and insincere. Not only does the comic incongruence of hard rock and tap dancing render Beers ridiculous; but in the context of a rock film discussing the issue of authenticity, Beer's volte-face behavior also robs him of his dignity and the audience's sympathy.

Another issue relating to masculinity in *Still Crazy* and *Almost Famous* is age. In *Almost Famous* 15-year old William Miller is thrown into the rock circus. As a rock journalist he fulfils the role of 'the Enemy' of the band Stillwater; yet at the same time they regard him as 'the Kid.' Due to his age and uncool looks, William is not taken seriously as a man and possible antagonist, which manifests itself for example in the fact that in the tour hotels William stays with the girls in the band aids' room. Nonetheless, in contrast to the band members, who have gone into the rock business to escape responsibility, William is ready to assume responsibility when required and thus, implicitly, to act like a man. It is him, and not the older and allegedly manlier Russell, who saves Penny Lane after her attempted suicide, because he is firmly rooted in what Penny Lane calls 'the real world.' In contrast, rock stars in films are often presented as juvenile or unable to cope with everyday life, which is always interpreted either negatively or to comic effect. Thus, in *Still Crazy* drummer Beano still lives with his mum and has a predilection for immature jokes based on body parts and farts, and lead singer Ray is fully dependent on his wife Astrid, whom he calls both his 'baby' and his 'mama.' Rather than his age and its implication of a loss of virility, it is Ray's incapability of mastering everyday life and of adapting to new circumstances, as well as his clinging to his former status as a stadium rock star, that takes away his dignity. Yet it becomes very clear why Ray feels so depressed when the film shows a young teen band receiving all the fan adulation and media interest that Strange Fruit have lost, while the veteran rockers can only look on with envy. *Still Crazy* repeatedly exposes the obsession of the music media, and especially music television, with the (rebellious) young and beautiful, and it shows the condescending attitude toward age projected by these media. However, just like the treatment of male homosexuality in *Rock Star*, this presentation can appear hypocritical in so far as the very premise of the film lies in the perceived incompatibility of middle or old age with the notions of virility and sexual excess associated with rock.[10]

Despite this subtext, manliness in *Still Crazy*, *Almost Famous*, and *Rock Star* is predominantly presented as defined by behavior rather than the body or sexual experience. The films imply that the real men are those who take on responsibility, give the best for a good cause and allow themselves to be directed by their sensitive side. In the context of rock films this also means that they find authentic expression in honest music. Thus, in *Rock Star* Chris Cole ultimately leaves the band Steel Dragon, cuts his hair, dresses in jeans and jumper instead of black leather, and goes on to sing his own, totally unaggressive songs. In order to create full viewer satisfaction, this domestication of the rebellious rock musician, which basically amounts to his self-reinvention as a New Man, also wins him back his girlfriend. The rock discourse of authenticity also prevails in *Almost Famous*, where Russell at the end 'turns real' and confesses to his unconditional love for music. Similarly in *Still Crazy*, the Fruits ultimately rediscover their old magic as musicians, which transcends the conflicts within the band and any issues of age and stardom. This celebration of authenticity and the debunking of the artificiality and vacuity of stardom and classic rock masculinities founded on a myth of virility are underlined by the historical distancing in the films, which implies a contrast to contemporary, post-feminist gender conceptions.

The issues of masculinity, rebelliousness, and authenticity are also inextricably linked in Todd Haynes's *Velvet Goldmine*, albeit seldom for comic effect. *Velvet Goldmine* focuses on the rather brief but influential period called 'glam rock' or 'glitter rock' due to the visual style of its stars and audiences. Glam rock, which is primarily characterized by its look, not by a specific musical style (Jensen 283),[11] lasted roughly from 1970, when Marc Bolan appeared with glitter on his face to perform 'Hot Love' on *Top of the Pops*,[12] until 1974. Its most famous exponent was David Bowie, whose stage persona Ziggy Stardust can be considered the epitome of the theatricality and artificiality embodied and celebrated by the artists associated with glam. This consciousness of the performative aspects of rock stardom – and in extension of life – also manifested itself in a deliberate play with gender roles and sexuality. Male artists like Bowie or Brian Eno consciously adopted styles of dress and make-up that were connoted as feminine, using glimmer as well as feathers or shining clothes to create an androgynous or feminized look. This trend was so pervasive that even artists outside the glam sphere proper adopted typical glam elements in their make-up and clothes, such as the Rolling Stones, Rod Stewart, Queen, and most obviously Elton John (Hoskyns 1998a: 51).[13]

In accordance with rock's anti-establishment stance and discourse of rebelliousness, several glam artists also stated that they were bisexuals or homosexuals, most famously again Bowie, a married man, who in 1972 told the *Melody Maker*: 'I'm gay and always have been' (qtd. in Gritten).

For many artists and fans, such a stance against the heterosexual norm may have been nothing but a rebellious pose, as a later comment by Bowie on his own admission of bisexuality demonstrates. Looking back, he claimed that 'It was probably the most provocative thing one could say in 1972. Drug talk was positively establishment, and it sort of felt like the era of self-invention [was] coming up' (qtd. in Gritten). Yet, even if these provocative statements on sexuality were partly calculating PR exercises, according to pop journalist Jon Savage, in the early 1970s, 'Glam was [indeed] finally some kind of free expression of male homosexuality in popular culture, five years after it had been partially decriminalized' (qtd. in Hoskyns 1998b).

This ambivalence of the treatment of sexuality and gender by glam rock is at the core of Todd Haynes's *Velvet Goldmine*, a period film about the rise and fall of the Bowieesque glam rock star Brian Slade and his relationship to fellow musician Curt Wild (a figure that combines traits of Iggy Pop and Lou Reed). The third main character is Arthur Stuart, a reporter of *The International Herald Tribune*, who in 1984 is assigned to investigate the hoax murder on stage of Brian Slade in 1974, which had led to the star's decline. This investigation is a painful process for Arthur because it confronts him with his own past, most importantly the break-up with his parents over his homosexuality. It is also a bewildering process, since Arthur – and thus the spectator – is confronted with continuously changing perspectives onto the past.[14] Brian Slade's first manager, Slade's ex-wife Mandy and Curt Wild provide him with their views on and their versions of Slade, and these merge with Arthur's own memories. Arthur's disorientation is mirrored in the film narrative, where all these memories and statements are presented in a non-linear, generically and stylistically hybrid and fragmented way. In contrast to *Rock Star*, *Almost Famous*, and *Still Crazy*, which follow a conventional linear and teleological structure, the narrative of *Velvet Goldmine* oscillates between the two time levels of 1984 and the early 1970s. It also mixes realistic and highly de-familiarized scenes, in which Haynes uses alienating techniques to draw attention to the constructed nature of both his film and Brian Slade's star persona. The narrative even includes scenes that have no immediate connection with the quest story and instead appear like authorial comments on the characters and events presented in the film. The spectator is persistently denied certainty, be it about the nature of the relationships between the various characters or about what really happened to Brian Slade. This refusal of certainty also extends to the film's discussion of ideas about art and aestheticism, stardom, theatricality, love, and sexuality.

A continuous string of intertextual references to Oscar Wilde[15] implies that Haynes interprets glam rock as one stage in a transhistorical arc of decadence in art (and life),[16] whose dominant elements are artifice, theatricality and the deliberate bending of gender roles. The latter takes place in the context of a firmly patriarchal and heterosexual framework, which in *Velvet Goldmine* is most impressively evoked by Arthur's secrecy toward his parents about his sexual tendencies and by the appalled reaction of Arthur's father when he discovers his son masturbating in front of a Brian Slade album cover. The 'heterosexual imperative' (Butler 2, 3) is also firmly in place in the rock world of the film, where management and the media coverage of rock are controlled by butch males like Jerry Devine (inspired by Bowie manager DeFries), who ruthlessly bullies Brian Slade's first (homosexual) manager out of business. Yet the film remains ambivalent about the liberating potential of glam. On the one hand, glam in the film contributes to Arthur's acceptance of and insistence on his homosexuality. On the other hand, the film also shows that many followers of glam only adopted bisexuality as a pose.[17] In hindsight and from a non-rock-fan point of view, such a stance is in danger of appearing banal because it over-fulfils the dominant rock discourse, and thus the dominant rock cliché, of rebelliousness.

This ambivalence is supported by the fact that the film denies, and therefore implicitly negates, any certainty about where performance ends and 'reality' begins. Whether it is the rock star's self-presentation on stage and in the media, his life off-stage within his rock entourage or his private life beyond the observing eyes of the public or semi-public – on all levels of the rock star's life that *Velvet Goldmine* presents, performance and true identity are inseparable. In the film's discussion of this idea, Brian Slade is pitted against Curt Wild.[18] Slade is the character who, with Oscar Wilde, propagates the authenticity of masks and multiplicity of selves. Wild, in contrast, does not hide behind a stage persona like Slade's Maxwell Demon. When he breaks down on stage, it is because he lives his songs, not because of a fake shooting. He bares himself on stage completely, also in the form of full-frontal nudity, which contrasts conspicuously with the tastefully contrived pin-up shots of Brian Slade on his album covers. In keeping with this, Wild also cultivates a more traditionally masculine stage appearance than Slade, whose stage persona Maxwell Demon is self-consciously androgynous. Wild performs in silver trousers, he covers himself in gold glitter and sports long hair and mascara; yet a modern spectator who is familiar with the glam-influenced hair and make-up styles of heavy-metal bands or musicians like Kurt Cobain, would not interpret this style as feminized. Most importantly, while stardom has come to Curt Wild without his seeking it, Brain Slade is the creation of his manager. He is a star because he knows how to behave like one. This becomes most obvious at Slade's press conferences, where he plays the role of the rebellious clown for the media establishment.

Due to Haynes's refusal of an unambiguous narration, the spectators are put in a similar position to Arthur, who tries to make sense of all the pieces of information he is able to collect about Slade: they are forced to interpret and to emplot. This act of sense-making essentially also mirrors the behavior of the fans (and the public in general) for whom the image the star projects is the starting point of various forms of interpretation and appropriation. Haynes thematizes this most obviously in a scene that shows us yet another version of the relationship between Brian Slade and Curt Wild. Here the two characters do not appear in the flesh but are represented by dolls. As we realize from their voices, they are being handled by two young girls playing out a romantic love scene between Slade and Wild which subverts traditional gender models and implicitly reflects on the nature of the relationship of star and audience. The dolls, which appear like feminized versions of Ken dolls or strangely masculine Barbie dolls, simultaneously exude and undermine the artificiality of the idealized bodies of these Mattel toys and thus reflect glam rock's play with sexuality and gender. They are recognizable as Slade and Wild due to their clothes and hair styles. In as far as the girls are the authors of the scene that the dolls are made to enact, as well as their owners and manipulators, this scene reflects the fate of the star, who is appropriated and becomes dependent on the public. Yet, in as far as the dolls are also extensions of the girls themselves and trigger off a creative act, Haynes also reflects on the role of the star as a possible model and catalyst for making sense of the world or even creating a new one. Here, the novelty lies not only in the fact that the two girls take on the roles of two men, but also that they apply conventions of romantic love scenes from literature and film (faltering declarations of love, wordless understanding, kiss) to a male couple. This constitutes a 'normalization' of gay love, in the sense of its inclusion into the norms of representing heterosexual romance, which Haynes himself self-reflexively underlines by filming the dolls' conversation in conventional medium and close shots, and which he possibly ironizes by ending the scene with a prudish dissolve on the 'kissing' dolls. An ironic intention behind this ending is especially probable in the context of films like *Rock Star*, *Almost Famous* and *Still Crazy*, where the depiction of sex is restricted to talk or suggestive visual allusions and where the spectator is always left with a fade-out or a dissolve just before the sex gets going. *Velvet Goldmine*, in contrast, confronts the audience with full-frontal male (and female) nudity, with masturbation, a sex orgy, and more than implications of gay sex. The doll scene thus provides a comment on cinematic conventions of presenting sex and romance in particular and the changeability of the conventions of presenting gender and sexuality in general.

The latter theme is also evoked by the historical distancing that pervades *Velvet Goldmine*. The film establishes a difference between the seventies setting and the present-day spectator as well as between the seventies setting and the Orwellian 1984 in which Arthur conducts his research, and where gray men regulate what can be said and written. It might appear as if this level of the story, with its gray world and dejected masses, supported, by comparison, a nostalgic picture of the glam rock era. After all, the film is a celebration of the period's music and of spectacle. Nonetheless, it is precisely the 1984 setting that exposes the potential emptiness behind glam rock's rebelliousness, for here we find with Arthur that after sinking into oblivion like Oscar Wilde's Remarkable Rocket,[19] Brian Slade seems to have re-invented himself as pop star Tommy Stone, a purely commercial performer with grotesquely artificial facial features and hair, who acts as a mouthpiece for the political powers that be. In contrast to Curt Wild who is an artist who 'looks at the world,'[20] Slade has given up rebelliousness, and thus the key legitimatory discourse of rock, in exchange for success, and he no longer tells the truth from behind his mask, possibly because Tommy Stone's face is his real face.[21] Eventually, the juxtaposition of Curt Wild and Brian Slade can therefore also be seen to relate to the distinction that most fans and critics make between rock and pop. In this distinction, rock is marked by poetic authenticity and an anti-commercial and anti-establishment stance as opposed to the commercialization of pop, its artifice, and banality. According to this logic, rock moreover aims at political significance, and its creators are in the first place artists, while pop provides private pleasure and is sold by stars for whom style is more important than substance.[22] However, as with all its various elements, and in contrast to *Rock Star*, *Almost Famous*, and *Still Crazy*, the film also refrains from an unambiguous message when it comes to evaluating Brian Slade. Tommy Jones is indeed an opportunist who loves the limelight and plays soulless music, yet the film does not end on this impression of Brian Slade but on that of his earlier days of glam glory when his emphasis on style and aestheticist statements were counteracted by his music.

The glory of glam rock music may thus be the only certainty at the center of an otherwise consistently ambivalent film, and the celebration of music may be one of the few qualities *Velvet Goldmine* shares with *Almost Famous, Rock Star*, and *Still Crazy*. The music is the true star of these films and is presented as enduring by the very same technique of historical distancing that is also used to lament the erosion of rock. Especially *Almost Famous* and *Still Crazy* celebrate a kind of prelapsarian state of rock before MTV and a process of commercialization that turned rock into an 'industry of cool' (*Almost Famous* 15.30). They hark back to an idealized era before rock became a business for making quick money as opposed to a form of authentic artistic expression. Moreover, all films are nostalgic for a time that many celebrate as a period of (sexual) liberation and most importantly a time before AIDS. However, the nostalgia refers less to the rock lifestyle and the gender models that come with it, than to a spirit of rebelliousness and artistic authenticity. The dominant versions of masculinity in the various fields of rock are, after all, either presented as a playful and insubstantial performance or pose in *Velvet Goldmine*, or they are – at least on a surface level – revised and debunked as reactionary in *Almost Famous, Rock Star*, and *Still Crazy*. These three films accordingly present male rockers as propagating gender conceptions that discriminate against women and homosexual men, yet they also present the musicians themselves as prisoners of an oppressive system. As a counter model to traditional rock star masculinities they suggest the supposedly more authentic New Man, thus implying that the search for a stable and unfragmented 'true self' is achievable. *Velvet Goldmine*, in contrast, makes for less comfortable viewing both narratively and ideologically because it denies any kind of closure and certainty and in accordance with performative notions of gender implies that life itself, and with it gender and sexuality, are constructed through continuous performance.

Notes

1. This has to be seen in the sense of Butler's notion of performativity: 'performativity must be understood not as a single or deliberate "act," but, rather, as the reiterative and citational practice by which discourse produces the effects that it names.... the regulatory norms of "sex" work in a performative fashion to constitute the materiality of bodies and, more specifically, to materialize the body's sex, to materialize sexual difference in the service of the consolidation of the heterosexual imperative' (2).
2. I wish to thank Paul Müller from the film club *Arbeitskreis Film Regensburg* for his advice on the selection of films for this essay.
3. All four films were inspired by real-life events and persons: *Velvet Goldmine* is saturated with allusions to events in the lives of David Bowie, Lou Reed and Iggy Pop; *Almost Famous* is an autobiographical film inspired by director

Cameron Crowe's experiences as a young reporter for *Rolling Stone* magazine; *Still Crazy* is based on an unsuccessful reunion attempt by the band The Animals; and *Rock Star* was inspired by events surrounding the band Judas Priest. Despite these references to real life, all four films are clearly fictional films since both the textual and the paratextual levels of the films present them as such. In this respect they differ from musical biopics, that is, films that are based on the lives of real musicians, whose textual and paratextual apparatuses usually imply historical facticity, regardless of the degree to which the filmmakers have dramatized and fictionalized the biographies that are the basis of the films.

4. The choice of films concentrating on rock stardom has led to the exclusion of rock films such as *The School of Rock* (dir. Richard Linklater, 2003), *Hedwig and the Angry Inch* (dir. John Cameron Mitchell, 2001), and *Detroit Rock City* (dir. Adam Rifkin, 1999).

5. See, for example, the films *Edgeplay* (dir. Victory Tischler-Blue, 2004) about the girl band The Runaways and *Electric Purgatory: The Fate of the Black Rocker* (dir. Raymond Gayle, 2005).

6. The visual conventions employed in rock films for the presentation of live performances support this impression. On the one hand, close shots of the musicians exhibit their virtuosity and commitment; they also create a proximity to the performers and thus an impression of immediacy and intimacy that is usually lacking in the concert experience. On the other hand, long shots across the audience and the concert venue show the communal experience and underline the sheer number of fans and thus the power of the musicians. Very often this power is also conveyed by low-angle shots of the musicians from the point of view of the audience members standing in front of the stage.

7. I use the term 'streamlined independent cinema' in a rather broad sense to describe films that are labelled as independent but are at the same time ideologically conservative. This may include films that are 'independent' in the sense that they are produced and realized outside an integrated and commercially oriented film industry. It may also include films produced by the so-called 'independent' branches of major film companies (for example, *Rock Star*), or studio films marketed as non-mainstream or independent films (for example, *Almost Famous*).

8. The term 'cock rock' was coined by Frith/McRobbie to describe 'music making in which performance is an explicit, crude, and often aggressive expression of male sexuality' (374).

9. This masturbatory quality is also emphasized by Simpson who sees 'cock rock' as a 'symphony to phallocentrism' (190) and points out phallic accessories like 'tattoos, muscles, and, of course, guitars hoisted between legs clad in skin-tight leather or rubber. The guitars are the key phallic trope and are played in a style that it would be something of an understatement to call masturbatory' (193).

10. The American poster and DVD cover of *Still Crazy*, for example, has as its central image a bent guitar, which, in keeping with the role of the guitar as 'the key phallic trope' of rock (Simpson 193), implies a limp penis.

11. In contrast to Jensen, Hoskyns also counts several musical specificities among the markstones of glam rock. Besides 'The orange "mullet" sported

by Ziggy Stardust' and 'The wide lapels of the satin jackets Marc Bolan wore on *Top of the Pops*,' for example, Hoskyns's list of glam signatures includes, among others, 'The fat sustain of the Gibson Les Paul guitar, as played by Marc Bolan, Mick Ronson, Johnny Thunders and Mick Ralphs,' 'The chamber-rock arrangements of Tony Visconti and Mick Ronson (T.Rex, Bowie), Bob Ezrin (Alice Cooper, Lou Reed), Queen and Jobriath, or 'The compressed, mechanical drum sound that dominated glam pop from T.Rex to Suzi Quatro' (1998a: xii).

12. According to Hoskyns, 'For thrill-starved juveniles the length and breadth of Britain, glam was born on that Thursday's *Top of the Pops*' (1998a: 18/19).

13. Hoskyns also points out the heritage of glam in the visual style of artists stretching from the New Romantics and Boy George, to Kurt Cobain, Marilyn Manson and U2's Bono Vox (1998a: 51, 112, 113). The influence of glam has even spread into spheres of rock which at first glance seem incompatible with it. Glam Metal, for example, incorporates stylistic elements of glam, although heavy metal appears in many ways diametrically opposed to it.

14. In this respect, Arthur's investigation mirrors that of Joseph Cotten's character in Orson Welles's *Citizen Kane*, a film which Haynes deliberately alludes to several times by copying striking instances of lighting and camerawork.

15. Not only are a lot of the dialogues in *Velvet Goldmine* directly quoted from Wilde's works or modelled on his epigrams and aphorisms, the film also deliberately plays with ideas about the dandy, the relation of fiction or art to reality, and the truth of masks, which are all key elements of Wilde's oeuvre. Haynes moreover evokes Wilde as the forefather of modern pop stars and, in the tradition of Sinfield, as the man around whom discourses on effeminacy and homosexuality crystallized to make him the archetypal queer, or at least the first in a line of artists whose art and self-realization are directly linked to their refusal of the norms of the heterosexual matrix.

16. See also Hoskyns, who states that 'dandyism of the self-conscious kind that glam would formalize had roots that went back still further: to the foppery of the Restoration and of Beau Brummell, to the obsessive aestheticism of Huysmans's *A rebours* and Wilde's *Picture of Dorian Gray*, to the silent-screen androgyny of Garbo and Valentino' (1998a: 11).

17. One rock fan in *Velvet Goldmine*, for example, claims in an interview that he likes both boys and girls: 'They are all great. No difference, is there?' Yet his deliberately provocative behavior exposes this as a pose as do statements by Curt Wild and others, who point out that claims of homosexuality or bisexuality are a fashion that few of those who make them will be able to live up to (12.07–12.53).

18. For Todd Haynes, the two characters of Brian Slade and Curt Wild also represent what he sees as the relationship between a British and an American element of glam rock: 'To me it's not ultimately about the relationship of Bowie and Iggy Pop. It's a distillation of the truly British element that inspired glam rock – the androgynous, self-conscious, ironic poseur, incredibly alluring to look at but dangerous at the same time – and that element's attraction to the American element: visceral, sexually violent, raw. That's what glam rock is – a romance between that British element and that

American element, and an infatuation that didn't last, didn't work, but produced something really resonant' (Haynes qtd. in Clover).

19. Like the arrogant and pathetic Remarkable Rocket from Wilde's story of the same title, which explodes by daylight without being noticed, Slade says of himself: 'I knew I would create a great sensation.'

20. See an exchange of Arthur and Curt Wild toward the end of the film (108.55–109.22):

CURT WILD: ...we set out to change the world; ended up just changing ourselves.
ARTHUR: What's wrong with that?
CURT WILD: Nothing. If you don't look at the world.

21. See Curt Wild's assumption, 'Well, I guess in the end he got what he wanted' (109.33).

22. See Tetzlaff's summary of the different conceptions of rock and pop as quoted in Jensen 234.

Works cited

Almost Famous. Dir. Cameron Crowe. Perf. Patrick Fugit, Kate Hudson, Billy Crudup and Frances McDormand. Dreamworks SKG, 2000.

Butler, Judith. *Bodies That Matter: On the Discursive Limits of 'Sex.'* New York and London: Routledge, 1993.

Clover, Joshua. 'A User's Guide to *Velvet Goldmine.*' *The Ziggy Stardust Companion.* Oct. 2002. Ed. Michael Harvey. 14 Dec. 2005 <http://www.5years.com/velvetfilm2.htm>.

Custen, George F. *Bio/Pics: How Hollywood Constructed Public History.* New Brunswick: Rutgers UP, 1992.

Frith, Simon and Angela McRobbie. 'Rock and Sexuality.' *On Record: Rock, Pop, and the Written Word.* Ed. Simon Frith and Andrew Goodwin. London and New York: Routledge, 1990. 371–89.

Gritten, David. 'Something Has Survived, Baby.' Rev. of *Velvet Goldmine.* *L.A. Times* Calender Issue, 27 July 1997. *Velvet Goldmine.* 1999. Ed. Eladio. 14 Dec. 2005 <www.geocities.com/Pipeline/3225/ Velvet/latimereview.html>.

Horrocks, Roger. *Male Myths and Icons: Masculinity in Popular Culture.* Houndsmills, Basingstoke: Macmillan, 1995.

Hoskyns, Barney. *Glam! Bowie, Bolan and the Glitter Rock Revolution.* London: Faber and Faber, 1998a.

——. 'What Do the Original Devotees Think of Ziggy, Bolan, Platform Boots and Glitter 25 Years on?' *Independent on Sunday* 13 Sept. 1998b. *The Ziggy Stardust Companion.* Oct. 2002. Ed. Michael Harvey. 14 Dec. 2005 <http://www.5years.com/ velvetfilm2.htm>.

Jensen, Heike. *Gendering and Sexualising Rock Stars: Star Cult – Genre Discourse – Mass Media.* Diss. Humboldt U Berlin, 2001. Berlin: MIK, 2001.

Metallica – Some Kind of Monster. Dir. Joe Berlinger and Bruce Sinofsky. Radical Media and Third Eye Motion Picture Co., 2004.

Rock Star. Dir. Stephen Herek. Perf. Mark Wahlberg, Jennifer Aniston. Warner Bros., 2001.

Sandahl, Linda J. *Rock Films: A Viewer's Guide to Three Decades of Musicals, Concerts, Documentaries and Soundtracks, 1955–1986*. Poole: Blandford, 1987.

Simpson, Mark. *Male Impersonators: Men Performing Masculinity*. New York and London: Routledge, 1994.

Sinfield, Alan. *The Wilde Century: Oscar Wilde, Effeminacy and the Queer Moment*. London: Continuum, 1994.

Still Crazy. Dir. Brian Gibson. Perf. Bill Nighy, Timothy Spall, Stephen Rea and Billy Connolly. Columbia TriStar, 1998.

The Doors. Dir. Oliver Stone. Perf. Val Kilmer, Meg Ryan. Imagine Entertainment et al., 1991.

The School of Rock. Dir. Richard Linklater. Perf. Jack Black. Paramount et al., 2003.

This is Spinal Tap. Dir. Rob Reiner. Perf. Michael McKean, Christopher Guest, Harry Shearer. Spinal Tap Prod., 1984.

Tina – What's Love Got To Do With It. Dir. Brian Gibson. Perf. Angela Bassett, Laurence Fishburne. Touchstone Pictures, 1993.

Velvet Goldmine. Dir. Todd Haynes. Perf. Jonathan Rhys-Meyers, Ewan McGregor and Christian Bale. Miramax, CiBySales, 1998.

Walk the Line. Dir. James Mangold. Perf. Joaquin Phoenix, Reese Witherspoon. Fox 2000 Pictures et al., 2005.

11
Histories of Violence – Fairytales of Identity and Masculinity in Martin McDonagh's *The Lieutenant of Inishmore* and *The Pillowman*

Wolfgang Funk

Abstract

By looking at two recent plays by one of contemporary Britain's most influential playwrights, this chapter attempts to retrace a shift in the configuration of male gender identities, a shift which is not restricted to Martin McDonagh's work only, but which could be read as symbolic for a larger transformation in the understanding of gender roles in general.

The Lieutenant of Inishmore still starts out from a traditional set-up, depicting the eponymous character as a lonesome warrior adored by the local girl. In the course of the play, however, this stock character of the male warrior is deconstructed and finally literally blown to pieces; along with it, McDonagh presents a range of male characters, who all represent different embodiments of failures of traditional male role ascriptions (such as fatherhood, strength, tactical acumen, analytic thinking, and so on).

The Pillowman, in contrast, focuses on the individual active configuration of (gender) identity through personal narrative. The narrative web that the protagonist Katurian weaves and is finally ensnarled in is analyzed in this essay in terms of narrative and interpretive authority, which has traditionally been associated with male virility; it will become apparent that eventually the stories defy any authorial control and become the producers rather than the product of narrative action, thereby at the same time obliterating conventional notions of activity and passivity in the creative process.

The shift this essay wants to reconstruct in the analysis of the two plays is from the deconstruction of the traditional male role by way of subversion of its accompanying attributes toward a new paradigm, where the notion of the gender role in itself has been made redundant and has been replaced by the free-flowing accommodation of individual narratives, which results in ever-changing and elusive configurations of the male.

In his Leenane-trilogy, Martin McDonagh has not only done his utmost to destroy Ireland's image as a country of peaceful peasants and sentimental pipe-dreamers, but has systematically brought down the three main pillars on which this image was grounded. *The Beauty Queen of Leenane*, McDonagh's 1996 debut on the European stage, did away with the notion of the 'family' as the ideological framework and foundation for any integrative national feeling by exposing the irreparable rifts between Mag and her daughter Maureen, who – in a final outburst of pent-up personal and sexual frustration – eventually kills her mother with a poker, the Freudian implications of which are as obvious as they are intended. Parallel to the breakdown of familial bonds and intimacy goes the severance of emotional ties between Ireland and her estranged children. Exiled Pato Dooley's claim about his home country that 'when it's there I am, it's here I wish I was. But when it's here I am... it isn't there I want to be. But I know it isn't here I want to be either' (McDonagh 1999: 22) is proof that the metaphor, essential and very pertinacious in traditional (self-) images of Ireland and the Irish, of the 'nation-as-family' (as articulated by Ciàràn Benson) has been collapsed amid both a post-modern plurality of identity markers, in the play poignantly symbolized by the omnipresence of television and consumer goods of various sorts (Wagon Wheels, Complan, Kimberleys, to name but a few), the incommensurability of the imagined homeland of Ireland (represented for example in Maureen's calendar, which she keeps as a constant reminder of good ole Ireland while she works in London as a cleaner) and the drab reality of living there. While the everyday cruelty and ultimate futility of Mag and Maureen's existence display little to no idiosyncratic Irishness, the definition of what it means to be Irish is relegated to sentimental memories of exiled Irishmen and women, images of a lost paradise to be hung on a wall.

The two other plays that make up the Leenane-trilogy, *A Skull in Connemara* and *The Lonesome West* (both premiered 1997), deconstruct in similar fashion other pivotal mainstays of the time-honored, stereotypical image of (especially the West of) Ireland as a country full of jovial, law-abiding, if occasionally poteened peasants. These are the Law and the Church as represented by Thomas, town policeman in *A Skull in Connemara* and Father Walsh/Welsh in *The Lonesome West,* who are both sincerely disillusioned with their station in life and whose aspirations to restore the esteem of their respective authorities end in failure, in the latter's case even in suicide.

While his first trilogy thus concerned itself mainly with the corre-lation of failed national identification and the consequences thereof on the interpersonal level, McDonagh's more recent plays mark a shift toward examining questions of a more general kind, which could for concision's sake be boiled down to the issue: 'How do the stories we tell and invent about ourselves constitute and/or challenge our personal identity?' In this context, he unavoidably touches upon issues of gen-der identity and the particular performances that configure individual gender formations. It seems as if McDonagh first had to brush aside the *grands récits* that form a collective (in this case Irish) identity in order to get down to analyzing individual patterns of identity-construction, a move I've tried to chronicle with this essay by investigating how these processes of identity configuration are mirrored in McDonagh's two most recent plays, *The Lieutenant of Inishmore* (first performed by the RSC on 11 April, 2001) and *The Pillowman* (premiered at the Cottes-loe on 13 November, 2003). The plays progress from the concrete to the abstract even in terms of their setting, which can be illustrated as follows (Table 11.1):

The concept of 'personal identity' is at best a shifty one, which on one hand lays claim to some inalienable traits and qualities that are supposed to set the individual apart from everyone else, while on the

Table 11.1

Play	Setting	Central Notions
The Leenane-trilogy	concrete, one location (West of Ireland)	destruction of national identity and consequent breakdown of social structures
The Lieutenant of Inishmore	concrete, more than one location (Inishmore, Belfast)	pointlessness of a personal identity based on political assumptions
The Pillowman	abstract	individual identity as product of narrative

other hand having to rely on the fact that these traits and qualities have to be grounded in a common framework of experience in order to be of signifying consequence in the first place.[1] The relative importance of the constituents comprising any identity (personal or collective) may vary according to the cultural and social context and discourse at any given time. While traditional heavyweights like one's religious inclination or inherited birthrights have more or less been relegated to the sidelines, nowadays structural categories like 'gender' (alongside and often over-lapping with 'race' or 'sexual orientation') are an intricate part of an individual's image of oneself and the classification of this individual in the global scheme of things. Accordingly, I will use issues of gender stereotypes and their inversions and in particular different constructions and narrations of masculinity in *The Lieutenant of Inishmore* to exemplify the volatility of identity-constructions in Martin McDonagh's dramatic universe, while in a second step tracing the effect of narratives as such on the possibility of identify formation in *The Pillowman*, where the (exclusively male) characters are constantly trying to revise their posi-tion both toward their own biography and their environment (and this is exactly what identity is supposed to add up to). One unifying *topos* bracketing the two plays, I would argue, is the treatment of violence (both real and fictional with regards to the internal event horizon of the plays) and its importance for the establishment of a stable (male) identity. As the underlying narrative forming the background of pro-cesses of identification in *The Lieutenant of Inishmore*, I would postulate the mythological interrelation of masculinity with war and violence, something that could for the sake of quotation be called the 'knight-in-shining-armor myth,' whereas in *The Pillowman* narratives of violence form the backdrop (or palimpsest, as I want to argue later on) onto which the ultimate futility of any quest for any stable personal and/or artistic identity is projected.

Shooting matches – inversions and reconfigurations of gender roles and identities in *The Lieutenant of Inishmore*

The shift of focus between the Leenane-trilogy and *The Lieutenant of Inishmore*, from portraying the impossibility of a common Irish identity assaulted and finally drowned in the face of a contemporary, hyper-real relativism and its subsequent interpersonal brutality and individual futility (symbolized – in *The Beauty Queen of Leenane* – by the prompting of cues and designs for life from the ubiquitous TV-set and the men-tal and physical torture of mother and daughter respectively) toward a more explicit interest in the interplay of political and personal identities, is reflected in the treatment of sexuality in the plays. In *The Beauty Queen of Leenane*, the failure to lead sexually fulfilling lives is used as a metaphor for the incompatibility of the myth of Irishness to a crude reality. Pato, for example, can only find marital (and one assumes sexual) bliss by leaving Ireland and moving to Boston. To remain in Ireland and have a satisfying love and sex life at the same time is not an option in McDonagh's Connemara. The same motif is taken up again in *The Lonesome West*, where a potential relationship between Girleen and Father Welsh is thwarted by the latter's suicide. Things alter noticeably in *The Lieutenant of Inishmore*, where destruction and violence are no obstacles for romance any more, but quite to the contrary 'terrorist violence is shown not to impede sexual expression but to facilitate it' (Lonergan 75). In the first part of my chapter, I will take a closer look at this transformed function of sexuality, arguing that it goes hand in hand with another development indispensable in view of McDonagh's swing from the national to the personal, that is, the unravelling of gender identities. It will become apparent that any stringent concept of masculinity in the West of Ireland is bound to falter with the characters in *The Lieutenant of Inishmore* covering the spectrum from dyed-in-the-wool chauvinist via effeminate sissy to gun-crazy tomboy, each of the designs depicted quite literally sawing or hacking away at a unified image of masculinity, until the stage is covered in blood and severed limbs, telling signs that not only bodies but also perceptions of bodies have been shredded in the process.

In order to substantiate this assertion and following Patrick Lonergan, who argues that the play's 'obsession with gender is revealed as an anxiety about the instability of sexual identity' (75), I will attempt a detailed analysis of the various masculine identities that are conjured up in the course of the play, only to be finally rejected and quite literally chopped to bits. The use of and attitude toward violence will by this means serve as the central parameter in relation to which the various images of masculinity are developed, interrogated, and ultimately confirmed to find wanting.

Much has been said, written and discussed about the birth-pangs of the play. Finished in 1996, it was turned down by both the National and the Royal Court, in the latter case – according to McDonagh – for alleged fear of halting the peace process in Northern Ireland, only to be salvaged for the stage by the RSC in April 2001. Aware of the huge potential for publicity that comes naturally with such high-flying rhetoric, the RSC lost no time in driving home the notoriety of the play and daring of its production in Stratford even to the most unruffled of spectators by stressing the dangers of seeing this ground-breaking *oeuvre* for pregnant women. The play itself has met with varied responses. While the audiences at large seemed to be taken in by the unusual depiction of political extremism in the guise of farce, shockingly violent, and tremendously funny at the same time, critics have either showered the play with contempt or highest acclaim. The main criticism, as exemplarily put forward by Mary Luckhurst, was that McDonagh fell victim to the lure of easy money by pampering to the English audiences' inclination to have 'Oirish' stock characters put on stage: dim-witted, blood-thirsty, emotionally challenged (to put it mildly), 'all victims of their own stupidity, ignorance and futility' (123) with no redeeming features and not even the depth to be a suitable subject for discussion, thereby perpetuating the colonial divide between the civilized 'tall kingdom over your shoulder' (to borrow Seamus Heaney's phrase) and the barbarian yokels inhabiting Hibernia, not fit for polite and enlightened society. Additionally, Luckhurst accuses McDonagh of trying to out-Kane *Blasted*, with the decided difference that Sarah Kane's 1994 masterpiece glories in its 'refusal to accept limits on naturalistic representation,' while 'his main objective with the play was sensationalism, was to get as much John Woo and Sam Peckinpah into theatre as possible' (122).

In the opposite corner we find critics like Catherine Rees, who situates the play comfortably in the tradition of 'In-yer-face-theatre,' described by Alek Sierz as being a form of theater dedicated to a 'ruthless commitment to extremes' (4) with its power lying 'in the directness of its shock tactics, the immediacy of its language, the relevance of its themes and the stark aptness of its stage pictures' (Rees 243). Even though the play's intention might be to make fun of the characters on stage, this ridicule, in Rees's view, serves a higher function than just the cosseting of late-colonial tastes, in so far as the play 'forces the audience not to laugh at the stupidities of the Irish but to confront their own approaches to the sentimentality of the Irish political movement' (237).

Questions of gender identity feature quite prominently on the agenda of several of the characters in *The Lieutenant of Inishmore*. Davey, for example, who is in the unenviable situation of being prime suspect number one in the killing of Wee Thomas, the beloved pet companion of the play's eponymous protagonist Padraic Osbourne, is constantly reminded of his girl-like behavior, hairstyle, and general appearance by none other than his little sister Mairead, whose notion of a real man is rather more in the vein of the shoot-first-ask-question-later-if-ever manifestation of Padraic. The self-styled freedom-fighter and committed splinter-group of his own is obviously not only secure in his political objectives, namely 'to free the North' (McDonagh 2001: 32), but also quite explicit about what he considers adequate behavior for the sexes. Activity, and in particular political activity, is the male domain, while the suitable aim for the weaker sex consists primarily in securing a decent husband and letting one's hair grow.

If we follow David Benedict's categorization of the play as being of the 'comedy-horror-genre' (qtd. in Worthen 155), this preoccupation with gender roles might seem odd at first sight, since the traditional blueprints for both of these genres depend heavily on the stability and subsequent high recognition value of gender roles, drawing their respective dynamics more from exaggerating gendered clichés than from seriously contesting them. The easily scared, passive, and altogether defenceless woman at the mercy of some horrifying monster, whose only chance is to be rescued by the knight (male, of course) in shining armor is the staple feature of horror-fiction from the mythical adventures of, for example, St George, via *King Kong* to the *Scream* films. I would follow Laura Eldred in this, who argues that – despite the fact that in the *Scream*-movies the killer is run to earth by a female character – the genre itself has a very conservative design, where the killer first punishes liberal transgressions (drinking, smoking, and shagging leading almost inescapably to being slashed, axed, or chain-sawed), only to be eventually deposed of by a hero character, who might be female, but is cast in a masculine role, so that these film 'ultimately vindicate masculine strength and resourcefulness through the masculine final girl's victory over a feminized villain' (202). In much the same way, comedy more often than not feeds on the contrast of the supreme logic and skill of the male with the confused and slightly hysterical behavior of the female. Cases in point range from *The Taming of the Shrew* to contemporary features such as *Sex and the City*.

While the indebtedness of the *Lieutenant of Inishmore* to both of these genres cannot be disputed, neither of these blueprints concurs with the events depicted on stage. The only female character is emphatically far from being helpless and the rational superiority of the members of the strong sex is doubtful, to say the very least. This is particularly apparent in the case of Padraic, the lieutenant of the play's title, whom Davey introduces as too mad to be allowed into the IRA (7) and who throughout the play does his utmost to live up to this description. We get an early impression of his rather idiosyncratic slant on the world when we first encounter him in a Belfast warehouse, where he has just ripped a couple of toenails from James, a small-time drug-dealer, hanging upside down from the wall. The reason why pushing drugs is immoral, Padraic's line of argument goes, is that it is '[k]eeping our youngsters in a drugged-up and idle haze, when it's out on the streets pegging bottles at coppers they should be' (12). Even James – and we must commend him for his outspokenness – finds time to remark on the intellectual shortcomings of his adversary: 'You've lost your train of thought? Uh-huh. As slow as that fecking train is, and you've lost it' (12). The scene in the warehouse not only acquaints us with the mindset of Padraic, but also establishes the subject of masculinity in no uncertain terms and images. Padraic is represented in the classical pose of the testosterone-fuelled warrior, his masculinity made evident by his assembled weaponry, a.k.a. phallic symbols, such as two handguns and a razor blade. The complementary role of the passive, and thus – in Padraic's patriarchal thinking – female, victim is assigned to James, whose relative gender status is confirmed both in word and deed, when Padraic, after disinvesting him of two of his toenails, thereby drawing first blood, accuses him of 'bawling like some fool of a girl' (14) and threatens to cut off his nipple, a consistent form of torture for the effeminate James. The cutting off of the toenails can be read as a primal way of establishing a binary gender relation, particularly since Padraic seems to specialize in such symbolic castrations; later on we hear that Padraic had once cut off the nose of one of his adversaries. His self-stylization as knight of the phallic and symbolic order is not limited to the area of conflict, but extends to his general outlook on gender configurations. When he first meets Mairead, he immediately subsumes her into the patriarchal scheme by identifying her with her father's name: 'You're not Seamus Claven's daughter?' (32). The hesitant nature of this inquiry is partly due to the non-normative appearance of Mairead, with cropped hair and a figure that prompts Padraic to acknowledge that she has grown '[u]pwards if not outwards' (33) since their last meeting five years earlier. Political and patriarchal convictions meet when Padraic blankly refuses Mairead entry into his INLA-splinter group (of which he is the sole member) for the simple reason that 'We don't be letting girls in the INLA. No. Unless pretty girls' (35), thereby in one broad sweep giving voice to his disapproval of Mairead's looks and informing her about the acceptable locus for the female in his scheme of things, that is, as an aesthetic and/or representational object. It comes as no surprise then, that his concluding advice on Mairead's future life might just as well be taken from a modern version of a nineteenth-century conduct book: 'Let your hair grow out a tadeen and some fella's bound to be looking twice at you some day, and if you learn how to cook and sew too, sure that'd double your chances.

Maybe treble' (36). Apparently, good looks and performing the role of the 'Angel in the House' is all he cares for in a woman.

One aspect usually thought to be a matter-of-course for the aspiring and confident male warrior is, however, lost on Padraic – the symbolic planting of his flag inside any female body crossing his way, an indifference explained rather unconvincingly by himself with the fact that 'there was work to be done ridding Erin of them jackboot hirelings of England's foul monarchy' (33).[2] Mairead, who is not only swift with an airgun, but also very quick on the uptake, latches on to that, instantly questioning Padraic's sexual orientation, no doubt driven both by an apparent tendency to be offensive and a certain amount of fear that his candid performance of masculinity might indeed cover up hidden homosexual inclinations. This imputation is immediately repudiated by Padraic with the words: 'I do not prefer boys! There's no boy-preferers involved in Irish terrorism. I'll tell you that! They stipulate when you join' (33). We are treated to a typical strategy of the cornered male. The contested identity marker is inflated and transported to the level of the political and impersonal, where the hazardous charge is summarily refuted by means of a contract. If Mairead suspects Padraic of protesting a bit too much, she certainly is on to something; Padraic's fictional self-image as the paragon of masculinity is destabilized from the outset. Before we even meet him, his father Donny tells us about the 12-year-old lieutenant *in spe*, wearing a 'girly scarf' (7). When his cousin laughed at that, Padraic made a cripple of him, laying down a very early example of his strategy of validating his challenged masculinity by means of violence. Nor is this the only crack to his façade. Just when Padraic is at his most masculine, torturing James with obvious relish, he receives a phone-call from his father Donny, who tells him that his beloved cat is 'poorly' (14), a piece of news that reduces him to tears in a matter of seconds. The comparative value of a cat's life to human existence in general is not only the yardstick with which McDonagh measures out the pointlessness of violence committed throughout the play, but also a dependable indication for the fuzziness of gender roles, in particular that of Padraic, whose eventual murder will be a fatal result of reasserting his masculinity by way of shooting Mairead's cat.

Diametrically opposed to Padraic's warrior-like, gun-toting version of malehood is Davey, whose description in the stage directions is given as *'Slightly overweight, long hair'* (2) and whose habitat on the passive, feminine side of the binary gender divide is made clear in the very opening moments of the play, when he brings the dead Wee Thomas home to Donny.

Davey	If he gave him an injection?
Donny (*pause*)	Have this injection, you!
Donny *steps back and kicks*	
Davey *up the arse.*	
Davey (*almost crying*)	What was that fer? (3)

The assignment to the non-male sphere (female or – even worse in
Padraic's philosophy – homosexual) is threefold – the threat of injec-
tion, the kick up the arse and the lachrymose nature of Davey's reaction.
Further corroboration of his dubious gender identity follows almost
immediately, when he presents his favorite means of transport: '*his
mum's bicycle (...) pink, with small wheels and a basket*' (5). It can hardly
come as a surprise to find Davey's appearance and behavior soon pen-
etrated further. Seemingly out of nowhere a bullet is fired at him and
gives him a bloody cheek, thereby acting out the defloration threatened
earlier. The bullet originates from the rifle of his sister Mairead, who goes
on to aim her weapon directly at Davey's face, triggering as a response
the classic female strategy of hiding behind the mother: '*Don't* now! I'll
be telling Mam on ya!' (17). Davey is quite aware of the fact that his
looks are not in keeping with traditional norms, when he informs his
sister, that 'I have as much concern for the cats of this world as you
do, only I don't go around saying it, because if I went around saying it
they'd call me an outright gayboy, and they do enough of that with me
hairstyle' (18). His long hair is again the focus of attention in the climactic Scene 8 of the play, when Padraic uncovers Davey and Donny's
admittedly rather obtuse plan of substituting Wee Thomas with another
cat, blackened for the occasion with shoe polish. The mad lieutenant,
after shooting the unfortunate cat at point blank, again makes use of
Davey's tresses to symbolize who is in charge, when he rubs Davey's face
in the blood of the slaughtered feline to stop his 'hysterical' (40) scream-
ing, thereby again using actual violence in a highly symbolic way to
sanction Davey's girlish (that is, hysterical) behavior. At this very point,
however, Padraic's system collapses. On the verge of being executed for
the murder of Wee Thomas, Davey comes into his own and confronts
Padraic head-on:

Davey (*angrily*)	Sure, I was only trying to save the feck was how I became involved!
Padraic	So me cat is a feck now, is he?

Davey   He is! And you are too, Padraic Osbourne! And I
don't care if you blow the head off me. You're a
mad thick feck and everybody knows that you are!
So there! (42)

Naturally, this outburst does not fit into Padraic's worldview and he
reacts by changing the outward significations of Davey's gender role by
'*roughly hacking off all of* **Davey***'s hair*' (42), thus rewarding him symbolically with a place in his male universe, if only to execute him as a worthy
opponent rather than a whining colleen, which might have been against
his code of knightly honor anyway: 'I'd be scared the bullets wouldn't
be getting through this girl's minge.' (42). But the execution is not to
be. A knock on the door interrupts the proceedings.

Entering in are three members of the INLA on a mission to casti-
gate Padraic for dropping out of the organization. In an earlier scene,
when debating the job that lies before them, these 'freedom fighters' are
introduced as faithful members of the phallic order and the audience
is treated to another manifestation of traditional masculine lore, when
Joey, accused of '[s]hitting his knickers,' ascertains that 'I've the balls
to take on any feck' (27), explaining his sulkiness with an objection to
shooting cats (they were responsible for Wee Thomas's untimely demise)
since they constitute no proper opponent. Further proof for their masculine certainty is given a few lines later when after quarrelling about
the pros and cons of shooting cats for achieving political objectives
they all point their guns at each other, proving their phallic upright-
ness. Even though the trio's disproportionate concern for cats might
hint at a latent obliquity both in their masculine façade and their political sense of judgment – Christy at one point asks his companions if 'the
cats of Ireland [won't] be happier too when they won't have the English
coming over bothering them no more?' (30) – they remain true to their
patriarchal values even in the face of death. Having been blinded by a
well-aimed volley from Mairead's rifle, their main concern is the sex of
their assailant:

Christy   Was it a boy or was it a girl?
Brendan   It was a boy with lipstick.
Christy   It was a girl with no boobs, sure.
Brendan   Oh, don't let me be killed by a girl, Sweet Jesus! I'll
never live it down. (51)

Quite. Faced with imminent loss of life, Brendan and Joey almost let themselves be seduced to showing unmanly affection toward each other only to be briskly reminded of the adequate performance expected from members of their sex by Christy, who commands them to 'stop that shite! Get firing, now!' (51). In vain they perform their ritual firing of the guns, as both their lives and their constructions of masculinity are obliterated in the wild shootout that follows.

This leaves us with Donny,[3] the remaining (biologically) male character, who as Padraic's father would be the logical reference point for his son's patriarchal worldview, but who never manages to present a proper role model for his son. He had to enforce his (supposedly natural) authority over the weaker sex by means of 'trampling on [his] mum' (25), an infirmity which in Padraic's opinion can never be forgiven and which has led to a complete loss of respect from the filial side, to the extant even that Padraic has no qualms about shooting his dad for the negligent care he bestowed on Wee Thomas. That his life is saved by the incursion of the INLA-hit squad and the ensuing showdown of (seemingly) successful masculine identity constructs adds to the confusion (both on stage and with regard to the gender identities performed) that makes up the last third of the play and that I will return to in more detail shortly.

There's one character left to examine. Mairead is in more than one way the only real man on stage, not only by virtue of her outward appearance, which is given as '*a girl of sixteen or so, slim, pretty, with close-cropped hair, army trousers, white T-shirt, sunglasses*' (17) but also due to her actual conduct. She is an excellent marks(wo)man (something that Padraic has still to verify, since his favored form of gun-use is the point-blank execution) and a veritable freedom fighter to boot, who demands respect for her very personal hero, Padraic, whom she calls 'a brave son of Erin' (19). She combines these two qualities in the exercise of shooting the eyes of cows, which she sees as her own modest contribution to bringing about the downfall of the meat trade and in due course the British Empire. Not only are her reasoning skills distinctly in the mold of Padraic and the INLA, but she also displays other poses and staple features of masculine behavior, such as the correct implementation of phallic symbols (when she puts her gun to her brother's head) and the attendant sanctioning of transgressive behavior. She also refuses to be subordinated to Padraic's binary categorization concerning gender roles. When he puts his gun to her head, she does likewise, indicating that they are on a par, a daring feat which elicits from him the appreciatory statement 'You have some balls anyway' (35), which almost amounts to her initiation into the phallic order. Almost, that is, because entry into his splinter group is still not on for her. This has to wait until she finally confirms her mettle in combat and (in a total reversal of stereotypical gender role allocation in the context of war) saves the hero's life by blinding his three would-be assassins.

The scene that follows is not only an exhibition of unadulterated theatrical genius with an obliging nod to Quentin Tarantino's *Reservoir Dogs* and Oliver Stone's *Natural Born Killers*, but the complete reversal of everything that has been built up so far in terms of deconstructing gender identities. At the very moment when a complete reversal of traditional gender configurations seems to have been accomplished, with the epic battle between Padraic and his killers practically at boiling-point, only to be decided by the shooting skills of a teenage girl, when the audience are apparently bereft of all signifying systems concerning gender roles, the greatest signifier of all returns with a vengeance – love. Padraic and Mairead enter the stage hand in hand and '*seem to almost glide across the room, their eyes locked on each other.* **Padraic** *caresses her hair and cheek, impressed beyond words at her ability with a gun*' (52). In time-honored fashion, this love makes them invulnerable to the aimless shooting of the blinded hit-squad and in an orgiastic dance of romance and violence the lovers kill and kiss and kiss and kill.

Once the gunfire has subsided, out of the blood mist emerges a happy couple, busily making plans for the future, even including marriage. Mairead, now that she has at last managed to officially join the ranks of the masculine order (Padraic has awarded her an second-lieutenantship in his splinter group), even dares to wear a dress and Padraic applies his newly garnered insights into the contingency of gender identities, when he acknowledges that 'you don't look like a boy at all' (58). One last stand of approximating Mairead to his ideal of a female companion (who happens to be Evie from the 1990s TV-series *The House of Eliot*) is shot down with Mairead's solid argument that Evie couldn't 'blind three fellas from sixty yards' (59). But apart from that, everything seems settled and so marriage is the inevitable destination. Or is it? Except for the rather unconventional proposal:**Mairead** Is it marriage you're proposing to me so, Padraic Osbourne?

Padraic   It is. After a biteen of a while I'm saying, now, (61)

the road ahead seems pretty clear. There is even a child to be christened already, even if it is only the new splinter group that is denominated 'Wee Thomas's Army' as from this moment on. Of course, there cannot

be a happy ending and the collapse of this idyll is once again triggered by the death of a cat. By accident, Mairead finds out that the cat,
which Donny and Davey used to stand in for Wee Thomas and that
was as a result killed by Padraic, was in fact her beloved companion Sir
Roger (as in Sir Roger Casement, the name being one more example for
Mairead's enthusiastic, if somewhat vague grasp of Irish republican history). Having been newly initiated into the phallic order, she follows the
example presented by her fiancé to set the life of a cat at a higher value
than that of any human being and accordingly shoots Padraic after a
long kiss good-bye. That she uses Padraic's favorite method of a point-
blank execution is owned as much to the circumstances as to her being
now part of the warrior caste. In order to dispel any doubts left about
who carries the banner of the phallic order in the end, Mairead deliv-
ers a succinct example: She *'places the barrels of both guns in* **Padraic's**
mouth' (66). That Padraic is finally hoist by his petard, that is, shot with
his own guns in his preferred manner of execution, confirms a suspicion that lies at the heart of a whole train of late twentieth-century
thinking, usually grouped under the generic heading of 'Queer Theories,' which claims that the eventual deconstruction of any binary
gender concept (be it masculine–feminine or heterosexual–homosexual)
is already invested in the structural setup of these dichotomies itself and
can be brought about by 'strategies of subversive repetition' (Butler 147).
In this respect, *The Lieutenant of Inishmore* can be seen as a collection of
these subversive repetitions of gender clichés and the ultimate question
left is: what does this fragmentation of gender roles signify in terms of
masculinity.

The representatives of the traditional, patriarchal class, who took
pride in their genuine masculinity (asserted and if need be defended
by means of gratuitous violence) are dead, their existences terminated
and their on the whole slightly unconvincing performances uncovered
and literally blown or hacked to pieces. The stage directions are quite
candid on that one: *'the blood-soaked living room is strewn with … body
parts'* (55). Survived have those, who from a patriarchal point of view go
beyond the scope of traditional gender allocations: Donny, whose failure
as a father rules him out as a positive reference point in the patriarchal
hierarchy; Davey, whose girlish façade and conduct have only ever been
used as a negative foil against which the proper masculinity of Padraic
could be displayed; and – most importantly – Mairead, who alone of all
the characters has actually undergone something like a learning process,
for, she states in the end, that she 'thought shooting fellas would be fun,
but it's not. It's dull' (66). The positive comeuppance for her might just

be the result of her flexibility concerning gender; she refuses to buckle under Padraic's initial attempts to integrate her into his global scheme of things, while at the same time carrying a female torch for the hero; she single-handedly rescues her idol from his foes, yet is not averse to entering into marriage with him afterward; on a political note, she remains faithful to her (however shadowy) liberationist ideals – after all, the last we hear from her is a patriot song – yet gives up on her plan to take the battle to the enemy and resigns herself to a living in Inishmore.

The successful strategy for survival in this violent world seems to be a protean ability to change not only alliances and splinter groups but above all not to maintain an altogether too stable identity (gender or otherwise), so as best to be able to deal with the vicissitudes of life.

Grim brothers and their household tales – how fictions influence male identities in *The Pillowman*

In a marked contrast to its predecessor, McDonagh's play *The Pillowman* features a cast of characters that is both entirely and (on the surface) rather uncontestedly male. Both the fragmentation of personal identities and the fragmentation of bodies are removed from the actuality of the events on stage and given a new realm – the narratives told by the protagonists. With a fleeting look to this book's overall subject, one could argue that while my analysis of *The Lieutenant of Inishmore* concentrated on the masculinity aspect of the title by showing how traditional concepts are used and abused in the process of forming individual and transgressive identities, my analysis of *The Pillowman* will put the emphasis on the performance aspect, illustrating how the performance (defining 'performance' in this context as the negotiation of the subject between fiction and reality) of internalized narratives and their rewritings (or 'subversive repetitions' to take up Judith Butler's dictum) create competing versions of reality that, when all is said and done, leave only the narratives themselves as the ultimate (?) arbiters of what is real, and a quest for stable configurations being as futile as it is abortive. The same contingency of identification holds true for the gender identities in the play, which I will analyze in terms of the control the protagonists exert over the narrative, as attributions of activity and passivity in the creative process have been used to identify the sexes since time immemorial.

In order to exemplify this, I want to investigate the function of violence in *The Pillowman*, used not as a means of protecting identities but as a narrative device that in itself becomes the subject of permanent reinterpretation and will thus eventually lead to a dismemberment of stable categories. Roughly speaking, and I know that this is probably an unseemly simplification, one could say that while violence – used as a means of safeguarding traditional styles of identity in *The Lieutenant of Inishmore* – ultimately fails and succeeds only in producing highly disruptive and non-normative gender identities, the violent stories engendered by the protagonists of *The Pillowman* form the framework and building set from which the characters assemble their distinct accounts of reality, thereby also implicitly questioning and reconfiguring their gender identities. To employ an artistic metaphor, violence is transformed from being a pen or a chisel, which tries to inscribe identities on the individual to occupying the role of a canvas or rather a palimpsest, on which the individual can create, efface, and recreate his or her identity.

In restricting myself to analyzing the interplay of the stories told by Katurian and the effects these stories have on both of the two brothers' respective rapport toward reality and the consequent configurations in terms of gender roles, I am more or less leaving out the actual setting and plot of the play, which concentrates on the writer Katurian Katurian Katurian (as the forger and creator of narratives quite aptly endowed with an access of signification in the shape of a treble naming, thereby foreshadowing the promise of multiple realities, which the play will make good on in due course), being interrogated over the murders of two, possibly three, children. These murders seem to have been inspired by Katurian's stories, since they were performed in the exact manner laid out in his writing, naturally promoting him to the unappealing position of prime subject number one. The investigation is conducted by detectives Tupolski and Ariel. Rather in spite of than owing to their examination techniques, it is revealed that the murders were committed by Katurian's retarded brother, Michal, who occupies the adjoining cell. His mental confusion seems to be the result of a vicious experiment, set up by Michal and Katurian's parents. While McDonagh's earlier plays abolished the nuclear family, a sure indicator for the stability of traditional gender roles, as an agency for stabilizing and integrating individual identities, it now seems to become the principal source of identification, as both the brothers' station in life (gifted writer and deluded psychopath respectively) and their coming to terms with it, are played out in stories that hearken back to the one initial event that I would identify as the primeval or master narrative of the play, from which all ensuing minor or personal narratives and the realities they create emanate.

The structural significance of this founding myth is accentuated by the fact that its re-enactment on stage takes up an entire scene (I, 2), in which Katurian narrates the story, which at the same time is played out as a dumb-show in the background. It is the story of a sinister experiment: Katurian's parents tried to cultivate their son's imaginative capacities by exposing him to a regime of mind-boggling terror. From the age of seven, Katurian is treated on a nightly basis to sounds of torture and 'the muffled screams of a small gagged child' (McDonagh 2003: 31) from the next room, noises that his mother puts down to his 'wonderful, but overactive imagination' (32). This imagination of his is kept on tenterhooks for seven years, until – just when he is on the brink of winning a story competition and the experiment thus about to yield first fruit – a note is slipped under his door saying 'They have loved you and tortured me for seven straight years for no reason other than as an artistic experiment which has worked. You don't write about little green pigs any more, do you? ... Your brother' (32–33). Katurian's first conscious brush with the master narrative leads him to axe in the door and find Michal, 'brain-damaged beyond repair' (34). His instantaneous reaction upon discovering this scenario is to murder his parents by suffocating them with a pillow. But the seeds are implanted and the experiment cannot be undone. The factual outcome is that Michal will remain brain-damaged and Katurian's imagination forever tainted by his childhood experience. The myth-machine of narrative identity formation has been set into motion, with the reality of Michal's ordeal being reconfigured by the parents' (narrative) authority into the foundation of Katurian's identity as a writer and producer of fiction (cf. Table 11.2), an identity he quite succinctly outlines as: 'That's my life. I stay in and I write stories. That's it' (14).

Analyzing this primordial event in terms of gender configurations, we have to acknowledge that this creation myth does not include a male creator God, but rather the bisexual entity of 'the parents,' while the (biologically male) brothers are conceived along traditionally gendered

Table 11.2

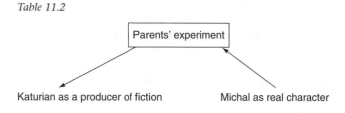

lines respectively: Katurian as the active and imaginative begetter of stories, a time-honored male sphere, which has been succinctly encapsulated in Sandra Gilbert and Susan Gubar's statement that the 'poet's pen is in some sense (even more than figuratively) a penis' (4); Michal as his muse, the unknowing and unknowable basis for Katurian's flights of fancy, and thus a role traditionally assigned to the female.

In view of his formative years, it is no surprise that the stories Katurian produces would center on the mistreatment of children. The most obvious narrativization of his childhood nightmares comes in the form of his short story 'The Little Apple Men,' where a little girl is maltreated by her father and kills him by tricking him into eating little men carved from apples, which she has fitted with razor blades. In an unexpected twist to this somewhat traditional Electra-meets-Cinderella revenge plot, the little girl is (by dint of Katurian's narrative authority) transformed from perpetrator to victim and is herself subjected to revenge from the apple men's brothers, who 'climb down their throat. She chokes to death on her own blood. The end' (13). Not quite the end, though, as Tupolski reveals to him that this story and another one (featuring a boy crippled by cutting of his toes in a macabre prequel to the *Pied Piper of Hamelin*) have evidently been used as blueprints for the actual murders of a child. While Katurian adopts a strictly aesthetic position, by stressing repeatedly (and quite incongruously in light of his upbringing) that his stories are pure fiction and have nothing to do with reality, someone must have taken them at face value. That someone turns out to have been his brother Michal, who confesses to the killings once the two brothers are on their own (48).

This is the next step in the workings of the myth machine: Katurian tries to put his experience into stories, while explicitly maintaining a clear discrimination of fiction and reality. For him, the claim to the absolute fictionality of his narratives is necessary for the upkeep of his identity, both artistic and personal, having been exposed to an excess of reality when uncovering his parents' experiment or in other words the realization that his literary career (if we may call it thus) is founded on a fiction that turned out to be viciously real. Michal, on the other hand, having been raised only as a functional character in the primeval fiction of the experiment has never had a chance to distinguish between real and fictional events. So, while Katurian fictionalizes real events, Michal turns the fictional narratives of his artist brother into a murderous reality (cf. Table 11.3).

In terms of gender configurations, Katurian is well under way on the established path of masculinity – or even patriarchy – in that he governs

Table 11.3

reality while or by inventing fictions. Michal, on the other hand, suffers from the affliction, usually assigned to members of the fair sex, not to be able to distinguish between fiction and reality, an alleged error of judgment, which has repeatedly been used as a pretext to prevent females from appropriating language as a signifying system. Lacan has transformed this notion into psychoanalytical discourse; he claims that women will never be able to become full members of the symbolic order or 'Law of the Father,' a system of reference which consist only of symbolic interaction. Instead, they retain a 'direct connection' to the pre-symbolic realm of 'the real,' which necessarily escapes any attempt of being successfully integrated into the male system of representation. Accordingly, Michal's murders can be read as a result of his inability to locate his brother's stories on the symbolic level and, consequently, prove to have direct repercussions in reality.

Katurian's creative impetus, however, goes one step further. His story 'The Writer and the Writer's Brother' is a fictional retelling of the master narrative. In this version, he discovers the decayed body of his brother years after the experiment's termination when revisiting his childhood home. In his hand, the dead brother holds 'a story, scrawled in blood ... the sweetest, gentlest thing he'd ever come across, but what was even worse, it was better than anything he himself had ever written' (34). As an ultimate means of empowerment over the overwhelming influence of the master narrative, Katurian challenges reality and rewrites it as fiction. By doing so, he not only discards his earlier claims about the purely aesthetic function of his writing, but tries to assert the superiority of fiction over reality. That he has to sacrifice his brother in the process is a logical consequence. By reproducing Michal as a fictional (if dead) character in his narrative, he takes an irreversible step toward establishing the autonomy of the artistic imagination, his attempt to erase or at least rewrite the master narrative of his and Michal's existence

Table 11.4

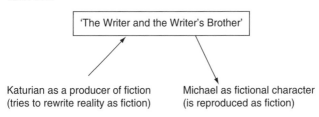

(cf. Table 11.4). Reconfiguring the violent treatment his brother had to endure, Katurian creates his own new identity as the sole arbiter of fortunes.

Intoxicated with his own creative powers and secure in his male role as judge on fiction and reality, Katurian is not content to only process and represent reality in his fictions, but aims to reconstitute it as he sees fit. Michal, on the other hand, is again assigned a feminine role, that is, that of the oblation, sacrificed symbolically at the altar of a supposedly superior male imagination. With him perishes the idea of his manuscript, which, as it was written in blood, could be said to have flowed directly from his body and could be read as a manifestation of an alternative system of signification, a notion akin to the feminist idea (brought forward by the likes of Luce Irigaray and Hélène Cixous) of an *écriture feminine*, a subversive since unrepresentable threat to the patriarchal order, based on corporeality and feminine *jouissance* (to use Lacan's terminology again). Katurian can only contest this threat by simultaneously writing it into existence and annihilating it together with its supposed originator.

Michal, however, is not dead. Katurian's fictional attempt on his life does not yet withstand the test of reality. So Katurian has to change his tactics once more and must grab reality by the horns. He *'takes the pillow and holds it down forcefully over Michal's face'* (67), killing him in much the same manner as he had killed his parents all those years ago. Interestingly enough, Katurian has – in the process of turning his fiction of a dead brother into reality – morphed into a fictional character himself: the Pillowman of the play's title and protagonist of a story he tells Michal shortly before. In this story, the Pillowman convinces people who are on the verge of suicide to travel back in time with him and kill themselves as children in order to avoid a whole lifetime of misery. By killing his brother, Katurian becomes part of his own fictional universe *and* succeeds in creating a new identity for himself. Katurian, the

Table 11.5

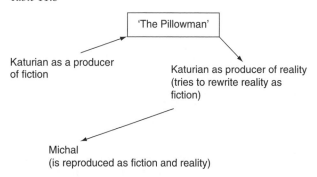

producer of fiction, has transformed into Katurian, the producer of reality, at the expense of Michal, whose fictional destiny finally catches up
with him (cf. Table 11.5). By wilfully blurring the boundaries of fiction
and reality, Katurian surrenders his narrative authority and subordinates
himself to the logic of the fictions he has created; the author, so to speak,
being engulfed by his own creations.

Katurian (read man) has by now assumed such an unassailable control over his fictions that he dares to relinquish the inaugural emblem
of his superiority, that is, the sovereign authority to distinguish between
fiction and reality. In order to irrevocably eradicate the threat posed by
Michal, he suits his actions to his words and kills him, smothering not
only the person of his brother, but with him the potential for alternative systems of signification. This victory in the contest between male
and female representation, however, is both complete and futile, since
it involves the renunciation of Katurian's status as creator of fictions to
become a fictional character (the Pillowman) himself.

On the event level in the play, Katurian finally gives in to the
supremacy of his narratives over his reality by striking a deal with his
interrogators. In exchange for a promise that they will not burn his
stories, he admits not only to the murders of his brother and parents,
but also to the murders committed by his brother. In a confession to
Tupolski and Ariel, he trades in the events of his real life (soon to be
terminated by execution) for the fictional universe created through and
in his stories, thereby ultimately giving up his quest of maintaining a
private version of reality outside of narrative. Yet, Katurian's narrative
authority makes one last stand; he has one more story up his sleeve.

After having finally been executed by Tupolski, the *'dead Katurian
slowly gets to his feet, takes the hood off to reveal his bloody, bullet-shattered*

Table 11.6

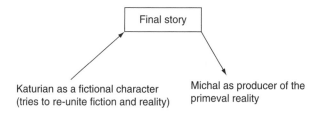

Final story

Katurian as a fictional character
(tries to re-unite fiction and reality)

Michal as producer of the
primeval reality

head...and speaks' (103). The story he relates is a final fiction about his brother, a fiction that is intended to reintegrate the narratives that Katurian has generated with the grim reality. Michal, so the story goes, had been visited by the Pillowman just before the gruesome experiment began, who faithful to his job description tried to persuade Michal to escape from his horrible fate by way of suicide. Michal denied the offer and accepted his fortune, "cos I think I'm going to really like my brother's stories' (103). It is significant that Katurian tells this, his final version of the master narrative, from beyond the grave. He has left the real space of events and returned as a fictional character himself[4] to reconfigure his brother as the original and deliberate creator of the master narrative, who had the chance to call off the entire experiment but decided to go on with it for the sake of the subsequent stories it would produce (cf. Table 11.6).

Has the ghost of Katurian's creative prowess returned from the grave to make amends for his sex as a whole by finally acknowledging that it had been the female principle all along that had triggered the whole succession of stories, that had suffered the mad tales of male imagination for their sheer drollness, safe in the knowledge that it had been the original *primum movens* all along? Or, is the resurrection of Katurian the ultimate self-elevation of the male imagination, which can control the borders of fiction and reality even from the other side of being?

These questions are left unanswered and it probably does not matter anyway, because Tupolski executes Katurian two seconds earlier than promised, thus not giving him enough time to finish his story. This leaves Katurian with only the fragments of his ultimate narrative to comment on:

Katurian The story was going to finish in fashionably downbeat mode, with Michal going through all that torment, with Katurian writing all those stories, only to have them burned from the world by a bulldog of a policeman. The story *was* going to finish that way, but was of course cut short by a bullet blowing his brains out two seconds too soon. And maybe it was best that the story didn't finish that way, as it wouldn't have been quite accurate. Because, for reasons known only to himself, the bulldog of a policeman chose not to put the stories in the burning trash, but placed them carefully with Katurian's case file, which was then sealed away to remain unopened for fifty-odd years. . . . A fact which would have ruined the writer's fashionable downbeat ending, but was somehow. . .somehow . . . more in keeping with the spirit of the thing. (104)

So, in the end the stories are all that is left. The records of the real events (the case files) plus Katurian's fictional versions of them rest side by side. The numerous gender configurations of activity and passivity that had been created and destroyed in the course of the play have all been uncovered as fictions and the audience is left with the sinking feeling that they are themselves probably not expected to distinguish between fiction and reality anymore. The narratives seem to have developed a momentum and authority of their own, making use of the characters and role configurations available rather than the other way around. A concluding summary of Katurian's masculinity, defined here by his creative authority, may exemplify and explain this claim. At the beginning of the play, he is depicted as a fervent believer in the autonomy of the male subject, whose authority rests on the power to clearly distinguish between fiction and reality, while the very end has him accept his position as a mere fictional character himself. Despite having put up a brave struggle, even he cannot escape from the realization that it is not the author that creates individual narratives, but individual narratives that create the author. This is paralleled by the resolution of the gender roles assigned to the two brothers, which seem to be fixed in the beginning, only to unravel completely in the transgressions and overlayings of the stories in which the creative subject becomes hopelessly entangled. The foil on which this replacement is displayed, I would argue, is the violence described, depicted, and alluded to in ever-changing ways through the various versions of the master narratives. The narrative of violence can thus be read as the palimpsest, onto which the futile quest for identity is inscribed and which ultimately is the only thing left and real, symbolized in the final moment of the play by the box filled with Katurian's stories and files, which officer Ariel (finally living up to his literary name) safely puts away.

Notes

1. A seeming paradox that can be highlighted by the fact that while it may be difficult to imagine two individuals aspiring to be designated 'identical identities,' these seemingly contradictory terms have the same etymological root, that is, Latin *idens* = 'the same.'
2. The format of this essay forestalls a discussion of the gendered aspects of colonial stereotypes. Let me refer you to Mária Kurdi, who claims that '[b]eing stigmatized as feminine and childlike in the colonialist discourse had sent the Irish male on a long-term fight to reclaim his masculinity, nationalist ideology itself linking the values of manhood with violence and positing sexual prowess as the opposite of weakness' (108).
3. The character of Donny, never far from the nearest bottle of poteen, incompetent, jovial but with a violent past, is the closest that McDonagh comes to putting a traditional 'Paddy' on stage. This claim can be substantiated by the fact that Donny gets most of the funny lines in the play, such as his dry observation when the INLA hit squad takes Padraic outside to shoot him that it is 'incidents like this does put tourists off Ireland' (50) or his reaction to Mairead and Padraic's declaration only to get married once Ireland is free: 'That'll be a long fecking engagement' (61).
4. ·I would like to refer you at this point to Ondřej Pilný's highly readable article about *The Pillowman* in the tradition of puppet theater. He argues that 'all characters in the play are puppets, swung around by their manipulative creator' (219), the marionette-like quality of the characters manifesting itself most clearly in the instant when the crouched figure of the executed Katurian is mysteriously brought back to life again.

Works cited

Benson, Ciarán. *The Cultural Psychology of Self: Place, Morality and Art in Human Worlds*. London: Routledge, 2001.

Butler, Judith. *Gender Trouble: Feminism and the Subversion of Identity*. New York & London: Routledge, 1990.

Eldred, Laura. 'Martin McDonagh's Blend of Tradition and Horrific Innovation.' *The Theatre of Martin McDonagh: A World of Savage Stories*. Ed. Lilian Chambers and Eamonn Jordan. Dublin: Carysford Press, 2006. 198–213.

Gilbert, Sandra and Susan Gubar. *The Madwoman in the Attic: The Woman Writer and the 19th-Century Literary Imagination*. New Haven et al: Yale U P, 1979.

Kurdi, Mária. 'Gender, Sexuality and Violence in the Work of Martin McDonagh.' *The Theatre of Martin McDonagh: A World of Savage Stories*. Ed Lilian Chambers and Eamonn Jordan. Dublin: Carysford Press, 96–115.

Lonergan, Patrick. 'Too Dangerous to be Done? – Martin McDonagh's Lieutenant of Inishmore.' *Irish Studies Review* 13 (2005): 65–78.

Luckhurst, Mary. 'Lieutenant of Inishmore: Selling (-Out) to the English.' *The Theatre of Martin McDonagh: A World of Savage Stories*. Ed Lilian Chambers and Eamonn Jordan. Dublin: Carysford Press, 116–29.

McDonagh, Martin. *The Lieutenant of Inishmore*. London: Methuen, 2001.

——. *The Pillowman*. London: Faber & Faber, 2003.

——. *Plays: 1*. London: Methuen, 1999.

Pilný, Ondřej. 'Grotesque Entertainment: The Pillowman as Puppet Theatre.' *The Theatre of Martin McDonagh: A World of Savage Stories*. Ed Lilian Chambers and Eamonn Jordan. Dublin: Carysford Press, 2006. 214–23.

Rees, Catherine. 'The Politics of Morality: The Lieutenant of Inishmore.' *The Theatre of Martin McDonagh: A World of Savage Stories*. Ed Lilian Chambers and Eamonn Jordan. Dublin: Carysford Press, 130–40.

Sierz, Alex. *In-Yer-Face Theatre: British Drama Today*. London: Faber and Faber, 2001.

Worthen, Hana and W. B. Worthen. 'The Pillowman and the Ethics of Allegory.' *Modern Drama* 49 (2006): 155–73.

12
'Ghosts of Sparta': Performing the God of War's Virtual Masculinity

Sven Schmalfuß

Abstract

Computer games, especially in their action-driven violent variety, are often associated with an unthinking attachment to traditional clichés of masculinity. The present essay shows that this assessment is far too simplistic. It explores in particular an adventure game franchise entitled God of War *to demonstrate that within chauvinist structures there is also evidence of often very radical subversions of traditional masculine norms. Patriarchy in the game is upheld as well as challenged. Macho sexual fantasies are acted out as well as evaded. Even the simulated bodies of the players' avatars do not simply correspond to clear-cut gender identities. Using a complex Lacanian model of analysis, the essay demonstrates that in the interaction of the game with the body and psyche of its player through the use of game technology, interesting gender revisions occur that resemble the concept of the cyborg identity famously proposed by Donna Haraway.*

Are the 'Ghosts of Sparta' the New *Dei ex Machina*?

In his spirited esoteric attempt to lay the foundations for a new 'masculinity,' Robert Bly tried to re-establish the link of modern men with their 'natural' selves as warriors. 'We could say that a third of each person's brain is a warrior brain; a third of the instincts carried by our DNA relates to warrior behavior; a third of our thoughts – whether we like it or not – are warrior thoughts. That is a sobering idea' (150). Finally, we can see our urge for violence and conflict in a sober light. We are warriors and we should feel proud rather than ashamed about it, since it is our nature. As much as this resembles a hopeless attempt at a backlash – even though Bly denies this – against the advances feminism has made over the last 40 years, his idea seems to have fallen on fertile ground in an area of cultural production commonly associated with 'masculinity' or even 'adolescent masculinity': digital games. In the virtual realms of digital games everyone can be a hero by being a warrior, using violence to reach her or his goal. At least, this is the public perception. Conflicts are predominantly solved through violent means, not through compromise reached by negotiation and diplomacy. From this warrior camaraderie and background of competition one can even derive positive social connections. In-game enemies can be best friends in the 'real' world. Gamers, male and female alike, seem to belong to a tribe of warriors.

This correlates with a newfound fascination with ancient Sparta in contemporary popular culture, ranging from Frank Miller's comic book *300* and its iconic filmic interpretation by Zack Snyder to digital games like *Spartan* or the *God of War* franchise.[1] In all these works heroic deeds are in the foreground – while the fascist elements of Spartan society are readily accepted and not even discussed. Historical Sparta was a totalitarian society ruled by a warrior caste, which had to focus all its powers on securing the state's wellbeing (cf. Baltrusch 2007). The lives of all members of the Spartan *polis* (even the slaves) were structured for the purpose of upholding the system and defending it against foreign influences of any sort. These fascist elements of Spartan society are often overlooked from a modern perspective, while heroic events in its history, for example the victory over the Persian Army at Thermopylae in 480 BC, are mythically heightened to examples of extraordinary bravery. An analogous development can be seen in the, necessarily simplified, presentation of political structures in digital games. This has special ramifications for the way 'masculinity' is constructed in games and perceived by the player through her or his performance of this 'masculinity' when playing a specific game. Just as much as 'female' game characters tend to be constructed along sexist images, 'male' characters are also confined to a very narrow stereotype.

At first glance the games of the *God of War* franchise seem to support this impression through the games' main protagonist Kratos's exaggerated 'masculinity.' On the other hand, this 'hypermasculinity,' focusing on rage and violence, is dismantled as a social construct by the performative nature of the player's action in the virtual world of mythical Greece. Unfortunately, this form of *pastiche* drowns in the sheer mass of 'over-the-top masculine' characters in games. As long as the 'ghosts of Sparta' regulate the internal dynamics of so many games, it seems hard to establish *pastiche* as a form of critique of the gendered norms prevailing in games.

The new god of war undermining the rule of Zeus

Kratos raises the Sword of Olympus. He is only moments away from driving it through Zeus's heart and thus killing the mighty leader and father of the Olympian gods. His own father, as Athena will tell him only seconds later after throwing herself into Kratos's blade to save Zeus. She sacrifices herself to secure Olympus' endurance, because, as she phrases it, Zeus is Olympus.

With this somewhat tacky and simplified Hollywood version of the Oedipal drama, *God of War II* is brought to an end, and the ground is laid for the battle to bring down Olympus and Zeus in the upcoming *God of War III*. The protagonist, and thus the character directly controlled by the player, in all different incarnations of the *God of War* franchise, is Kratos, the so-called 'Ghost of Sparta.' Spartan warrior turned God of War, turned mortal again, Kratos made himself a slave of Ares to win a battle, leaving his fate with the gods, who use him as their brutal and ruthless executor on Earth. Ares even tricks him into killing his own wife and daughter. Ten years later he is offered the opportunity to revenge himself, when Athena asks for his help to defend her city against Ares. Kratos turns his rage against Ares, destroying him and becoming the new God of War. But still tormented by the nightmares of his deeds, and redemption being denied by the gods, he turns his anger against Zeus himself, siding with the Titans to wage war against Olympus.

As pretentious and underwhelming as this may sound to an educated reader, the game still works for most people. Of course this simplistic version of Greek mythology is used to motivate the player to engage in an extended sequence of gory fights. However, it does so with such technical excellence and gameplay smoothness that it gets nearly everyone hooked, as player reactions and reviews show. The technical slickness of such games on a gameplay, audiovisual and code level, which enables marketing to employ them as showcase applications for their respective hardware platform, also adds to *God of War*'s reputation as a series of 'guy games.' As the shortened and condensed version of the series' storyline above shows, the desire for technical perfection is not the only 'masculine' stereotype catered for in the game. From the first moments of production onward Kratos was designed as the very opposite of a wise and diplomatic leader. David Jaffe, the first game's director, characterizes him as 'brutal, nasty, violent, antisocial, angry, fuck-you' ('Making-Of God of War' video on *God I*). In other videos the design team describes Kratos as 'primeval' ('Heroic Possibilities' on *God I*) and a 'badass' ('Kratos: Concept to Completion' on the bonus disk of *God of War II*'s German special edition; *God II* bonus disk: 0:29).[2] Kratos was even stripped of most of his armor to underline his 'animal character' visually (Jaffe in 'Making-Of God of War' video on *God I*). All symbolic trappings of culture were taken away, and he was left with his muscles as the only form of armor to protect his body and its integrity against the backdrop of his tormented soul. The protagonist was designed to make 'the player feel *he* could unleash *his* dark side.... [The developers wanted to] let players go nuts and unleash the dark fantasies they have' (Jaffe in 'Heroic Possibilities' on *God I*; my emphases). This is strongly reminiscent of Bly's *wild man* whom we have to find in our soul (Bly).

Yet Kratos does not use his wild side to serve a 'masculine' order. Instead he sides with the much older female Titan Gaia to bring chaos to the patriarchal structure of Olympus and to bring down Zeus, the namesake of Bly's Zeus energy, 'which encompasses intelligence, robust health, compassionate decisiveness, good will, generous leadership. Zeus energy is male authority accepted for the sake of the community' (Bly 22). Kratos seems increasingly destined to escape from his slavery to the patriarchal Olympian gods. Rumor has it that *God of War III* will even explain why there are no Greek gods anymore.

Potential players become aware of the protagonist's driven nature from the moment they see him on the games' covers. All cover artworks feature Kratos's muscular figure and his grim and determined look. On the first game's European cover he is shown in action in an exposed place, surrounded by enemies whom he is fighting off using his chained swords and the Medusa's head. The cover shows remarkable similarity to the cover artworks for two other iconic games, which are often regarded as the figureheads of a sort of 'digital masculinism': *Doom II* and *Duke Nukem 3D*. These two games also position their respective heroes on top of a rock, fighting off massive waves of enemies.

God of War, *Doom*, and *Duke Nukem* present their main protagonists not as men of word but of action. They are on a mission to face a whole army of monsters by themselves. There is no doubt that the player will take their position and thus perform this heroic task him- or herself. On *God of War II*'s European cover we see Kratos from the left and from the rear, facing the temple of the Fates (with its monumental statues of Zeus and Chronos). This time no enemies are visible, implying that Kratos's quest and not his enemies will be his greatest obstacle. *Chains of Olympus*, while still focusing on Kratos's powerful features and stressing his determined and grim glance at the viewer, also allows, at least partially, the personal dilemma awaiting Kratos in the games into the artwork. The close-up on Kratos's head and upper-left torso make visible the details of the layer of ash now covering his whole body as a sign of his subaltern status as a slave to the gods' will. This layer of ash is the last remnant of the fire that has consumed the bodies of his wife and daughter, who had been slain by his own swords. The ash actually gives Kratos the nickname 'Ghost of Sparta' in the game's world. Kratos is directly looking out from the cover artwork, challenging the player with his intense gaze. He has turned his back on the phallic pillar holding the world in the background. He has also turned his back on the gods, here represented by Helios's light illuminating Kratos's head from behind his left shoulder. It was this light that had led him into the underworld and that now stands between him and Zeus.[3]

The pillar, a symbol of Zeus's absolute power that holds the world together, is the location of the game's showdown. Kratos has to defeat Cassiopeia and Atlas to keep them from destroying the pillar and throwing the world into ultimate chaos. This victory does not matter to Kratos anymore. His mission has finally turned into a personal crusade to overcome his own torment. He will forever be separated from his wife and daughter. And he is bound to make the Olympian gods pay for what they have done to him. In this respect the games seem to offer what a 'real guy' should expect from a digital game: machismo par excellence. But are the *God of War* games really unquestioning fulfilments and reproductions of stereotypes that are commonly thought to be especially appealing to male players? Or is it rather the other way around: do games like the *God of War* series and our performance in them shape our perception of an in-game, virtual masculinity, which is then experienced as an augmentation of our 'real world' social gender role, be it 'masculine' or 'feminine'?

Performing virtual gender roles

Judith Butler contests identity as a mode of 'being,' a stable idea of oneself, and instead sees our sex or gender roles and our sexual identities as fluid concepts that we perform (Butler 1999: 175).[4] This performance is an ongoing act which is continuously repeated and renegotiated (178), but which is also 'socially constituted, where 'constitution' carries both the enabling and violating sense of 'subjection'' (Butler 1993: 123). The social networks we inhabit restrict and enable the extent to which this performance is possible. Through the appropriation of the act of performance, these limits can be tested and extended. For this purpose Butler utilizes the literary *pastiche*, the 'imitation that mocks the notion of an original' (Butler 1999: 176).

> As the effects of a subtle and politically enforced performativity, gender is an 'act', as it were, that is open to splittings, self-parody, self-criticism, and those hyperbolic exhibitions of 'the natural' that, in their very exaggeration, reveal its fundamentally phantasmatic status. (187)

Butler's model of the *pastiche* can be seen as a politically appropriated version of Baudrillard's *simulacrum* (cf. Baudrillard 1994). The copy 'creates' our perception of the 'original,' which has never existed. If we use this copy to achieve political ends, we can change the definition of this 'original.' Or, to use an idea I will return to below, 'gender' can be seen as 'gender play.' In a field demarcated by certain rules, gender can be performed individually.

This comes very close to Roger Caillois's continuum between 'play' or *paidia* and 'game' or *ludus* (13). 'Play' is a form of 'free play' that is bound to nearly no restrictions[5] whereas 'game' is, literally, ruled by 'arbitrary, imperative and purposely tedious conventions' (13), that is, rules. The same 'force field' determines gender in between the drive for free personal expression and social constraints. We have internalized this struggle in the competition between the *super-ego* and the *id* in our psyche. It becomes most visible in situations of 'virtual drag,' where the genders of the player and of the virtual avatar differ, for example, if a 'female' player plays a 'masculine' avatar.

Butler's concept is closer to Lacan than to Freud in this respect. *I*, the subject, is always determined through the *Other*. *I* recognize myself through the Other. In the *mirror stage* of psycho-sexual development (16th–18th month) (Pagel 23) the *I* begins to recognize 'itself' as an individual subject through its reflection in a 'mirror.' This only seemingly autonomous *I* becomes the *ego ideal*: the perceived recognition of unity that is only anticipated in the 'mirror image' but which is not yet corporeal (25).

Through the drama of the *mirror stage* two desires are triggered. The first desire is to become like our imaginary *ego ideal*; the second is what Lacan calls *jouissance*, the phantasmatic identification and longing for this identification with the unity with the mother's body (cf. Butler

1993: 70). Therefore male *jouissance* is directly linked to the imaginary place of the phallus, while female *jouissance* seems to be unrestricted and omnipresent. So, while male *jouissance* is satisfied through the means of the *symbolic order*, female *jouissance* is directly linked to the pre-symbolic state.

To compensate for this desire, male children are introduced to the *symbolic order* by their father. The *symbolic order* serves to establish order by creating the illusion of security in a symbolically charged context on the one hand, while on the other hand it is an order of men, an exclusive club (cf. Pagel 66). Women can never be fully accepted within this order, as the bonding agent of the club is language. Language is used to hand over the *phallus* from an older generation of men to a younger one in a *phallogocentric* society. *Phallus* for Lacan does not refer to the penis, but it is the means of power, transmitted through language, in patriarchy (Pagel 94, 100–101). Women, in Lacan's view, can only 'be' this phallus.[6] 'To "be" the phallus is to be the "signifier"[7] of the desire of the Other and *to appear* as this signifier. In other words, it is to be the object, the Other of a (heterosexualized) masculine desire, but also to represent or reflect that desire' (Butler 1999: 56; original emphasis). A dominant group, men, needs another group, women, to define itself. The hegemonic power of the dominant group is socially constructed through language. The correlation to Butler's concept of gender is obvious, although Butler defines it in much broader terms, not only focusing on 'masculine' and 'feminine' gender roles, but also breaking up this dichotomy.

By definition, games are bound to a fixed symbolic order, that is, rules. Consequently, games serve as mirror and *symbolic order* at the same time. The player can recognize and misrecognize certain aspects of her or his self through the performance of virtual gender roles. This is set in an environment created through symbols, rules and, in the case of digital games, code. Only in this environment is the existence of this specific mirror possible – and it can only be used by those who have been allowed access to the symbolic order, that is, those familiar with the rules. Even on the story level a connection to the *God of War* series is visible. Kratos has to act as an agent of the gods' will, especially of the will of his father Zeus. He thus enforces the *symbolic order*. Yet he cannot find satisfaction in this; he longs for a state of mind that precedes the one he is in. He experiences a form of *jouissance*, a longing to reunite himself with the female part of his family, his wife, and daughter.

Do cyborgs dream of ancient Greece?

Butler takes a step away from the body, focusing more on the social forces that have an impact on the body. Therefore, her means of political action are those of the individual in a social group. Donna Haraway, with her background in Socialist and Radical Feminism, maps the way to political action in her seminal 'Cyborg Manifesto.' Haraway appropriates the fictional concept of the 'cyborg,' a life form created out of organic and mechanical components, for Feminism. 'Cyborgs are hybrid figures composed of elements which are both one and the other simultaneously – part human, part machine; part natural, part cultural construction; part fiction, part reality' (Smith 37). Cathy Peppers reminds us that,

> [w]hile Haraway's utopian image of a subject who takes pleasure in boundary confusions sounds charming, it also sounds suspiciously like the deconstructionist's eagerness to embrace a 'dissolved' subject in order to avoid the disruption of feminists' concerns with gendered subjectivity. (165)

Following Peppers, Haraway unites parts that cannot actually be united. Still this seems inevitable if one wishes to reach the political ends Haraway is aiming for. Haraway's Cyborgs are not really a unity, but rather a cybernetic network. Therefore the Cyborg is neither singularly gendered nor 'postgender' (165), as Peppers claims. The Cyborg[8] is not troubled by the heterogeneous quality of our gendered selves and identities; it sees this as its specific source of power. The Cyborg uses external inscription on its body as a powerful tool for political action. It is the only form to really challenge what Haraway calls the *Informatics of Domination*, the cybernetic, post-modern form of hegemony that has replaced the older 'grand theories' (cf. 523). This concept of the *Informatics of Domination* is heavily reminiscent of Lacan's *symbolic order*, Foucault's *dispositif*, or Butler's *heterosexual matrix*.

Cyborgs are not linked through identity but through coalition and affinity (519). 'So [Haraway's] cyborg myth is about transgressed boundaries, potent fusions, and dangerous possibilities which progressive people might explore as one part of needed political work' (519). The cyborg acknowledges its 'constructedness' – its 'fracturedness'[9] – and uses it for political action in fusion with other fractured entities. It is, if one likes, Butler's *pastiche* lifted to a social, 'interrelational' level. The cyborg associates with other cyborgs, which feature similar fragments in their fractured selves through a cybernetic network of attraction.

Digital games present the opportunity to experience a quasi-cyborg existence. In many games a 'real world' player controls a virtual avatar on her or his way through a virtual world using a form of human–computer interface. The interface translates the player's commands into actions that the avatar then executes. In this respect the avatar is her or his extension into the virtual world. The avatar and the player constitute a sort of 'entity' with a 'real world' end and a virtual world end that interact. The player is mostly free to choose her or his virtual representation and how she or he wants it to react in the framework created by the game's rules. She or he is performing in virtual space.

This performance is not executed directly, but in a mediated form. The player is sitting in front of her or his PlayStation 2 (or PlayStation Portable or a mobile phone for that matter[10]), which is connected to the TV set, playing *God of War* with a combination of controller button pushes and analogstick movements. The program interprets these commands as a multitude of movements or attacks of Kratos and visualizes them on the screen. Even though the player is limited in her or his actions by the game's rules and the code it is running, she or he still has a direct influence on the narrative of the game. She or he is manipulating a machine in the 'real' world with her or his 'real' body to perform as a virtual character in a virtual environment. The player thus has to react to audio-visual and tactile stimuli created by the game.

> [G]ame worlds and code are designed to maximize the sensory experience of the gamer based upon how much sensory information can be conveyed in each sensory 'channel' – the visual, aural, and finally, tactical sensory 'channels'. Because humans can take in the most information visually, those aspects of game design are given the most attention. Sound design – from the soundscape and soundtrack of a game to its special sound effects – is the second most important of this [*sic*] sensory channels.
>
> (Murphy 234)

Most games can be played mute without losing so much information that the game becomes unplayable. There are only few exceptions to this, for example Nintendo's experimental *Soundvoyager*, which relies completely on the aural information for the player (cf. also Röber and Masuch).[11] *God of War* is no exception to this. Some enemies can be heard before they are seen, but ultimately the game only diminishes in atmosphere when the volume is turned down. Even *God of War II*'s invisible Perseus can either be detected via surround-sound or via his visually traceable movements in the water basin. The same seems to be true for the tactile information conveyed to the player through the vibrating force-feedback motors of the *DualShock 2* joypad. Neither sensory channel, aural and tactile, is essential to the gameplay, but if one of these information systems is left out, as, for example, in *God of War: Chains of Olympus* because of the *Playstation Portable*'s lack of a force-feedback system, something seems to be missing. The experience is different. Through this sensory input and the player's reaction two interlinked feedback-loops are created, one centered on the player and the other centered on the game. Both, the player and the game, process information received from the other and create a certain output for the other. The player and the game are to some extent 'merged' in this circle. The player becomes part of the game, and the game becomes a part of the player.

As a 3D action-adventure game, most of the gameplay in *God of War* is made up of spatial exploration and fighting. Even the riddles included now and then are of a spatial, architectural nature. These two gameplay elements, exploration and fighting, require the avatar, Kratos, to function as a kind of prosthesis for the player in the virtual world of ancient Greece. Kratos is the player's representation in the virtual world. He becomes a part of the player through the input-output-circle, as much as the player becomes a part of him. Through the use of a virtual marionette, the player is performing as Kratos. So while she or he is sitting in her or his 'reality,' she or he is at the same time Kratos in the virtual, fictional world of Greek mythology. The player and Kratos have formed a cyborgian 'entity,' if it is possible to talk about an entity in connection with a cyborg. This cyborg is part human (the player) and part machine (the computer running the game, but also the game in itself, with all its rules and mechanics), but also part real and part fictional. The avatar is the virtual, thus fictional, representation of the 'real' world player.

Nevertheless the player and the game protagonist are not in an easy, direct connection with each other. Digital games in general,[12] *God of War* included, tend to use a rather complex translation of the input via keyboard, mouse, joypad, or joystick into the on-screen action. So, for example, while the player moves Kratos in *God I* with the use of the left analogstick, pressing the x-button triggers a jump. Other movements like swimming or climbing need analogstick commands and other buttons to be pushed. Fighting is controlled through a combination of the square-, triangular- and L1-buttons. The circle-button starts context related actions. So the controls of the game have only a very small, one could say metaphorical, connection with the actions of the game's protagonist. Control schemes of games have to be learned, as they cannot be deduced from the movements an action would actually require. Once these schemes are learned, they appear perfectly natural to a gamer. She or he has accepted the cyborgian connection with the game and has mastered it, expanding her or his power in the virtual realm. This is a continuous process, since different games, genres, and gaming platforms require different controlling methods.

While digital game controls have to be learned like any other tool we use, they are still not completely alien to us, as they can, in their cybernetic-mechanical make-up, also be seen as a mirror image of the way we execute an action in the 'real' world. A cognitive, and for this purpose cybernetic, decision for a specific action, is transported through an array of electrical connections, our neural system, to a mechanical apparatus, our bones, joints, and muscles, executing this task. So when the player decides to push the analogstick upward, an impulse is sent through her or his nerves to her or his hand pushing the stick. The computer registers this mechanical impulse and converts it into an electrical impulse to send the information from the joypad to the main computer in the console, which interprets this impulse through a cybernetic system, that is, the program, into the command for Kratos to step forward. The player then again registers the audio-visual representation and reacts accordingly. The two feedback loops, in a simplified view, actually seem to be a mirror image of the respective other. So the cyborgian 'entity' of the player/avatar is itself and its own mirror image at the same time. To speak in Lacanian terms, the player recognizes her- or himself in the game's protagonist, but she or he also misrecognizes her- or himself in it, since it is no direct representation of the player, but a complexly mediated one. The Cyborg, in Haraway's definition, is aware of the fictional quality of this misrecognition, but does not fall into a melancholic state and instead uses these multiple levels of interpretation of its body as a powerful extension of it.

So far the gendered dimensions of this cyborgian 'entity' have not been illuminated. Bryan-Mitchell Young argues that in a state of immersion, that is, one's perception being fully absorbed by the games action (cf. Newmann 16ff.; McMahan 68–69), 'both the physical body as well as the virtual body become backgrounded to the (virtual) physicality of the action itself' (3):

[N]ot only does the intensity of the action within the game render the physical body of a ... player 'invisible', but so too is the ideal body within the game so that the player can concentrate more fully on the actions of that body. That both the physical body and the virtual body can so easily be ignored while playing a game seems to indicate that rather than something tied directly and essentially to any physical biology, masculinity is a set of behaviors and a mentality that one can act out. (3)

Young, writing about First-Person-Shooters, considers the fights in these games to be 'physical, aggressive, hyper-masculine conflicts' (3). He sees the constructed nature of gender roles underlined by a First-Person-Shooter's *un-corporeality*.[13] All the player can see of the avatar's body in most First-Person-Shooters is, to use Robert Bly's term in a way he would not like, *Iron John*'s phallus (the gun in the hands of the protagonist) penetrating the enemy's lines. This phallic power tool has no apparent connection to the protagonist's or the player's body. Even the protagonist's arms we see seem to be more attached to the gun (functioning as tools to reload it) than to the protagonist/player. From the action on screen we conclude that the protagonist might be 'male.' Therefore players often seem confused when they find out that the protagonist is actually 'female,' as for example in the case of *Portal*. The same mechanics of misrecognition are at hand when the protagonist, while being seen on the screen, has her or his gender rendered indistinguishable by armor, clothes, and so on. For example, many players were puzzled by the fact that *Metroid*'s Samus Aran is revealed as 'female' during the death and victory animations. Young argues in the quote above that this state of *un-corporeality* is heightened in moments of immersion, when we forget about our own body in front of the machine we are playing with.

This also applies to games like the *God of War* franchise in which the protagonist is visible all the time, from the front ends main menu throughout the game to the end credits. In moments of high immersion, the player seems to focus singularly on the burning circle of the Chaos-Blades, Kratos's two swords chained to his forearms, whirling through the enemy formations in a hopefully flawless motion. The player forgets about Kratos's and her or his own body. On the other hand, the player is made painfully aware of the virtual and the 'real' body in scenes where this immersion is broken. The Hades level of *God I* is a good example. It features a now infamous tower of blades, a cliff that Kratos – and thus the player – has to climb, which features many rotating saw blades.

This seems to be only surmountable with much luck and a good deal of trial-and-error.

In situations of unfair game balancing like this the cyborgian connection between player and avatar seems to dissolve, opening up the possibility for the avatar to be personalized as a different character. For a game to be used as a form of *pastiche* it is important to break the connection once in a while, to let the player reflect on her or his and the avatar's status and their hierarchical relation to each other. If the immersion is too complete, the player will not see the frictions. On the other hand, if there is no immersion at all, the player will see nothing but frictions, resulting in a feeling of disempowerment and being at the program's mercy. I will return to these notions below.

The *God of War* franchise has the dubious fame of featuring a scene of specific *un-corporeality* in each iteration of the series (apart from *Betrayal*): the sex-scene. Digital games, despite being sexualized most of the time, normally tend to circumvent the depiction of explicit sex. The *God of War* series does feature sex, even though it is executed in the most immature and chauvinist way. *God I*, *God II*, and *Chains*[14] all feature a scene, very early in the game, in which Kratos meets two women. These two bare-breasted ladies, who have seemingly enjoyed the 'blessings' of modern-world plastic surgery, await Kratos in a separate (and thus safe) environment. Without much ado they invite Kratos to a threesome – an invitation he does not turn down. While Kratos falls into the arms of the women, the camera zooms in on a nearby object, which serves as a clumsy metaphor for the sexual activities the player only hears during the following mini-game. These objects are a vase on a sideboard, which falls off its stand when the mini-game is solved in *God I*, a *Manneken Pis*-style water-fountain spraying water at completion in *God II* and, most plainly of all, a candle supported by a candleholder in the shape of a naked woman, whose flame is extinguished and releases a cloud of smoke at the climax of the mini-game in *Chains*. During the mini-game these objects are shaken by the force of the sexual act taking place nearby.

The mini-game asks the player to execute a certain number of input commands in the correct rhythm. There is only one way to solve this game, through the input of the commands asked by the program. There are no alternative ways or different goals. This mirrors the teleological structure of a chauvinistic 'masculine' sexuality. These commands are meant to be representations of the movements of Kratos during sexual intercourse. The final goal of the mini-game is to bring Kratos and the two women to an orgasm. This is at least what the player is supposed to deduct from the visual, metaphoric representation of the sexual act in the aforementioned objects, and the groans and teasings she or he hears from the two women, which grow more and more ecstatic. For the completion of this task, the player is offered a high amount of health and experience orbs, the games 'currencies' to replenish Kratos's health and level-up his weapons and magic spells. If the player fails to solve the mini-game, the women comment disapprovingly on Kratos's stamina. From Kratos the player hears the same grunts he makes when fighting, implying, together with the shaking of the metaphorical objects and a rumbling effect of the controller, the violent nature of this sexual act. Thus, a misogynist exploitation of these women (to gain orbs) – which functions in an analogous way to the, far more graphically explicit, mini-games to violently 'finishing-off' enemies in the game (which also supports Kratos with more orbs than he would get through normally killing them) – is covered up on a superficial level with the excuse of satisfying these women's sexual appetite.

This positions these scenes even more closely to the 'language' of pornography by presenting sex-hungry 'vixens' – who in the case of *Chains* even conform to the porn stereotype of the *damsel in distress*, as those women have been incarcerated by an evil Persian general and now want to thank their savior in an unmistakeably physical way. Even the metaphorical phallic objects seem to be taken directly from pornographic iconography. *God I*'s intro video tries to explain Kratos's sexual escapism with his wish to forget the nightmares of slaughtering his wife and daughter. The violence of the (implied) sexual act also correlates with the character's animalistic side. Still all this seems at odds with Kratos's reactions when he actually meets his family in the Underworld or even when he just sees them in visions. The sex-scene in *Chains* therefore seems to undermine the whole finale of the game, which shows Kratos choosing between saving the world or staying with his daughter and seeing the world and the Underworld turn into chaos.

On the other hand, all three sex mini-games are optional. The player can choose not to play them. It is up to the player if she or he wants to explore this dark side of Kratos's character or stay away from it. It is a moral decision, which – unlike *BioShock*'s exploitation of the Little Sisters – has no influence on the rest of the game and thus should rather be compared with *Call of Duty: Modern Warfare 2*'s infamous airport-level. This moral irrelevance combined with the *un-corporeality* of the whole scene, which stands in harsh contrast to the vividly graphic fights, gives these scenes a flavor of boyish, immature 'fun.' This stands in diametrical opposition to the scenes' nature and the theme of the rest of the games. Kratos is not just a young lad toying with his sexuality; he uses these women to divert his thoughts from his nightmares but fails to accomplish this. Why then does he serve (seemingly following the logic of pornography) the sexual needs of these anonymous 'mistresses'? Why are these scenes not visualized, analogous to the fights, as what they are: rape? If Kratos is designed to be a 'badass' anti-heroic character, why refrain from presenting him as dark and aggressive also in a sexual way? This would certainly be a morally dubious design decision, but all this is already contained in these scenes, merely hidden under a layer of immature 'fun' without consequences. In my eyes these sex-scenes are far more problematic than the, equally immature, infamous *Hot-Coffee-Mod*[15] to *Grand Theft Auto: San Andreas*, which was a hidden feature, but caused a witch-hunt in the USA (cf., for example, Chapter 4 in Brathwaite).

So if corporeality is to some extent dissolved, what happens in moments of cross-gender play, or as I have called it above, *virtual drag*? Sheri Graner Ray proposes the problematic theory that 'male' gamers feel more at ease playing a 'female' character than 'female' gamers playing a 'male' character because of the *pyramid of power* (95–100). Following this theory, members of a group of a certain social status feel more 'comfortable' (which does not mean 'enjoy') acting within an environment corresponding to their own status or below than in an environment of higher social rank. This model, however, is far too simplistic. The problems already arise in Graner Ray's own example. She claims that a baron can easily fulfil the task of a baker, while a scullery maid would feel very uncomfortable in the role of a queen (97–98). The baron

> would probably not be happy with his lot, but he would understand the social rules associated with the tradesman's class and be comfortable functioning within those parameters. However, [the maid] would be very uncomfortable; she would not understand the societal rules that define that position. (97–98)

First of all it seems awkward to use a historicized example containing a simplified idea of early modern society to underscore one's argument. And even in the logic of this (fictional) cosmos it seems highly doubtful that a baron would be familiar with the skills or the knowledge needed to organize life in the lower ranks effectively. It seems more like a question of how far up or down one will step on the pyramid. One feels quite at ease in an environment similar to one's own, and intimidated in alien surroundings. Another factor for the comfort experienced in such a role is the permeability of the borders between these social strata. Often it is socially more acceptable for a person of higher rank to step down than for a person to step up. Comfort seems to be more dependent on the social acceptance of this move than on one's personal knowledge or abilities. This again shows the socially constructed 'nature' of the glass ceiling and the performativity of our roles, virtual or 'real.'[16]

The greater problem of this theory is its traditional essentialist view of gender. It acknowledges only two genders, which are linked with the biological sex of the respective person, implying that all persons of one sex make the same experiences of empowerment (if 'masculine') or disempowerment (if 'feminine'). Feminist authors like Judith Butler have shown this as a far too simplistic, and in many cases completely wrong, description of the gendered system we live in. 'Men' are also situated in a stratified 'masculine' pyramid of power. Differences occur also, but not exclusively, along the lines of race, sexual preference, or levels of income. Consequently, different 'men' make different experiences, which also have an important influence on their level of comfort when performing a 'differently' gendered role.

Still Graner Ray's example of a quality assurance test session for a Fantasy Role-Playing Game seems striking (99–100). A test crew for this game consisted of 20 male and 3 female test players. The game tested allowed the player to decide over the avatar's gender. All test players, male and female, picked a 'female' character as their virtual representation. When the male testers were asked why they were using the 'female' avatar,

> [t]heir answer was almost always, 'because she is prettier and nicer to look at.' When the female members of QA [Quality Assurance] were asked why they were using the female avatar, their answer was usually, 'I always play female characters. Playing a male character just doesn't feel right.' (100)

These statements are surely not universally valid; still I myself have to admit that I, considering myself 'male,' tend to play a 'female' character if a game offers me this choice. In a Beat'em Up fighting game this can be rationalized as a choice of special fighting styles and thus of a specific way of playing a game.[17] In Role-Playing Games, however, these considerations are often impossible. They usually offer classes of characters (for example, warrior, mage, and so on) in a 'male' and a 'female' form, with only slight variations in their character statistics. The way the game can be played varies only to a very small degree. The choice merely seems to be one of taste and of visual representation. Apart from these pleasures, *virtual drag* also allows for a socially accepted form of gender play, which can therefore be tried out in a 'safe place': the virtual realm. The tasks in most games could be described as only allowing for a traditionally 'masculine' solution, as 'competition' – however defined – is commonly seen as a 'masculine' way of solving problems.[18] This would entail that a version of *virtual drag* already exists on a game level for the 'female' characters, even before the player enters the scene. Despite being labelled 'female,' they have to perform a role commonly defined as 'masculine' to accomplish the game's goals. Violence, for example, as the only way to resolve a problem, is traditionally associated with 'masculine' thinking. In Butler's terms, an outburst of violence executed by a 'girl' in all its gory 'splendour,' as, for example, in *American McGee's Alice*, could be seen as a *pastiche* of this allegedly 'masculine' behavior, uncovering the constructed nature of the gender label attached to this behavior, thereby re-assessing this 'gender boundary.'

A reduction to *scopophilia*, the pleasure of looking, that is, the *male gaze*, again seems too simple an answer. The male player can find enough of what gamers like to call in a sexist fashion 'eye-candy' in the side characters of a game when playing a 'male' character. This does not mean that the looks of a character have no influence on the player's choice. It is hard to find any character in a digital game that looks at least somewhat 'natural.' 'Male' and 'female' characters have exaggerated body features. 'Female' characters are mostly styled in a hyper-sexualized way, with exaggerated breasts and waspish waistlines. 'Male' avatars in nearly all games feature an exaggerated torso and arm muscles and a very narrow waist, presenting them as born fighters.[19] Kratos fits this definition perfectly. Over the last few years some 'older' but still very fit heroic 'masculine' characters have been introduced (for example, Sam Fisher of the *Splinter Cell* franchise and Solid Snake in *Metal Gear Solid 4*). Yet 'older' heroic 'female' characters still seem unthinkable. It cannot be denied that this calculated sex appeal of 'female' characters is used to attract 'male' gamers. Still a reduction to the passivity of the gaze seems insufficient to explain why 'male' gamers enjoy playing 'female' characters so much.[20]

This passive *scopophilia* is supplemented by the active pleasure in taking control over somebody. Many scholars from an essentialist background would argue that 'boys' like the problem-solving aspect of games most, while 'girls' like to play around, that is, act freely in a specific environment offered by the game. Even though this is a very simplified and deterministic point of view, it seems plausible in our traditionally conditioned society. In this narrowly defined descriptive field it would explain the above-mentioned phenomenon of character choices by 'male' and 'female' players. 'Female' players would see the 'female' avatars as a direct fictionalized representation of themselves in the virtual world. It would amend their 'real' world personality with a virtual element. The 'male' gamers on the other hand would see the avatar as a tool they possess to achieve a certain goal, that is, winning the game. They would not really identify with the avatar, but control it, using and abusing it according to their own will. Sheila C. Murphy cites from an interview with a 'male' gamer:

> With third-person [perspective], especially if the controls are difficult to operate (thus making me feel much less strongly identified with the character and much more fighting to make the character obey my will; intuitive controls = greater identification), I'm more likely to blame my failures on the character. The usual shout is, 'move, you asshole!' or 'move, you fuck!' Tellingly, Lara [Croft of *Tomb Raider*] is invariably a 'bitch,' and when she's particularly stubborn and clumsy she's probably a 'whore.' Characters who are prone to falling off cliffs receive the most abuse. (231)

It seems unlikely that the same player would use the same abusive terms to scold himself. Still these characterizations in broad strokes seem to be self-fulfilling prophecies. They see gendered behavior in games, as we would expect it from our experiences in the socially constructed framework of the so-called 'real' world. This model, for example, does not account for the huge popularity of Open World/Sandbox games like *GTA IV* with male gamers. It also has a blind spot for the massive female market for genres like Adventures or Role-Playing Games, which rely on constant (narrative) progress and thus on problem solving. Identification also seems more connected to a certain degree of immersion, as has been argued above, than to a difference in the functional approach. The gendered expectations a player has, coming from a specific 'real' world context, can have an influence on the level of immersion of the player in the game, and thus her or his identification with the protagonists. The visualization of the action through a third-person 'camera' perspective, as in *God of War*, diminishes the identification with the game's protagonist to a certain extent. Kratos is seen less as a virtual representative of the player than as the player's virtual slave, prone to fulfil her or his task of overcoming the obstacles and finally finishing the game. The player is not so much directly playing Kratos than swinging a virtual 'whip' driving him on. This would support Young's thesis of the virtual body being dissolved in the player's perception during intense scenes of fighting. Still the cyborgian connection to, and thus the identification with, the avatar is never really lost. This becomes evident especially after a tough fight or a hard passage requiring spot-on jumping, for example, the above-mentioned Hades Level from *God I*. When the player overcomes these obstacles, she or he feels a relief close to the one the character would feel at this moment. In this respect the player's avatar is in itself also a cyborg existence. The avatar is a representation of the player and the player's slave-like tool at the same time. It is the factual means to an end in the framework of the game's mechanics and at the same time the fictional representation of the player.

Cyborgs versus the innumerable army of Spartans

The concept of this two-fold cyborg, player/avatar and representation/slave, is not *per se* gendered, and therefore might be a way out of the trap of a gender dichotomy. Tradition considers the two genders it acknowledges prone to a specifically gendered way of acting. Even though we have internalized this ideological gender system on a very deep level and act accordingly, all our actions already include an element of the differently gendered action. Hence, it is impossible to play *God of War* without identifying at least a little with Kratos, a character far removed from the 'normal' experiences of most players; while on the other hand it seems equally impossible to play the game without seeing him at least in hard passages as a tool to reach a certain goal. The ambiguity of the cyborg allows for the incorporation of these differences in one concept.

> The cyborg body exists in instances of contradictory experience, a temporal snapshot of continually shifting parameters. The space it inhabits becomes therefore a site of confrontation and transgression. The cyborg is an ambiguous and multiple subjectivity implicating a vast horizon of possible meanings.
>
> (Smith 37)

The cyborg draws its power from the ambiguity of this seeming contradiction. The cyborg is an ironic concept and thus depends on an ironic basis, the connection of two seemingly different concepts, which are traditionally considered impossible or wrong to combine.

The cyborg is able to perform a sort of free gender play only limited by the borders created by the game's rules. Consciously having more than one identity at any time, it can disrupt the boundaries of traditional gender concepts. The cyborg could even be a form of Butler's *pastiche* in a game. In the form of *virtual drag*, the player can play a character of the supposed 'different' gender, which in turn is an over-stylized and simplified representative of this 'other' gender. Butler sees the political potential in the conscientious, playful performance of an oversimplified gendered identity. Unfortunately, absurdly hyper-sexualized or hyper-masculinized characters are the norm and not the exception in most games. Gamers are so used to this form of gender representation that it is regarded as the rule. Thus, even the slightest attempt of presenting a 'normal' gendered character, 'natural' in form and not shaped by 'masculine' fantasies, is striking. As a consequence it seems important to introduce more 'realistic,' that is, differentiated, characters to games, thereby underlining the possibility for the player to identify with the character, enabling her or him to understand and appropriate the 'virtual drag' involved. This could finally result in 'a conscientious retooling of... games not to consolidate gender, which of course means far more than "sex", but to fracture and fragment and disperse difference/s' (Castell and Bryson 254).

Notes

*"Parts of this essay are abridged sections of my hitherto unpublished M.A.-thesis " 'How is One to Find Her Way?' Gender Roles in the Alice-Works of Lewis Carroll, Walt Disney and 'American McGee' ". I'm indebted to Alexandra Knott and Martin Decker for their valuable comments on earlier drafts."

1. *God of War* (PlayStation 2, (*God I*)), *God of War II* (PlayStation 2, (God II)), *God of War: Chains of Olympus* (PlayStation Portable, (Chains)), *God of War: Betrayal* (mobile phones, (Betrayal)), *God of War III* (PlayStation 3, 2010).
2. Interestingly enough, Charlie Wen reveals in the same video that for some time concepts also explored the possibility of Kratos as a 'feminine' character ('Kratos: Concept to Completion' on the bonus disk of *God of War II*'s German special edition (God II bonus disk: 0:45)). Unfortunately the designers never went down that road.
3. From the first presentations of *Good of War III* one could deduce that Helios would be one of the first Gods to be destroyed by Kratos (cf. the links to the trailers in Shuman, 2009.).
4. To underline this performativity while still securing readability, I will mark all gender roles with inverted commas.

5. Caillois actually defines it as 'an almost indivisible principle, common to diversion, turbulence, free improvisation, and carefree gaiety' (13). Today it is interpreted in a narrower sense, as a form of 'free play' based only on a minimum set of rules (Frasca 229).

6. Most feminist theorists, and especially his own pupils Hélène Cixous, Luce Irigaray, and Julia Kristeva, would doubt this view. They see a potential for 'women' to satisfy their *joussance* through a link to the *pre-symbolic*. This link is said to find its expression in *écriture féminine* and the *parler femme*.

7. Lacan deliberately uses Saussure's terminology to highlight the socially constructed nature of this power structure.

8. I will use Harraway's form of 'Cyborg' with a capital 'C' when referring directly to her concept as a programmatic political means. In all other cases, I will use 'cyborg' with a lower-case 'c,' even though this distinction is not always clear-cut.

9. Haraway's indebtedness to Irigaray seems obvious.

10. I will only refer to the PlayStation 2 control scheme in the following, as the differences to the other two platforms are too nuanced (even the quite different control scheme for *Betrayal*) to be relevant for my argument.

11. Even rhythm games like the *Bemani* (*Beatmania*), *SingStar*, *Guitar Hero*, and *Rock Band* franchises rely on the visual indicator for the different tunes the player has to hit. Most of these games seem impossible to play blindfolded.

12. Some Wii and Nintendo DS titles, Racing Games that can be played with a steering wheel controller, and Lightgun Shooters aside.

13. Most digital games featuring a first-person perspective do not display body parts of the player's protagonist apart from her or his hands. The most famous exception to this might be the First-Person-Platformer *Mirror's Edge*.

14. Interestingly enough, during the latest interviews (as of May 2009) for *God of War III*, it was still under debate if the game would feature these sex-scenes too or not, but Stig Asmussen, *God of War III*'s director, would only consider cutting them for reasons of redundancy (cf. Shuman).

15. *Hot-Coffee* allowed the player through a cheat code to participate in a sex mini-game every time the protagonist CJ brings home a girlfriend. When this became public the games US age-rating was changed and major supermarkets took it from the shelves. Finally, Take2 published a new version of the game without the code for the mini-game.

16. Graner Ray participates in this construction with her essentialist views on gender in her book. This is even obvious from the above-quoted example. The members of a gender group (baron-baker; scullery maid-queen) only swap positions with a member of the same gender group who is of different rank.

17. Though there are, as always, exceptions to this rule.

18. For a discussion of the gendered aspects of 'competition', see Jenson and Castell (770).

19. This is turned into a parody in the hilarious *Earthworm Jim*. Here an earthworm is turned into a superhero by just crawling into a muscle-packed fighter suite from outer space using his worm-body as a whip.

20. It should be mentioned that this does not apply to all male players. An editor of the German PC game magazine *GameStar*, summarized these anxieties, in the extremely chauvinistic phrase: 'If I wanted to play being a woman, I would sit down to pee' (*GameStar* DVD: 03:21).

Works cited

God I. Sony Computer Entertainment, Santa Monica Studio. *God of War* (digital game). Sony Computer Entertainment, 2005.

God II. Sony Computer Entertainment, Santa Monica Studio. *God of War II: Special Edition* (digital game). Sony Computer Entertainment, 2006–2007.

Chains. Ready at Dawn. *God of War: Chains of Olympus* (digital game). Sony Computer Entertainment, 2008.

Betrayal Javaground. *God of War: Betrayal* (digital game). Sony Online Entertainment, 2007.

Other digital games cited (sorted by title; only the relevant or the first part of a series is included)

Rogue. *American McGee's Alice* (digital game). Electronic Arts, 2000.

2K Boston & 2K Australia. *BioShock* (digital game). 2K, 2007.

Id Software. *Doom* (digital game). Id Software, 1993.

3D Realms. *Duke Nukem 3D* (digital game). GT Interactive, 1996.

Shiny. *Earthworm Jim* (digital game). Playmates Interactive, 1994.

Rockstar North. *Grand Theft Auto IV* (digital game). Rockstar, 2008.

Rockstar North. *Grand Theft Auto: San Andreas* (digital game). Rockstar, 2004.

Harmonix. *Guitar Hero* (digital game). RedOctane, 2006.

Kojima Productions. *Metal Gear Solid 4: Guns of the Patriots* (digital game). Konami, 2008.

Nintendo R&D 1. *Metroid* (digital game). Nintendo, 1986.

Digital Illusions CE. *Mirror's Edge* (digital game). Electronic Arts, 2008.

Infinity Ward. *Call of Duty: Modern Warfare 2* (digital game). Activision Blizzard, 2009.

Valve. *Portal* (digital game). Valve, 2007.

Harmonix. *Rock Band* (digital game). MTV Games, 2007.

Sony Computer Entertainment, Studio London. *SingStar* (digital game). Sony Computer Entertainment. 2004.

Skip. *Soundvoyager* (digital game). Nintendo, 2006.

Core Design. *Tomb Raider* (digital game). Eidos, 1996.

Ubi Soft. *Tom Clancy's Splinter Cell* (digital game). Ubi Soft, 2003.

Creative Assembly. *Spartan: Total Warrior* (digital game). Sega, 2005.

Works cited

Baltrusch, Ernst. *Sparta: Geschichte, Gesellschaft, Kultur.* 1998. 3rd ed. Munich: C.H. Beck, 2007.

Baudrillard, Jean. *Simulacra and Simulation.* 1981. Ann Arbor: U of Michigan P, 1994.

Bly, Robert. *Iron John, A Book about Men.* New York: Vintage, 1992.

Brathwaite, Brenda. *Sex in Video Games.* Boston: Charles River, 2007.

Butler, Judith. *Bodies That Matter, On the Discursive Limits of 'Sex.'* New York & London: Routledge, 1993.

——. *Gender Trouble, Feminism and the Subversion of Identity.* 1990. 10th Anniversary Edition. New York & London: Routledge, 1999.

Caillois, Roger. *Man, Play and Games.* 1958. Urbana & Chicago: U of Illinois P, 2001.

Castell, Suzanne de and Mary Bryson. 'Retooling Play: Dystopia, Dysphoria, and Difference.' *From Barbie to Mortal Kombat, Gender and Computer Games.* Ed Justine Cassell and Henry Jenkins. Cambridge, MA and London: MIT Press, 2000. 232–61.

Frasca, Gonzalo. 'Simulation versus Narrative, Introduction to Ludology.' *The Video Game Theory Reader.* Ed Mark J. P. Wolf and Bernard Perron. New York and London: Routledge, 2003. 221–35.

GameStar DVD. 'Testcheck.' *GameStar* (July 2008). IDG Publications.

Graner Ray, Sheri. *Gender Inclusive Game Design, Expanding the Market.* Hingham: Charles River, 2004.

Haraway, Donna. 'A Cyborg Manifesto, Science, Technology, and Socialist-Feminism in the Late Twentieth Century.' 1985. *The New Media Reader.* Ed Noah-Wardrip-Fruin and Nick Montfort. Cambridge, MA and London: MIT Press, 2003. 516–41.

Jenson, Jennifer and Suzanne de Castell. 'Girls and Gaming: Gender Research, "Progress" and the Death of Interpretation.' *Situated Play, Proceedings of DiGRA 2007 Conference.* Ed. Akira Baba. Tokyo: U of Tokyo, 2007. 769–71. See also: <http://www.digra.org/dl/db/07311.36536.pdf>. last accessed 16/5/09.

McMahan, Alison. 'Immersion, Engagement, and Presence, A Method for Analyzing 3-D Video Games.' *The Video Game Theory Reader.* Ed Mark J. P. Wolf and Bernard Perron. New York & London: Routledge, 2003. 67–86.

Miller, Frank. *300.* Milwaukie: Dark Horse, 1999.

Murphy, Sheila C. "Live in Your World, Play in Ours': The Spaces of Video Game Identity.' *Journal of Visual Culture* 3.2 (2004): 223–38.

Newman, James. *Videogames.* Abingdon & New York: Routledge, 2004.

Pagel, Gerda. *Jacques Lacan Zur Einführung.* Hamburg: Junius, 1989.

Peppers, Cathy. ' "I've Got You Under My Skin": Cyber(sexed) Bodies in Cyberpunk Fictions.' *Bodily Discursions: Genders, Representations, Technologies.* Ed Deborah S. Wilson and Christine Moneera Laennec. Albany: State U of New York P, 1997. 163–85.

Röber, Niklas and Maic Masuch. 'Playing Audio-Only Games, A Compendium of Interacting with Virtual, Auditory Worlds.' *Changing Views – Worlds in Play: Proceedings of DiGRA 2005 Conference.* Ed Suzanne de Castell and Jenson Jennifer. Vancouver: U of Vancouver, 2005.See also: <http://www.digra.org/dl/db/06276.30120.pdf> last accessed: 16/5/09.

Shuman, Sid. 'God of War III: Q&A with Stig Asmussen.' <http://www.gamepro.com/article/features/208896/god-of-war-iii-q-a-with-stig-asmussen/>. 17/2/2009 last accessed: 17/5/2009.

Smith, Zoe. 'Technological Bodies: Feminist Cyborg Constructions.' *Convergence, The International Journal of Research into New Media Technologies.* 3.2 (1997): 36–42.

300. Dir. Zack Snyder. Warner, 2006.

Young, Bryan-Mitchell. 'Gaming Mind, Gaming Body: The Mind/Body Split For a New Era.' *Changing Views – Worlds in Play: Proceedings of DiGRA 2005 Conference.* Ed. Suzanne de Castell and Jenson Jennifer. Vancouver: U of Vancouver, 2005.See also: <http://www.digra.org/dl/db/06278.12199.pdf> last accessed: 16/5/09.

Index

Note: The letter 'n' following a page number indicates an endnote.